CONNECTING NATIONS

CONNECTING NATIONS

Politico-Cultural Mapping of India and South East Asia

edited by

ACHINTYA KUMAR DUTTA
ANASUA BASU RAY CHAUDHURY

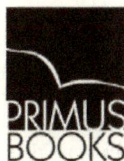

PRIMUS
BOOKS

PRIMUS BOOKS

An imprint of Ratna Sagar P. Ltd.
Virat Bhavan
Mukherjee Nagar Commercial Complex
Delhi 110 009

Offices at

CHENNAI   LUCKNOW

AGRA   AHMEDABAD   BANGALORE   COIMBATORE
DEHRADUN   GUWAHATI   HYDERABAD   JAIPUR   JALANDHAR
KANPUR   KOCHI   KOLKATA   MADURAI   MUMBAI
PATNA   RANCHI   VARANASI

First published 2019

ISBN: 978-93-5290-269-9 (hardback)
ISBN: 978-93-5290-268-2 (POD)

Published by Primus Books

Laser typeset by Guru Typograph Technology
Crossings Republic, Ghaziabad 201 009

Printed and bound in India by Replika Press Pvt. Ltd.

Contents

Illustrations

Figures

Maps

Tables

Acknowledgements

THE PRESENT collection is the result of an international conference held in December 2013 at the Department of History, University of Burdwan in collaboration with the Department of South & South East Asian Studies, University of Calcutta; and Indian Association for Asian and Pacific Studies. The idea of this conference on 'India's Look East Policy: Gleanings from the Past to the Present', was conceived by Lipi Ghosh, Professor at the Department of South & South East Asian Studies, University of Calcutta. She visualized the initiative of holding a collaborative conference where scholars of national and international repute could gather, talk about, and shed light on the relevant aspects of the theme that has received immense historical importance and international recognition in the recent past. We are grateful to her for her valuable advice and cooperation, without which this conference would not have been possible.

We are also very thankful to the Indian Council of Social Science Research, New Delhi and to the collaborators for funding the conference and making it a success.

We offer our heartfelt thanks to all the participating scholars and contributors who have thrown new light on India's looking to the South East Asian countries with their learned contributions and extended their cooperation throughout the making of this collection.

Our colleagues at the Department of History, University of Burdwan; Department of South & South East Asian Studies, University of Calcutta; and Indian Association for Asian and Pacific Studies deserve a special thanks for their moral and mental support in making our drive successful.

We hope that the present collection of essays will generate further interest amongst scholars and researchers interested in this field and the work would be useful to the teachers and students at the university level.

ACHINTYA KUMAR DUTTA
ANASUA BASU RAY CHAUDHURY

Introduction

India-South East Asia
Connectivity through the Ages

Achintya Kumar Dutta
Anasua Basu Ray Chaudhury

Historical Overviews

LOOKING TOWARD the East constitutes an important aspect of India's foreign policy since the 1990s and henceforth, India has been looking to the East and South East Asian neighbours to consolidate ties of friendship and mutual understanding. The initiation of the Act East Policy, 2014 is a harbinger of a positive approach in India's foreign policy towards South East Asia. The roots of India's Look East Policy can, however, be traced to India's past history and tradition dating as far back as the period preceding the Christian era.

Since time immemorial, Indians have had a close trading connection with different regions of South East Asia. References to South East Asia appear in Indian literature as early as the sixth century BCE. The *Ramayana* refers to *Suvarna-dvipa* and *Yava-dvipa* (*dvipa* means peninsula or island, while *suvarna* means gold and *yava* means barley). Moreover, in the third century BCE, King Asoka sent Buddhist missionaries to Subarnabhumi (land of gold). Although it is difficult to identify the exact location of such place-names, they are believed to be parts of South East Asia. Land routes through east Bengal, Assam, and Manipur transported the Indians further east. Indians travelled to Upper Burma through various passes in the Manipur Hills, and to Lower Burma through Arakan. They also managed to reach places such as Malay, East Indies, and Indochina by crossing the Bay of Bengal.[1]

As a consequence of close trade and cultural connections with the South East Asian countries since ancient times, India managed to leave its cultural imprints on South East Asian society and culture. Although the South East Asian people developed a society and culture of their own much before it reached them, India's cultural influence was widespread and deep-rooted and came in a number of waves through the centuries.[2]

The process of this cultural diffusion is said to have been preceded by a commercial connection. Indian trading activities enormously increased in South East Asia during the first three centuries CE. This commercial contact might possibly have brought South East Asian traders close to Indian merchants, and inspired them to acquire knowledge about India's language, religion, and culture. But Indian culture could not reach there until the brahmins were invited to the courts of South East Asian rulers.[3] Since Indian seafarers and traders belonged to the vaisya varna, they had no right over the knowledge of the shastras and were not in a position to transport social, religious, scriptural, or administrative knowledge to this region. It was the brahmins who monopolized the knowledge of sacred lore, rites, rituals, customs, and laws. Thus, the Indian culture spread to South East Asia only when the brahmins visited this region at the invitation of the rulers cum traders to serve as priests, astrologers, or advisors. The brahmins introduced Indian court customs, the theory of monarchy, administrative organization on Indian patterns, laws based on Manu's code, Indian epics, the *Ramayana* and the *Mahabharata*, and also other works on a variety of subjects such as philosophy, medicine, mathematics, and religious lore. This period of cultural diffusion lasted from around the beginning of the first century until the end of the twelfth century.[4] This resulted in a certain degree of acculturation. In fact, acculturation takes place only when each of the two distinct cultures have the elements of accommodating and absorbing each other. South East Asia's indigenous culture was no exception. The people representing this culture did not contest the inclusion of foreign cultural elements into their indigenous culture. As Indian culture was welcomed and accepted, it implies that cultural assimilation did take place. It is argued that 'The superior cultural endowments of the immigrants, often basically similar to those of the local people, assured the newcomers of a welcome'.[5]

It is often argued that Indian culture took root in various parts of South East Asia on account of the comparative wealth and prestige of Indian traders.[6] However, before making such observations, it is essential to comprehend the underlying historical processes behind the spread of India's cultural influence in South East Asia. Interestingly, of the two significant Asian cultures, Chinese and Indian, the latter was found to be more attractive and popular with the South East Asian rulers and elites.

Vietnam, with its cultural inclination towards China, was an exception. The syncretic character of Indian culture is said to have been successful in striking roots in the South East Asian region when the local elites and rulers were assured of not losing their identity. The relative acceptability of Indian culture is further attributed to the geographical and cultural commonness and relative lack of Indian political ambition in the region. Geographically, India and South East Asia share the tropical monsoon climate that led to a way of life based on irrigated agriculture and wet rice cultivation.

No wonder, therefore, when Aryanized Indians migrated to South East Asia in the first millennium of the Christian era, the indigenous people discovered among them a similar cultural base, a shared substratum; some of the traits were pre-Aryan and common to all peoples of monsoon Asia.[7] Therefore, the perception that Indian rule was established in South East Asia or a process of 'Indianization' being initiated in the region does not hold ground, especially in the light of new historical and archaeological sources, that present a different picture altogether. Apart from the solitary instance of invasion of the Srivijaya Kingdom in Sumatra by the Indian King Rajendra Chola in the eleventh century CE, there is no concrete evidence of any colonial expansionism by the Indian rulers in neighbouring South East Asia or direct Indian intervention into the political affairs of South East Asia.[8]

Indian Colonization or Indianization in South East Asia

For a long time, nationalist historians tended to view India's influences in South East Asia through the prism of political and cultural colonization of the latter. So extensive were the signs of India's cultural influences, as evident in language, inscriptions, architectural remains, religious ideas, and other artistic forms such as the borrowing of the Sanskrit epics: the *Ramayana* and *Mahabharata*; that many saw it in the pre-Second World War period as the result of Indian emigration to and colonization of South East Asia or of actual conquest and wrote of South East Asia as 'Greater India' or 'Further India' or 'Hindu Colonies'. As early as 1912, an Indian historian Radhakumud Mookerjee spoke of Hindu imperialism. The Hindu rulers were shown as occupying the shores and hinterlands of 'Further India' and Indonesia through the course of the centuries. Later, this was criticized as nationalistic self-exultation by scholars.[9]

Another Indian historian R.C. Majumdar became the chief proponent of the concept of ancient Indian colonization in South East Asia, although Indian sources did not support such a view. He put forward this theory first in 1927 and reiterated it subsequently in the 1940s and even in the 1960s when contrary views were already being expressed by other scholars like J.C. van Leur (the English translation of his work was published in 1955) which also grabbed the attention of the historians. In 1940, Majumdar observed that the Hindu colonists in South East Asia brought with them their culture and civilization that was transplanted there completely.[10] Again in 1963, in the second edition of his book, titled *Hindu Colonies in the Far East* (the first edition of the book was published in 1944), he discussed how the Indian colonial kingdoms were continuously being strengthened by fresh streams of immigration from the motherland, and grew up in different parts of Indo-Chinese Peninsula and the East Indies from the beginning of the Christian era.[11]

European scholars like C.C. Berg and N.J. Krom have argued along Majumdar's line, although not in its entirety. They used the term 'Indianization' (which was also subsequently criticized and rejected by the scholars) instead of 'Greater India' or 'Hindu Colonies', and argued that Indianization was the result of military conquest and commercial expansion, respectively.[12]

However, this theory of Indian colonization or 'Indianization' has been contested by scholars like Paul Mus, Leur, and F.D.K. Bosch. Mus argued that a common, primordial substratum of belief and culture existed in both the Indian and South East Asian societies and when Hinduism and Buddhism became widespread, there was a local basis in South East Asia for the acceptance of these beliefs and for their absorption into the local culture.[13] Rejecting the hypothesis of Indian colonization and cultural influence carried by trade, Leur argued that particular aspects of Indian culture found a ready home in South East Asia where the people deliberately borrowed many of the Indian ideas, artistic styles, and modes of political organizations which were absorbed into the local culture. He also observed that South East Asian trade was basically a pre-capitalist, peddling trade which could not have been the means of transmitting those elements of Indian culture that were absorbed into the local scene.[14] Indian influence was likely to have been the result of borrowings by the South East Asian rulers of those features of Indian culture which were of use in emerging kingdoms of the region. Therefore, India did not impose itself on indigenous cultures. Leur also throws light on the notion of autonomy. If Indian influence were to be seen as borrowed or absorbed, it allowed continuing independence and authority to local cultures which might otherwise be seen as subject to or conquered by external pressures.[15]

Bosch's argument supported Leur's view, adding that there is an absence of references to Indian conquest in any inscriptions and that the signs of Indian influence were strongest in inland kingdoms, not coastal ones, as might have been expected if the culture had been carried by commerce.[16] H.G. Quaritch Wales argued that there was intense Indian grip on many parts of South East Asia but that was purely cultural, and asserted that there was never any military conquest or annexation by the Indians.[17] Another European scholar G. Coedes also speaks of 'Indianization' and 'transplantation' of Indian culture into South East Asia but asserted that there was never any military conquest or annexation by India. While discussing introduction of Indian culture in Indochina, he holds

. . . nor was India ever introduced for political purposes, as was the case with the Sinicization of Vietnam, which was conquered by China and then administered for several centuries as a province of the empire; whereas none of the Indochinese States of Indian type was ever a dependency of an Indian metropolitan power.[18]

Recent researches reveal that the concept of 'Indianization' seems to have neglected South East Asian initiatives towards cultural assimilation or accommodating alien culture and civilization. It is also argued that Majumdar ignored the process of interaction between the Indian immigrants and the indigenous population and rejected any role for local creativity in adopting and adapting to the Indian culture.[19]

Of late, Hermann Kulke, the celebrated German historian, has studied the politico-cultural connection between India and South East Asia, suggesting a cultural convergence of early kingdoms in both regions in the middle of the first millennium. He has illustrated that early state formation in South East Asia under the Indian influence in the late fourth and fifth centuries took place almost simultaneously with a similar development of early state formation in India. In the post-Satavahana period, eastern, central, and southern India, too, followed similar 'trajectories' of political and socioeconomic evolution and a new kind of local state formation was found in contemporary South East Asia.[20] He added that similar processes of socioeconomic changes and cultural transformation including the process of early state formation occurred on both sides of the Bay of Bengal in the early centuries of the

Christian era. These new processes influenced and accelerated indigenous processes of early state formation in South East Asia. It was during that time that the South East Asian rulers felt the need to invite brahmins from India 'to their little courts, in order to legitimize and strengthen their claim to superior authority and power through their advice,' which indigenous traditional institutions were unable to fully provide.[21] Kulke, thus, observed a similarity and even convergence of politico-cultural evolution on both sides of the Bay of Bengal in the middle of the first millennium CE. He holds that it was the nearness among the societies in the coastal regions of the Bay of Bengal rather than the social distance between imperial Indian states and emerging early kingdoms of South East Asia, which made the Indian model so attractive to South East Asian rulers. The process of 'Indianization' implies a social distance as a major cause of acceptance of Indian influences in South East Asia, the convergence theory postulates social nearness as the primary factor in promoting and accepting sociocultural changes under Indian influence in South East Asia. The Hindu model of a 'limited universal kingship' was initially taken over by early local rulers of South East Asia from the early kingdoms of southern and eastern India and not from the Imperial Guptas of northern India, a model that did not fit the requirements of contemporary South East Asian rulers.[22] Arguably, then what happened, there was not the 'transplantation' but the transfer of Indian culture in South East Asia and consequently a process of cultural assimilation. In this process, South East Asia was an active agent, not a passive onlooker.

Of all the South East Asian nations, Burma has always been regarded by the nationalist historians as one of the earliest places in South East Asia to have received Indian influence. Since time immemorial, Indians and Burmans have maintained close contact in the spheres of trade, commerce, religion, and culture. Buddhism further strengthened cultural ties between the two countries. The friendship between the Indians and Burmans continued in the nineteenth and the twentieth centuries also. During the colonial period, Burma played a major role in the emerging Asian solidarity and relations between Delhi and Rangoon (present day Yangon). A large Indian population in Burma provided substance to this relationship. Considerable trade dealing in Burmese teak, rice, and gems flourished between the Indian eastern coast and Rangoon. India provided considerable support to Burma in the years following its independence when the state had to deal with insurgencies and subnational militancy.[23] The bond between the people of the two countries during the colonial rule is further evident from the references to the Indians residing in

Burma and engaged in the literary productions of the nineteenth and twentieth centuries. [24]

Apart from Burma, India and Siam (present day Thailand) had reciprocal cultural contacts since ancient times. Indian contact with Siam is said to have begun in the third century BCE in the course of propagation of Buddhism by King Asoka. The history of the successive waves of Indian arrivals, with traits of Hinduism, in Siam can be identified since the pre-Sukhothai period, i.e. Dvaravati period (tentatively from ninth to eleventh centuries), when present day Thailand is a good compatriot of India's linkage. In the fifth and sixth centuries, the first group of brahmin priests went to Pegu and then to Siam, and they became the first brahmin settlers there.[25] Subsequently, Ayuthian kings maintained and even strengthened Siam's relations with India, and this did not originate from any politico-cultural pressure from the latter. Many of the regions in Siam, being influenced by the Indian culture, adopted Sanskrit names. It was during this period that the *Ramayana*, better known to the Thais as *Ramakien*, gained popularity in Siam. Interestingly, the Chakri kings have always called themselves as Rama [as Mongkut (1851–68) was known as Rama IV, Chulalongkorn (1868–1910) as Rama V], the great hero-king of the Indian epic, the *Ramayana*.[26] Siam's support for India's freedom struggle was substantial. Indian revolutionaries from Malay moved to Siam and carried on their activities from there. They moved to Siam because unlike Malay, the former was independent and nurtured strong anti-British feelings and hence, considered to be safer than the latter. Interestingly, during the Second World War, the Thai prime minister assured that the Indians in Thailand would face no difficulties or problems as far as the Thai Government was concerned.[27]

Champa was the Sanskrit name of a kingdom in South East Asia and the kings of Champa assumed the Pallava style, their names ending with varman, like Bhadravarman who built the first temple of the Hindu god Shiva.[28] In fact, religions from India deeply influenced the people of the East and South East Asia. Along with Hinduism; Buddhism, both Mahayana and Theravada, spread from India to Funan, Angkor, Sumatra, and Java in the first millennium CE. After the eleventh century, Theravada spread rapidly in Mainland South East Asia and became the dominant faith of the people of Burma, Siam, Laos, and Cambodia.

Similarly, the kingdoms, like Srivijaya, Sailendra, and Mataram in Island South East Asia were deeply influenced by Hinduism and Buddhism. The city of Palembang in Srivijaya was an important centre of Buddhist learning; the Borobudur Temple in Sailendra was an example of Indo-Javanese art; and the Mataram rulers built numerous temples dedicated to Hindu gods.[29] Even Islamic culture became acceptable to South East Asians only when it came through Indian intermediaries. Islam also appealed to South East Asian people because, like earlier Hinduism and Buddhism, it came in a relatively peaceful fashion.[30] Thus, India not only received valuable commercial goods from farther east and south-east, but also offered the benefits of its rich culture to the people of this region. It is true, however, the age-old practices and beliefs of the South East Asian people, in general, were not fundamentally changed under the influence of Hindu culture. Animism, ancestor-worship, and agricultural rituals meant more to the South East Asians than the imported cult of Buddha, Shiva, or Vishnu.[31] Still, Indian influence left an indelible mark on South East Asian culture.

As discussed in this essay, Indian influence in the region cannot be associated with the idea of the extension of Indian political power. India accommodated diverse elements of foreign cultures that entered the subcontinent in ancient times, and laid the foundation of a civilization which is centred in a sense of oneness. Needless to say, India successfully established bonds of relationship with foreigners and turned them into friends. India unhesitatingly entered into the minds and lives of others and assimilated elements from outside. It is with this mission that King Asoka sent his emissary to South East Asia. India has had a long history and rich heritage of relations with the other countries of Asia. Streams of culture have not only entered into India from the East and the West but also flowed from India to distant parts of Asia.

The ties of friendship and mutual understanding between the two regions of Asia were maintained through the centuries. Medieval and modern periods witnessed further intensification of this relationship through multiplication of trading activities, and import and export of goods between India and South East Asian countries. In the medieval period, commercial connections were maintained through the sea route with the Malay Peninsula. Detailed evidence of commercial and cultural interactions are available from contemporary books and travelogues. Under the Mughals, interaction through river and sea routes was facilitated by the active and prosperous ports. Though for a long time during the colonial rule, India was almost isolated from its neighbouring friends, the historic bonds between the Indians and South East Asian people did not break. Even during this phase, Indians continued to attach significance to the East and tried to bring the East closer to India. Rabindranath Tagore embarked on a three-and-a-half-month tour to South East Asian countries (1927) in order to reinforce cultural ties with the region. He was warmly received in different countries in the region and was successful in connecting the cultures of India and South East Asia.[32] He is regarded as a pioneer in reviving intra-Asian relations in modern times. Tagore considered the South East Asian region as a home away from his home, and therefore, considered his tour to this region (Singapore, Malaya, Java, Borneo, Sumatra, and Indonesia) as 'Bharat Tirtha', i.e. a pilgrimage to India beyond its modern political boundaries. Tagore's visit to Burma was a part of his effort to preach the principles of peaceful universalism maintained by Asia, of which India was a prominent leader as against to the narrow power-centric nationalist tendencies of Europe.[33]

Indian minorities were also found in many countries of this region—Burma, Malay, and Singapore—during that time. After 1800, Indians arrived here mostly as labourers. They remained confined to the British territories and did not assimilate with the South East Asian themselves. Nevertheless, the vestige of India's historical bonds with the region was preserved to a great extent in this period by Indian Muslims who had traded in the South East Asian waters for generations.[34] More importantly, the British colonial rule in the region created a demand for English educated Indian clerks, hospital dispensers, lawyers, teachers, merchants, and moneylenders who started settling in South East Asia and formed a small professional middle class, subsequently influencing the course of history in the countries like Burma and Malay.

Decolonization, India, and South East Asia

The process of decolonization set in motion after the Second World War and subsequently the forces of globalization and liberalization provided a new impetus to India's relationship with its South East Asian neighbours. In the post-independence period when a new power equation developed on the heels of Asia's emergence as a centre of international power-politics, this relationship between India and the countries of South East Asia called for further investigation.

However, the ideal of mutual understanding and cooperation was also reflected in India's foreign policy in the post-1947 period. Jawaharlal Nehru as the first prime minister of India laid stress on peaceful coexistence of countries with different ideologies, differing systems, and pluralism. To this end, he outlined the five principles of peaceful coexistence or Panchsheel for conducting relations among countries in Asia.[35] There was mutual respect for each other's territorial integrity, sovereignty, non-aggression, and non-interference in each other's internal affairs, equality, mutual benefit, and peaceful coexistence. Interestingly, these principles were accepted by the South East Asian countries in a conference held in Bandung, Indonesia in 1955. Even before that, with India's independence imminent, Nehru took the lead in organizing a conference (March 1947) of Asian countries those were free or still under the colonial rule. The purpose of organizing the conference was to rekindle the spirit of mutual progress, well-being, and friendship; and promote the interaction between India and its Asian neighbours.[36]

Thus in the 1940s and 1950s, India had a close rapport with the South East Asian countries, while in the 1960s, its engagement with the South East Asian countries was gradually replaced by periods of isolation. A clash of ideologies and superpower dynamics kept the geographically contiguous regions on opposite sides of the Cold War divide. It has been argued by the scholars like C. Raja Mohan that

... the enduring consequences of the subcontinent's partition, and the conflict with China over Tibet and the boundary, tied down India to deal with conflicts within its own neighbourhood. India's insular socialist policies resulted not just in India's relative economic decline, but also saw the erosion of historic trade links with the neighbouring regions in Asia. ... Although India's Third World activism meant taking positions on all global issues, these degenerated into mere posturing against one or both superpowers, and the inability to come to the aid of friendly nations in conflict with their neighbours.[37]

While India was preoccupied with its problems with China and Pakistan during the 1960s and early 1970s, South East Asia was also going through turbulent phases with increasing communist insurgency within the region. Insecurity among the countries from the pro-Western camp of South East Asia heightened particularly in the 1960s, with Britain's decision to withdraw from the east of Suez, Nixon's Guam Doctrine of 1969, and intra-regional conflicts. These disturbances pressed the countries of South East Asia to build a regional identity to strengthen the cooperation among the states. As a result, the Association of South East Asian Nations (ASEAN) was formed in 1967 out of the Chinese threat perception.

It is to be observed that during the Cold War days, most of the South East Asian countries perceived India to be in the camp of the former Soviet Union.[38] Apart from Vietnam to an extent, there was very little political interaction. Strategic links were virtually non-existent and economic bonds were of low importance. On the other hand, the intensification of the US involvement in Vietnam led to polarization within South East Asia. More so, in the aftermath of the oil shocks in the early 1970s, India's main concern was to secure uninterrupted oil supply to meet its increasing energy demand. As a consequence, India tilted towards the West Asian regions and its close relationship with the West Asian countries kept India away from South East Asia.

In the late 1970s and the early 1980s, India's attention was drawn again towards South East Asia. The reason was the Chinese attack on Vietnam for the latter's military intervention in Cambodia in February 1979. India, being the only non-communist country, supported Vietnam. Therefore, the status of ASEAN dialogue partner granted to India in May 1980 was quietly withdrawn the next month to punish India for its pro-Vietnam policy on the Cambodia issue.[39] Against this backdrop, India's revival in relations with its South East Asian neighbours was a result of two main factors: first, post-Cold War apprehensions about China moving in to fill the vacuum following the US withdrawal from the region and second, the constraints of liberalized economy under intense globalization.[40]

India's Look East Policy Revisited

The sudden collapse of the former Soviet Union in 1991 resulted in the emergence of a new global, political, and economic scenario which prompted a paradigm shift in India's strategic world view, including the countries of South East Asia. The economic reforms, coupled with the integrative forces of globalization, frustration with the process of integration within South Asia, and the renewed concern about the powerful China and its growing assertiveness in the Asia-Pacific region made India rethink the basic parameters of its foreign policy.[41] India, under the given circumstances, advocated a policy of new regionalism towards the South East Asian countries and later in East Asia and beyond, which occurred in response to the prevailing international environment after the demise of the Cold War. To cope with this evolving global milieu, in July 1991, New Delhi, under the leadership of the then Prime Minister P.V. Narasimha Rao, announced its new economic policy which was guided more by economic imperatives and less by political rhetoric. It is indeed true that the groundwork for this foreign policy shift was prepared by the Rajiv Gandhi regime during the late 1980s and moves were made by the Rao government soon after its coming to the power in 1991.

At this juncture, Indian foreign policy had threefold objectives: to maintain the territorial integrity of India; to ensure its geopolitical security by creating a durable environment of peace and stability in the region; and to build a framework for the well-being of the people by encouraging a healthy external economic environment.[42] During this phase, India's strategic world view clearly shifted from an emphasis on 'moral speak' to 'realpolitik' based on acquiring and exercising economic and military power.[43]

The Look East Policy was officially launched in the year 1991 during the tenure of Prime Minister Rao, although the term 'Look East' was mentioned for the first time in the *Annual Report of the Ministry of External Affairs* in 1996.[44] In this context, a statement by I.K. Gujral is worth mentioning, 'What Look East really means is that an outward looking India, is gathering all forces of dynamism, domestic and regional, and is directly focusing on establishing synergies with a fast consolidating and progressive neighbourhood to its East in Mother Continent of Asia.'[45]

In fact, Gujral referred to the importance of ASEAN and India to the geopolitical complex to which they belonged and to each other in their own right. He affirmed that historic linkages, economic complementarities, and policy coherence had meant that ASEAN-India relations would henceforth be predicated on intrinsic value. The context of Pan Asian, Asia-Pacific, and South-South Cooperation dynamics was invoked.[46]

The shift in India's overall economic reforms and market liberalization policy attracted many countries of South East Asia to develop better economic linkages with India. India's Look East Policy took off at the time when South East Asian countries started heading towards West. India's aim at improving economic ties with its South Eastern neighbours encouraged it to be a sectoral dialogue partner of the ASEAN in 1992, full dialogue partner in 1995, and also a member of ASEAN Regional Forum (ARF) in 1996; demonstrating several other gestures of solidarity with its South East Asian neighbours. A host of literature have already emerged outlining the origins and ideological underpinnings of India's Look East Policy.[47]

However, during this long journey of India's Look East Policy, in the initial years, New Delhi had transitorily lost the rhythm of continuing its fraternal ties with some countries (mainly the Indochina States and Myanmar) of South East Asia. The major rationale behind this low profile towards these countries centred on New Delhi's sluggish pace of economic reforms, the lack of stable governments in New Delhi, and the 1997 financial crisis faced by ASEAN members. Further, the impact of globalization and slow adjustment of the Indochina states with reference to the socialism-oriented economy greatly obstructed the flowering of better ties between India and the Indochina states. Hence, India's Look East Policy towards these less developed countries of South East Asia in the early 1990s clearly reveals a feeble priority area of Indian foreign policy.

Fortunately, this lack of initiative of India towards these countries was short-lived. The progression of better linkages with these countries by New Delhi was already underway before the Look East Policy Phase II was announced in September 2003 on account of the inclusion of Myanmar within ASEAN in 1997, the formation of the Bay of Bengal Initiative for Multi-Sectoral Technical and Economic Cooperation (BIMSTEC) in June 1997, and the Mekong-Ganga Cooperation (MGC) on 10 November 2000 at Vientiane. These events were naturally aimed at broadening and intensification of the joint efforts in economic cooperation between India and ASEAN in the Mekong Basin, and thereby New Delhi's economic interests, national security, and strategic imperatives towards these countries recuperated their momentum, and the countries of South East Asia recommenced and restored the ancient propinquity, in addition to re-establishing the kinship that both civilizations have experienced since the days of yore.

In a nutshell, in these last twenty-five years, India's Look East Policy has crossed two important phases. While the first phase extending from 1991 to 2001 laid particular accent on cementing greater ties with the developed ASEAN members, in consonance with the focus on subregionalism as well, augmented by India's sincere initiatives in establishing subregional organizations like BIMSTEC and the MGC forum; the second phase (2002–11) embraced New Delhi's involvement with the late entrants of ASEAN (Cambodia, Laos, Myanmar, and Vietnam) and trod further east, as enunciated in the doctrine of 'Moving East' towards China, Japan, South Korea, Australia, and New Zealand. Furthermore, the announcement of India's Maritime Doctrine in 2004 (revised in 2009), destined to develop a blue water naval capability, augmented the strategic domain of the Look East zeal, and thereby provided a holistic and pivotal shape to the anthology of India's Look

East Policy. In fact, India-ASEAN relations were upgraded to a Summit Level Partnership in 2002. India became one of the four ASEAN Summit Level Partners along with China, Japan, and Korea. At the 2nd India-ASEAN Summit in October 2003, India and ASEAN signed the Framework Agreement on Comprehensive Economic Cooperation, leading to the creation of a free trade area by the year 2011 and India's accession to the Treaty of Amity and Cooperation in South East Asia. Following the trend of India-ASEAN cordial relationship, it can also be said that after 2012, the Government of India continued to work towards what it called the third phase that was termed as an 'Enhanced LEP'. This new re-engagement policy of India with the countries of South East Asia, East Asia, and Asia-Pacific has been envisioned based on expediency and progressive self-interest.[48]

This Look East Policy essentially represents a multi-pronged approach, encompassing political, strategic, and economic aspects. By virtue of the geographical situation as well as the civilizational contacts in culture, religion, language, and trade; the growing business and investment in contemporary times, and the presence of large Indian diaspora; India is placed on a high pedestal. Having realized ASEAN's strategic importance, India tried to use the ASEAN platform as a springboard for its further successful integration within Asia. With regard to the expectations of India in the emergence of Asia as Asian Century, New Delhi intended to deal with Asian economic and security cooperation keeping the Asian powers such as China, Japan, and South Korea and external powers, such as Australia, the US, and Russia in mind.

It is worth observing that India-ASEAN functional cooperation is diverse and includes cooperation across a range of sectors, such as trade, science and technology, agriculture, environment, human resource development, space science, new and renewable energy, information and communication technology, telecommunications, transport and infrastructure, tourism and culture, and health and pharmaceuticals.

Though in recent times many scholars have already analysed in different ways how India's Look East Policy has strengthened India's bilateral relationships with the states of South East Asia in general and India's engagement with the ASEAN in particular, it is important to note that at the 7th India-ASEAN Summit held in October 2009, India announced a contribution of US$50 million to ASEAN-India Cooperation Fund to support implementation of the India-ASEAN Plan of Action 2010–15 which envisages cooperation in a range of sectors in the political, economic, and sociocultural spheres for deepening and intensifying India-ASEAN cooperation. This was in addition to the India-ASEAN Science & Technology Fund, set up in 2007 with an initial corpus of US$1 million, and the India-ASEAN Green Fund, established in 2007 with US$5 million, for funding pilot projects to promote adaptation and mitigation technologies in the field of climate change.[49]

At the India-ASEAN Commemorative Summit in December 2012, the leaders welcomed the conclusion of the negotiations on India-ASEAN Trade in Services and Investment Agreements. The India-ASEAN Trade-in-Goods Agreement was signed on 13 August 2009 at the India-ASEAN Economic Ministerial Meeting in Bangkok and became fully operational from 1 August 2011, when the process of ratification by all the ASEAN countries was completed. The total trade between India and ASEAN was increased by 37 per cent in 2011–12. It had reached US$79.3 billion by surpassing the trade target of US$70 billion by 2012.[50]

Cooperation between India and ASEAN is also being reinforced in the cultural, educational, and academic fields, through the promotion of people-to-people contacts and ongoing initiatives such as the Youth Exchange Programmes, Media Exchange Programmes, Special Training Courses for ASEAN Diplomats, and Eminent Persons Lecture Series. India has established Centres for English Language Training (CELT) and Entrepreneurship Development Centres (EDC) in Cambodia, Lao PDR, Myanmar, and Vietnam (CLMV countries).[51]

While emphasizing regional integration, reform, and liberalization of India, the policy also stressed on rapid economic growth and development of the north-eastern region of India. Therefore, engaging the north-east of India in the process of various regional and subregional cooperative initiatives became one of the important features of India's Look East Policy. The experts argue in this context that no longer is India's north-east seen as a remote and dangerous frontier zone; rather, many view it as 'gateways of opportunities of international trade and commerce'.[52] Some have gone to the extent of saying that this new 'strategic vision' could be a 'game-changer' for Asia, especially because it has the potential to bring China, India, and South East Asia together in a single rope. Various multilateral initiatives across borders, such as the Bangladesh-China-India-Myanmar (BCIM) and BIMSTEC are seen as holding 'promises of historic proportions for trans-national region-building in the area.'[53]

However, the fact remains that though this policy brought India closer to the ASEAN nations, India could not fully reap the benefits of such relations. India's north-east has remained deprived of most of the benefits that could have been accrued from the policy being followed in earnest.[54] The challenges that were faced by ASEAN internally and the financial crisis that it faced, also kept Indian businesses and policymakers hesitant about the Look East Policy being taken seriously as a policy.[55]

Experts have argued that India's Look East Policy has yielded 'mixed results' for the north-east. It has benefited traders, industrialists, and highly qualified professionals but it has not met the expectations in the field of employment generation. The movement of general people and skilled labours remain still constrained or is open only to select sectors.[56]

Act East Policy: New Vista in India-South East Asia Relations

It is indeed true that India's Look East Policy has gained momentum through the newly furnished and more focused Act East Policy during the India-ASEAN Summit in Myanmar in November 2014.[57] The foundation and objective of the Look East Policy remain the same but to provide impetus and increase its importance and focus on it, the policy has been upgraded. The Act East Policy of India is to strengthen its interaction with its south-eastern neighbours in three important domains: commerce, culture, and connectivity.[58] In this process of relinking with south-eastern countries especially with Myanmar and Thailand; physical and infrastructural connectivity by road, rail, air, and water through India's north-east—a strategic point of India—for the promotion of economic links and activities with the countries to the east and south-east; has been a topic of major concern for the government.

Indian Government's commitment to the stability in the South Asian neighbourhood will not necessarily come at the expense of East Asian engagement. India's north-eastern states cannot be easily accessed from the mainland without Bangladesh's cooperation, so positive relations with India's South Asian neighbours will also be crucial to enhance its land connectivity with South East Asia. Moreover, from the beginning, the top political leader has advocated a 'Look East, Link West Policy', pointing to a broader Indo-Pacific conceptualization of India's region.[59]

In this context, the Vision 2020 initiative by the Government of India, especially for the development of the north-eastern region of India, is worth mentioning. It aims at the achievement of 13 per cent annual growth rate of GSDP. In order to accomplish higher development in this region, the Government of India is encouraging the public sector to invest more. Experts argue that this is required to ensure self-sufficiency in basic areas such as availability of food.[60] Three key projects that are being undertaken as part of the Vision 2020 plan are the Kaladan Multimodal Project, the India–Myanmar rail linkages, and the Trilateral Highway project between India, Thailand, and Myanmar.

Considering all these facts, this collection comprising nine comprehensive essays intends to analyse various facets of India's connectivity, historical as well as contemporary, with South East Asian countries encompassing importance of India's north-east, the re-discovery of Indian imprinted culture (mainly Buddhism and other religions) in the South East Asian region and beyond, the involvement of the Indian diaspora in economic development, implementation of various agreements signed by India with these countries, etc. These have been covered to varying degrees in the essays collected in this book. The authors here have studied them with a new thrust and attempted to arrive at innovative conclusions. The essays deal with the analytical method of historical linkages between India and South East Asia, with critical observations of contemporary dynamics of international politics.

The first three essays focus on India's linkages with South East Asian countries from a historical perspective. Suchandra Ghosh explores the influence of early Indian political culture on the polity of the Indrapura dynasty of Champa (Vietnam) in ancient times. Looking at the inscriptions of the Champa rulers found in Central and South Vietnam, the author examines the functioning of their monarchical polity comparable to early Indian monarchical structure. She has investigated the influence of Kamandaka's *Nitisara*, a Sanskrit text on polity, on the political culture of this dynasty, dealing with the nature of the relations between the king and the ministers or nobles, and the position of the royal officers in the political structure of the kingdom. Ghosh has studied the content of the inscriptions speaking about the ruling elites or the high officials, and the power and position enjoyed by them that was largely derived from a close connection with the royal family. It is known that some of the high officials were as powerful as the king, had profound knowledge in political affairs, advised the king in administering the kingdom, and had matrimonial relations with the royal house. The families of these high officials equalled the rulers in social position, virtues, and riches as well. They were highly lauded by the rulers of the Indrapura dynasty and received many accolades from the latter. The author further analyses the reasons behind the importance given to the nobilities by the rulers and illustrates that the formation of the monarchical polity of Champa along with the bureaucratic machinery, particularly the idea of maintaining a friendly relation between the king and his courtiers, was a result of its interaction with India.

The search of the Bengali intellectuals in the first half of the twentieth century for a Greater India in South East and East Asia, and the continuity of this search even in postcolonial times, have been highlighted by Sarvani Gooptu who argues that since the 1920s, a group of Bengali intellectuals was trying to explore the presence of India's cultural influence in South East Asia. The influence of India's art, architecture, music, and religion was found there through the ages. It has been pointed out that Indian cultural traits that existed there cherished the hope for the present that Indians could create a brighter future. The essay throws light on the various strands of thought that shaped Bengali intellectual activity for a Greater India to South East Asia, with the noble intention of broadening India's cultural and spiritual linkages. Tagore, one of the celebrities of modern India, was an exponent of that idea that was propagated and popularized through journals like *Prabasi* and *The Modern Review,* which were widely acclaimed. Another important journal, *Bharatbarsha* also made similar attempts. The essays and travelogues, written by the literary men including Tagore, Kalidas Nag, Jadunath Sarkar, etc., published in these journals talked about the ancient and contemporary cultural links between India and Asia. The author argues that the intellectual movement of the 1920s and 30s that looked forward to the friendship and cultural ties between India and South East Asia can be upheld as the best-illustrated example of India's effort to reawaken the historical linkages with South East Asia.

The principal theme that figures in the third essay is the migration of Indians to colonial Burma, the underlying causes of the migration, and their role in the economic development of Burma. Stating the fact that there were close cultural ties between India and Burma from ancient times, Aparajita Dhar explains that a large number of Indians migrated to Burma in the nineteenth century when communication between the two countries developed as a result of the emergence of steam navigation companies. Indians were attracted by the opportunities for trade and jobs in cultivation, railways, and commercial firms in colonial Burma. She examines how Indian labourers, predominantly illiterate and unskilled adult males engaged in agricultural production and processing industries, contributed to the development of the colonial economy in Burma. Moreover, Indian financiers, particularly chettiar moneylenders, were found to provide the required working capital for agriculture and commerce. At the same time, an investigation has been made into how

Indian immigration caused overcrowding and problems of housing and unsanitary conditions in the coolie lines, resulting in the spread of communicable diseases from the late nineteenth century. It became a matter of concern for the colonial administration and consequently, health measures were adopted to tackle the situation. However, the relations between the Burmans and the migrated Indians gradually turned to be strained and the essay portrays that story from the 1930s when Indian immigrants were blamed for the economic distress of the Burmans and the slogan 'Burma for the Burmans' was repeatedly chanted. This ultimately resulted in a huge exodus of Indians from Burma to India.

On the other hand, the rest of the essays concentrate on various aspects of India's Look East Policy from the perspective of contemporary inter-country relationships. Man Mohini Kaul in her essay has focused on the contours of India's transition from Look East to Act East Policy by examining the dynamics of India-ASEAN engagement that evolved since the 1990s. She delves into the factors that accounted for ASEAN's success as a 'successful and sustainable' regional organization. Her essay also throws light on ASEAN's economic engagement with China, while also underscoring the threat posed by China in recent times by the constant muscle-flexing in the South China Sea. India has also been described here as the new entrant in the South China Sea imbroglio. Thus, this essay identifies the broad trends that have emerged in South East Asia in recent times and also the nontraditional security threats that could dismantle the stability of the region. Interestingly, the author suggests ways in which India could sustain its Act East Policy by placing its engagement with ASEAN on a 'high-growth trajectory'.

The achievements of India in its attempt to promote greater regional integration with ASEAN through the Look East Policy has been discussed by Tridib Chakraborti, focusing the areas such as trade and defence where India was successful. India's engagement with the ASEAN countries at the East Asian Summit, which was first held in 2005, was lauded. Equally commendable was India's participation in the Initiative for Asian Integration (IAI). He has identified the areas, such as piracy and trafficking, where India and the ASEAN countries can cooperate and highlighted the obstacles to India's ambition to become a major player in Asian politics. Some of these were China's hostile attitude towards India and India's lack of political will to lend added weight to its relationship with Myanmar. The essay ends with the author's recommendation for a more 'pragmatic, practical, and effective role' to be played by India in South Asian and South East Asian geopolitics.

Jatindra Nath Saikia looks into how the expanding bilateral ties between India and Thailand could strengthen the foundation of India's Look East Policy and Thailand's Look West Policy, respectively. He highlights India's north-east and its connectivity with Thailand that could promote India's integration with South East Asia. He delineates the present nature of engagement between India's north-east and Thailand. By harping on the cultural similarities between the Thais and the people of Assam, in particular, the author suggests ways in which India's north-east and Thailand could cooperate in forging meaningful cultural and economic ties and also recommends collaboration in areas such as sports, services, technical and job-oriented educations, food processing, etc.

Suthiphand Chirativat and Kornkarun Cheewatrakoolpong examine the nature of Thailand's trade with the South East Asian neighbours, especially with the four neighbouring countries of Cambodia, Laos, Malaysia, and Myanmar. They point out how Thailand's trade with Myanmar, in particular, could open up new avenues of trade and connectivity with South Asia with special implications for India and its north-east, thus promoting both India's Look East Policy and Thailand's Look West Policy. Pondering on the ways in which Thailand could strengthen its economic linkages with India's north-east, the authors underline certain obstacles, such as lack of proper transport and logistics, customs procedures, the absence of sufficient infrastructure in the north-east, and most importantly, lack of awareness of the business practices on both sides.

Looking toward the east constitutes an important aspect of India's foreign policy since the 1990s and henceforth India has been looking to the East and South East Asian neighbours to consolidate ties of friendship and mutual understanding. It is against this backdrop that Anasua Basu Ray Chaudhury delves into how north-east India can play an important role in building up connectivity and cooperation with eastern and south-eastern neighbouring countries. The author here lays stress on physical infrastructural connectivity by road, rail, air, and water through India's north-east, which is one of the key strategic points of India and could help the geoeconomic links with the countries to the east and south-east. The initiatives taken in launching the projects and programmes in this regard by the Government of India and assistance provided by an international monetary agency like Asian Development Bank (ADB) have also been discussed. Taking into account that physical connectivity would strengthen bilateral and multilateral ties among the nations, the author has examined the importance of the Asian Highway Network that would connect India through its north-eastern region with East and South East Asia. She adds that the transborder road connectivity would promote economic development through quick and easy movements of people and goods, along with enhancing exports, development of industry and tourism, etc., giving the central argument that India's Look East Policy would be highly successful if India looks at east through its north-east.

In the last essay, Rajen Singh Laishram argues that India should prioritize overland connectivity with South East Asia through its north-east. Considering overland connectivity as an 'intrinsic component' of India's engagement with the East Asian and ASEAN countries, the author demonstrates how overland connectivity could promote greater trade and economic cooperations with the South East Asian countries, besides facilitating greater cultural ties through sports, tourism, and academic and medical researches. It is also argued that cooperation emerging from increased physical connectivity with South East Asia will enable easy movement of people and goods across borders, buttress regional production networks, attract greater investment, and also contribute significantly to poverty alleviation. These will, in turn, reduce regional development gaps and minimize regional conflicts.

The contributors of these essays highlight some of the important yet neglected aspects of India's relation with South East Asian countries in a rational and objective manner. A great deal of work remains to be done in respect of India-South East Asia connection through the ages. This collection aims to supplement the general findings by politico-historical studies about different facets of India-South East Asia relation and provide the stimulus to further enquiry. This may be useful as a core text at all colleges/universities teaching international relations, political science, and history. More so, it may grip the attention of the research centres and Non-Governmental Organizations (NGOs)/International Non-Governmental Organizations (INGOs) working in India and South East Asia, specially with Myanmar, Thailand, and Vietnam.

Notes

1. A.D. Pusalkar, 'Cultural Interrelation between India and the Outside World before Asoka', in *The Cultural Heritage of India*, vol. I, ed. Suniti Kumar Chatterjee et al., Kolkata: Ramkrishna Mission, 2013, p. 157.
2. Dong-son civilization, a bronze-using civilization dating around 300 BCE, which was developed, though not homogeneous and evenly spread, in the mainland deltas and low-lying plains of Java, when the people built up a

society of their own, based on irrigated cultivation, sharing the benefits and problems common to the inhabitants of monsoon Asia. D.R. Sar Desai, *Southeast Asia: Past & Present*, 4th edn., New Delhi: Harper Collins, 1997, p. 14.

3. Ibid.

4. D.J.M. Tate, *The Making of Southeast Asia*, vol. I, Kuala Lumpur: Oxford University Press, 1971, p. 10.

5. H.G. Quaritch Wales, *The Making of Greater India*, 2nd edn, London: Bernard Quaritch, 1961, p. 26.

6. Brian Harrison, *Southeast Asia: A Short History*, 3rd edn, New York: Macmillan, 1967, p. 12

7. For details, see G. Coedes, *The Making of South East Asia*, tr. H.M. Wright, London: Routledge and Kegan Paul, 1966, p. 52; Sar Desai, *Southeast Asia*, p. 17.

8. Sar Desai, *Southeast Asia*, p. 1; Tate, *The Making of Southeast Asia*, vol. I, p. 11.

9. For details, see Debarati Ganguli and Suchandra Ghosh, 'The Greater India Society and R.C. Majumdar's Perception of India-Myanmar Relations', in *India-Myanmar Relations: Historical Links to Contemporary Convergences*, ed. Lipi Ghosh, New Delhi: Paragon, 2016, pp. 75–86.

10. For details, see Hermann Kulke, 'The Concept of Cultural Convergence Revisited: Reflections on India's Early Influence in Southeast Asia', in *Asian Encounters: Exploring Connected Histories*, ed. Upinder Singh and Parul Pandya Dhar, New Delhi: Oxford University Press, 2014, pp. 3–19.

11. For details, see R.C. Majumdar, *Hindu Colonies in the Far East*, 2nd edn., Calcutta: Firma K.L. Mukhopadhyay Agents, 1963, pp. 8–16.

12. For details, see J.D. Legge, 'The Writing of Southeast Asian History', in *The Cambridge History of Southeast Asia*, vol. I, ed. Nicholas Tarling, Cambridge: Cambridge University Press, 1992, pp. 1–50.

13. Legge, 'The Writing of Southeast Asian History', p. 7.

14. For details, see J.C. van Leur, *Indonesian Trade and Society: Essays in Asian Social and Economic History*, The Hague, 1955, pp. 95, 103; cited in Legge, 'The Writing of Southeast Asian History', pp. 8–25.

15. Legge, 'The Writing of Southeast Asian History', pp. 8–25.

16. Ibid., p. 8.

17. Wales, *The Making of Greater India*, p. 27.

18. Coedes, *The Making of South East Asia*, p. 50.

19. For details, see Ganguli and Ghosh, 'The Greater India Society', p. 82.

20. For details, see Kulke, 'The Concept of Cultural Convergence', p. 8.

21. Ibid., pp. 8–9.

22. Ibid., pp. 9–10.

23. For details, see Lipi Ghosh, ed., *India-Myanmar Relations: Historical Links to Contemporary Convergences*, New Delhi: Paragon, 2016, pp. 12–15.

24. Ibid., 'Introduction', pp. 3–4.

25. Lipi Ghosh, ed., 'Introduction', in *Connectivity and Beyond: Indo–Thai Relations through Ages*, Kolkata: The Asiatic Society, 2009, p. xiv.

26. Sunait Chutintaranond, 'Indian-Thai Relationship in Cultural Dimension: The Issue of Indianization vs Localization', in *Connectivity and Beyond: Indo–Thai Relations through Ages*, Kolkata: The Asiatic Society, 2009, pp. 78–87.

27. Lipi Ghosh, 'Indian Revolutionaries and Subhas Chandra Bose in Thailand: The Era of Plaek Phibul Songgram', in *Connectivity and Beyond: Indo–Thai Relations through Ages*, Kolkata: The Asiatic Society, 2009, pp. 154–179.

28. Sar Desai, *Southeast Asia*, p. 25.

29. For details, see J.G. De Casperis and I.W. Mabbett, 'Religion and Popular Beliefs in Southeast Asia before c. 1500', in *The Cambridge History of Southeast Asia*, ed. Nicholas Tarling, Cambridge: Cambridge University Press, 1992, pp. 276–340.

30. Sar Desai, *Southeast Asia*, p. 58.

31. Harrison, *Southeast Asia: A Short History*, p. 18.

32. For details, see Lipi Ghosh, ed., *Rabindranath Tagore in Southeast Asia: Culture, Connectivity and Bridge Making*, New Delhi: Primus, 2016, pp. 1–20.

33. Ghosh, ed., *India Myanmar Relations*, pp. 3–4.

34. For details, see Tate, *The Making of Southeast Asia*, vol. 2, Kuala Lumpur: Oxford University Press, 1979, pp. 19, 23.

35. Bipan Chandra et al., *India since Independence*, New Delhi: Penguin, 2008, p. 191.

36. For details, see Ramchandra Guha, ed., *Makers of Modern India*, New Delhi: Penguin, 2010, pp. 340–3.

37. C. Raja Mohan, 'India's Geopolitics and Southeast Asian Security', *Southeast Asian Security*, Singapore: Institute of Southeast Asian Studies (ISEAS), 2008, p. 48, see http://www.jstor.org/stable/27913351, accessed 26 June 2016.

38. G.V.C. Naidu, 'Wither the Look East Policy: India and Southeast Asia', *Strategic Analysis*, vol. 28, no. 2, April–June 2004, p. 332.

39. S.D. Muni, ed., 'Review of Baladas Ghoshal', *India and Southeast Asia: Challenges and Opportunities*, New Delhi: Konark (in association with India International Centre), 1996; *Contemporary Southeast Asia*, vol. 19, no. 2, September 1997, pp. 209–12.

40. See Frederic Grare and Amitabh Mattoo, eds., in *India and ASEAN: The Politics of India's Look East Policy*, New Delhi: Manohar, (in association with Centre de Sciences Humaine, New Delhi, Institute of Southeast Asian Studies, Singapore, and Centre for the Study of National Security Policy, New Delhi), 2001, p. 93.

41. Thongkholal Haokip, 'India's Look East Policy: Its Evolution and Approach', *South Asian Survey*, vol. 18, no. 2, 2011, p. 248.
42. Ministry of External Affairs, *Annual Report 1991–2*. New Delhi: Government of India, 1992, p. ii.
43. Grare and Mattoo, eds., *India and ASEAN*, p. 93.
44. Ministry of External Affairs, *Annual Report 1996–7*, New Delhi: Government of India, 1997, p. 118.
45. Statement by I.K. Gujral, Minister of External Affairs of India, ASEAN Post Ministerial Conference, Jakarta, 20–21 July 1996, see http://www. aseansec.org/4308.htm, accessed 10 July 2009.
46. Joint Press Release, The First ASEAN-India Joint Cooperation Committee Meeting New Delhi, 14–16 November 1996, see http://asean.org/?static_ post=joint-press-release-the-first-asean-india-joint-cooperation-committee- meeting-new-delhi-14-16-november-1996, accessed 10 June 2016.
47. See Kripa Sridharan, *The ASEAN Region in India's Foreign Policy*, Aldershot: Dartmouth, 1996; and Christophe Jaffrelot, 'India's Look East Policy: An Asianist Strategy in Perspective', *India Review*, vol. 2, no. 2, 2003, pp. 35–68.
48. Vinod Anand and Rahul Mishra, 'India's "Act East" Policy: A Perspective', Vivekananda International Foundation, 20 November 2014, see http://www. vifindia.org, accessed 14 June 2016.
49. Ministry of External Affairs, 'India-ASEAN Relations', Government of India, New Delhi, 2013, see https://www.mea.gov.in/Portal/ForeignRelation/ India- ASEAN_Relations.pdf, accessed 14 June 2016.
50. Ibid.
51. Ibid.
52. Subir Bhaumik, 'Look East through Northeast: Challenges and Prospects for India', *ORF Occasional Paper 51*, New Delhi: Observer Research Foundation, June 2014, p. 1.
53. Ibid.
54. Dhrubajyoti Bhattacharjee, 'India's Vision on Act East Policy', New Delhi: Indian Council for World Affairs, 2016, pp. 2–3.
55. Ibid.
56. Ibid.
57. Narendra Modi, 'Media Statements by Prime Minister of India and Prime Minister of Vietnam in New Delhi', 28 October 2014, see http:// www.mea.gov.in/incoming-visitdetail.htm?24143, accessed 10th June 2016; Narendra Modi, 'Opening Statement by Prime Minister at the 12th India-ASEAN Summit', (speech, India-ASEAN Summit, Nay Pyi Taw, Myanmar, 12 November 2014), see http://www.mea.gov.in/incoming- visitdetail.htm?24143/.
58. Yaduvendra Mathur, 'India's Look East-Act East Policy: A Bridge to the Asian Neighbourhood', Symbiosis Institute of International Studies, International Relations Conference 2014, see http://www.irconference.in/ assets/IRC_conference_proceedings.pdf, accessed 11 June 2016.

59. 'India Needs Policy to Look East, Link West: Narendra Modi', *Deccan Herald*, 25 September 2014, see http://www.deccanherald.com/content/432698/india-needs-policy-look-east.htm, accessed 12 June 2016.

60. M.P. Bezbaruah's comments on 'Northeast Region of India within India's LEP', *India's Look East-Act East Policy: A bridge to the Asian Neighbourhood*, Proceedings of International Relations Conference, Symbiosis Institute of International Studies, Symbiosis International University, Pune, 2014, p. 59.

1

Representations of Ministers and Functionaries in the Epigraphs (*c.*909–19 CE) of Indrapura Dynasty of Champa (Vietnam)

Influence of Early Indian Political Culture?

Suchandra Ghosh

Introduction

D IVERSE INTERPRETATIONS have been offered by scholars regarding the nature of interaction between different regions of India and South East Asia in the early periods of history.[1] Religious monuments, images, inscriptions, and archaeological material appearing from the first millennium CE have been interpreted as showing distinctly 'Indian' traits in the adoption of Brahmanical and Buddhist cults, political ideologies, and a ritual language. Scholars are unanimous regarding the recognition of the presence of Indian inputs in regions of South East Asia in whatever form it might be. In order to understand the interaction in the sphere of polity, we intend to narrow the focus to a very important region of early South East Asia, located on a narrow strip of land that runs for more than a thousand kilometres along the coast of Central Vietnam, known as the Kingdom of Champa.[2] It is a generic name occurring in a sixth century inscription of one Sambhuvarman, and is used to describe a series of small coastal kingdoms that developed in Central Vietnam during the first millennium CE.[3] Compressed between the mountain and the sea, the entire area consists of small regions of flat terrain that are difficult to access, except by sea. Given such geographic fragmentation and the constrained nature of the coastal plains, exchange and communication along this coast were easily undertaken by sea. To the west lay the Truong Son Range, which provided a major obstacle to communication with the Mekong Valley, save for three passes. This long coastline was nevertheless strategically placed, particularly as the pace of maritime commerce accelerated with the Chinese interest in a southern route to India and the Roman Empire.[4] Trade and exchange acted as an agency of change in South East Asia, and Vietnam in particular, bringing forth large scale transformations in the existing societies. The adoption of Sanskrit and Brahmi scripts; of Indian philosophic, astronomic, and calendrical systems of knowledge; of brick temple construction; of ideas concerning sacred and secular space; and the adoption of Indian religious iconography and concepts attest to the intellectual connection with India during the first millennium CE.[5] It has to be mentioned here that the earlier notion of several provinces within a homogenous state of Champa has been questioned, and it is more likely that the political organization of Champa was fluid and changed with time.[6]

Much of the information on the culture of Champa after the fourth century CE is derived from inscriptions found in Central and Southern Vietnam. A majority of them are stela inscriptions placed in temple complexes constructed by the rulers. Later from the last quarter of the ninth century CE, a short portion in Cham language began to appear at the end of the inscriptions, the purpose being to convey to the local people the royal order of land grant contained in the Sanskrit portion of the inscriptions. Being court documents, they are useful in understanding the kingship and polity in the region concerned. They tell us about different ruling families in Central and Southern Vietnam that often coexisted with one another and still claimed themselves uniformly as the rulers of Champa. Comparison with scripts current in early India may throw light on the particular region which provided the inspiration to adopt this script. This may be again useful in understanding the network of the interaction.[7]

The inscriptions of the Champa rulers clearly bring to light the functioning of a monarchical polity which could be compared to some extent with early Indian monarchical structure. This essay attempts to suggest how prescriptions of a Sanskrit text on polity, Kamandaka's *Nitisara* (*NS*) which could be placed between *c.*500–700 CE, had some bearing on the political culture of a dynasty of Champa known as the 'Đồng Dương' or 'Indrapura dynasty', which was the so called sixth dynasty. M. Vickery links the re-emergence of the north through this dynasty to another change in international trade routes from China to Indonesia and India.[8] The political culture of Indrapura relates to the position of the ministers and nobles in the courts who were called the 'eyes' or even 'mind' of the king.[9] The essay seeks to understand the reciprocal relation between the king and the ministers/nobles in the courts of the kings of Champa, taking recourse to three inscriptions dated from 909–19 CE. These inscriptions form a part of the 25 inscriptions ascribed to Indrapura. In the words of Vickery, they delineate a coherent area from Quảng Nam to Quảng Bình and include the only epigraphy in the published corpus found north of Huế. Thus, Đồng Dương or the Indrapura dynasty expanded its area northwards. The epigraphs that have been studied are the Hoa-Que Stele Inscription of Bhadravarman dated 909/910 CE,[10] Nhan-Bieu Stele Inscription of Indravarman II dated 911/912 CE,[11] and Lai-Trung Stele Inscription of Indravarman II dated 918/919 CE.[12] An attempt has been made to move beyond the kings and understand the position of the royal officers in the political structure of the kingdom. Unfortunately, there are limitations to the sources and one could only locate three inscriptions of a given period and geographical space, which belonged to the Đồng Dương dynasty.

Đồng Dương was known as Indrapura and for about a century it was the centre of power of Champa, the Nagara Champa. A look at the chronology of the rulers of Indrapura, following Schewyer,would show that the first ruler of this dynasty, Indravarman, assumed the title *champadhipa*, *maharaja*, and *rajadhiraja*; and came to power in 875 CE.[13] His lineage is said to be from Bhrigu. His territory, according to the epigraphic material, extended from Chau Sa in the south to Bac Ha in the north, near Port de Annam. The next ruler, a nephew of Indravarman I from matrilineal descent, Jaya Simhavarman's territories extended also from Chau Sa in the south to My Duc, a little far from Annam. Bhadravarman was an indirect cousin and his territory comprised all of the areas between Kon Klor at further south and Nhan Bieu in the north. The inscriptions of Indravarman II were mostly concentrated in the central region.

Content of the Inscriptions

First, we take note of what the inscriptions say about the ruling elites. We begin with Hoa-Que Stele Inscription of Bhadravarman dated 909/910 CE. Line 19 of the inscription refers to a minister called Ajna

Mahasamanta, owner of various riches, who obtained wealth and riches through the favour of his king. This minister was honoured by the king with a garland on his head, the forehead being marked by a tilak. He was also granted ornaments for the ears, earrings; a pair of robes; a golden girdle string; an excellent dagger with a golden sheath; a vessel; a *chiranda*, white as silver; an umbrella made of the feathers of a peacock; a multitude of pitchers and vases; and a palanquin with a silver staff. The inscription clarifies that this kind of honour was very difficult to receive and it was only possible for the *mahasamanta* because of his faithful performance of the royal command. This *mahasamanta* had two brothers who were also ministers. One was Ajna Narendra Narpavitra, who was versed with all sacrificial ceremonies and all treatises dealing with the Saiva religion; and the youngest was Ajna Jayendrapati, who was well-versed in all the shastras and renowned in the world like Angirasa for his intelligence and fortune. Jayendrapati also had the caliber of understanding the messages sent by kings from different countries by instantly looking at them. He was also a poet and like the eldest brother, he too received a palanquin, a parasol decorated with peacock feathers, a golden sheath of a sword, vases, pitchers, silver vessels, girdles, earrings, a *chiranda*, a pair of robes, etc.[14]

Their father was Ajna Sarthavaha who was the brother of the Chief Queen of King Sri Indravarman I. From the inscription, we further learn that these three brothers along with their sister erected an image of Maha Rudradeva in imitation of the features of their father. A similar image of Bhagavati was erected by them in their native place in imitation of their mother. Moreover, the youngest son Ajna Jayendrapati also established, in his native place, the god Sri Mahasivalingesvara for the worship of Siva and the sake of his own glory. Thus, we come across a family of high officials, having ties with the royal family, so powerful that one of its members could erect a temple for his glory and get it inscribed.

The second inscription is the Nhan-Bieu Stele Inscription of Indravarman II dated 911/912 CE. It introduces us to another family of high officials that had also marital relations with the royalty. The inscription gives us a detailed account of Pov Klun Pilih Rajadvarah who was the son of the cousin of Tribhuvanadevi, the Queen of King Jayasimhavarman. This Rajadvarah was the favourite captain (*ati vallabho nayaka*) of the King Sri Jaya Simhavarman who could have riches to his desire. We learn that he was sent to the capital of Yava-dvipa on a diplomatic mission, which he successfully completed (siddha yatra) and thus gained substantial wealth. The inscription then talks about the prosperity of Champa during the reign of Sri Jaya Simhavarman, and Rajadvarah continued to enjoy a high position. Sri Bhadravarman succeeded to the throne and Rajadvarah obtained the title of Pov Klun Sudandavasa. He was again sent to Yava-dvipa for the second time and attained success in his mission. As a prize, King Bhadravaman gave him agricultural fields/land in the villages of Sudan and Kumuvel. Rajadvarah further received the title of *akaladhipati* from the next ruler Indravarman II for the zeal he showed in serving the king. It appears from the inscription that his knowledge in political affairs enabled him to advise the king. Thus, he was truly performing the role of a confidante and since he served the earlier kings with integrity, King Indravarman took him into confidence. His eldest son (brother?) was called Sukrti Pov Klun Dharmapatha and he was a favourite of Indravarman. Along with his son, Rajadvarah established the temple of Devalingesvara as well as a monastery called Sri Vrddhalokesvara in the village of Chikir which was his as well as his mother's home.[15]

The third inscription, Lai-Trung Stele Inscription of Indravarman II dated 918/919 CE describes a noble man, a governor, who was the lord of Amarendrapura and was in the service of Sri Jaya Indravarman. Thus, according to William A. Southworth, within the kingdom of Indravarman, there is presence of another centre known as Amarendrapura which was ruled by the dignitary Po Yan pov ku Danay Pinan.[16] Amarendrapura was obviously distinct from Indrapura and could be Lai-Trung itself. It was located in the district of Hue. The qualities of Danay are described in a eulogistic manner. It is said that he possessed all the qualities of Siva, performed meritorious work for which the sages were happy. He acquired fame, knowledge of scriptures, and riches; and among other things his praise was sung by all the learned men in all the regions. He established the temple of Siva in order to emancipate himself and his parents from this ocean of existence. Incidentally, Danay Pinan was also referred to in the Chausa Stele Inscription, datable to *c.*893 CE. Thus, he continued to be an important dignitary for a long period.

Interpreting the Inscriptions

The three inscriptions when studied together suggest the making of ministerial families who practically equalled the rulers in virtues as well as riches. From the same dynasty, there is an earlier inscription, the Ban-Lanh Stele Inscription of Jaya Simhavarman I dated 898 CE, where an officer in charge of coercive measures (*dandavaso*) is described as virtuous, wholly devoted to his master (*pati bhakti*), an asylum of glory arising from his prosperity, and famous as an ocean of intelligence. He is also said to have had a fortune superior to that of the king, full of nobility, well-practised in meritorious deeds, with a celestial face superior to that of the sun as it carried the entire Lakshmi day and night. Moreover, he received three names from the king—Isvarakalpa, Sivakalpa, and Srikalpa. Such kind of epithets and praise for officers is unique to the rulers of Indrapura. In the earlier inscriptions, there were scattered references to officials, e.g. there is mention of one senapati Par or a minister Ajna Manichaitya. But the reference was minimal and apart from these inscriptions, none of the other epigraphs were so eloquent about the families of ministers or dignitaries. It is clear that these inscriptions were actually issued by the ministers in the name of their kings. While we do not suggest that silence about nobility amounts to their non-existence, what is intriguing is their sudden visible existence in Indrapura. We know that inscriptions of Champa, in general, do not give us much information about bureaucracy. The question here arises as why the functionaries were given such importance. The detailed descriptions in the inscriptions of the bestowal of riches to these nobles or them being referred to have accumulated wealth are noteworthy. Was there any political compulsion on the part of the rulers to adorn these people? A reading of the inscriptions might lead us to some answer, however, inconclusive it might be.

This essay concentrates on certain terms used in the epigraphs. Interesting is the usage of the word *rajadhiraja*, which is used separately from *maharaja* or *champadhipa*. Literally, *rajadhiraja* means king of kings. This is a title which has been used in India by different rulers, e.g. *rajati raja* by the Kushanas. When there is such an expression 'king of kings', there might be an indication that there were subordinate minor kings around and one ruler reigned supreme over them. Though there is not much evidence, at least two cases show that there were local chiefs within the kingdom of the rulers of Indrapura who were practically independent, owing perhaps just a nominal allegiance to the ruler. Here we can cite the case of Danay Pinan, the ruler of Amarendrapura, who was a dignitary in *c.*893 CE and later on paved his way to become the lord of Amarendrapura. Another example is that of King (*nripa*) Mahindravarman ruling in Kon Klor in the province of Kontum during the period of the rulers of Indrapura. In the opinion of Schewyer, he enjoyed a kind of autonomy. This is evident from the fact that he established the image of Mahindraokesvara. Moreover, the reference to Ajna Jayendrapati as having the caliber of understanding the messages sent by kings from different countries by instantly looking at them suggests that the kingdom was in constant diplomatic interaction with other neighbouring rulers who could be friends or foes, and this minister was able to read the underlying messages of these rulers.

Considering the location of the kingdom of Indrapura that was exposed to attack from the Dai Viet in the north and other neighbouring rulers, the rulers of Indrapura had to be well prepared for the safety of their kingdom. Thus, they kept their ministers/close confidantes in good humour. This is evident from the gifts that King Bhadravarman offered to Ajna Mahasamanta and his youngest brother Ajna Jayendrapati. The use of the term *ajna* is interesting. *Ajna* may be a short form of *ajnadharaka/ajnaparipalaka*, an executor of the royal order, which is used in the sense of an officer or minister.[17] Here, it acts as an honorific and is distinguished from Sri, which is used for kings and gods. The use of the term *mahasamanta* as a proper name is also intriguing. The tendency to use these official titles as proper names was also seen in an earlier inscription. The Bakul Stele Inscription, found near the village of Chung My in the valley south of Phanrang, ascribes the meritorious act to a *nayaka* who was famous by the name of Samanta.[18] *Mahasamanta* is generally translated as the 'great chieftain' or a vassal chief, sometimes holding the post of a minister or a governor.[19] It appears from the description in the inscription that he was a minister. Could it be that *samanta* or *mahasamanta* was so famous in his official designation that these came to be used as proper names?

These inscriptions betray a clear knowledge of the early Indian political system. Here attention is drawn to a Sanskrit text on polity, Kamandaka's *Nitisara*,[20] which could be placed between *c*.500–700 CE. Kamandaka's treatment of the king's relationship with his courtiers or discussion on court protocol largely follows Kautilya's dictum *Arthasastra* (5.4).[21] It is interesting to note that some of the enumerations of the *Nitisara*, regarding courtiers, to some extent fit well with the kind of information the Champa inscriptions offer. The *Nitisara* talks about seven types of people associated with the king, of which there was a category called the king's own men (*nija*).[22] This category included his courtiers (*anujivis*), to whom he was tied with complex ties of reciprocity. The *anujivin* was to be conversant with what was appropriate to place and time, and be an expert in interpreting the king's gestures, appearance, and movements. The summary of their duties included giving the king good counsel and dissuading him from inappropriate acts (*NS* 5.8.50).[23] A corroboration of such a situation was found where Rajadvarah, who was given the title of *akaladhipati,* was said to have the capability of advising the king as to what was good and what was bad (*ishta-anishteshu naradhipasya*). In fact, ministers were expected to direct the king away from any faulty action, which could arise from weaknesses like pride, anger, or conceit. The use of phrases like *ativallabha* in relation to the ruler indicates that the relative status of these courtiers were determined by the level of proximity to the king. This is clearly manifested in the case of Ajna Mahasamanta who is also said to have been seated next to the king in the palanquin, apart from being given gifts. This suggests the exalted status of *mahasamanta*. There is an interesting example of one *padaraksha* known to be an officer of King Bhadravarman, who founded the temple of Dharmalingesvara between 908–17 CE. *Padaraksha* can be literally translated as one who protects the feet of the king, which means he protects the territory on which the king rules. Such a designation is quite unique.

Another title used was *nayaka*. *Nayaka* was the title of a subordinate ruler or could also be used in the sense of a feudatory chief. When Rajadvarah was referred to as *ativallabha nayaka,* it signified that he was very close to the ruler and this was particularly the reason for choosing him as an emissary to Yava-dvipa, which could be a potential threat to Indrapura. This relationship between the king and his courtiers was no doubt rooted in the contemporary political context—specifically in the need for the king to create a group of capable and loyal courtiers around him. It is interesting to note that Indravarman I claimed his descent from the Bhrigu lineage. Claim of descent from a high lineage was the first step towards seeking legitimation or asserting the legitimate right to rule. Lineages in Champa had become purely political references and there was no more an ethnic connotation.

Before concluding, a few words about the name 'Sarthavaha' would perhaps not be out of place here. In the Hoa-Que Stele Inscription, there is a reference to Ajna Sarthavaha as the father of the three important dignitaries, and whose sister was the queen. Like the proper name Mahasamanta, use of *sarthavaha* as a proper name is unique and interesting. *Sarthavaha* generally means a merchant, a caravan trader to be more precise. This would imply that this Sarthavaha was rich enough to be socially acceptable for his sister to be married into the royal family. He could have been a royal merchant, having a place among the councilors. There are instances from India about the importance of *sreshthis* in the royal court and *Prathama Sarthavaha,* meaning the head of the *sarthavahas*, acting as a signatory in land sale deeds in the Gupta period.[24] We know that economically, this region was gaining supremacy. It was linked to international trade routes. The production centres of Gio Linh and Vinh Linh were both linked to trading centres at the river mouths to mountain routes which brought in rare forest products. A case in point is the growing demand of aloes wood from Champa in the international market. According to Schewyer, the centre of amassing such riches was the citadel-capital of Da Nghi-Nhan Bieu. Hence, in this milieu of politico-economic ascendance and connecting trade networks, the position of a trader was very high in the royal court and, thus, could be considered a member of the core group of the ruler. Gradually, his sons would attain higher positions in the court. It is also interesting to note that the children of Ajna Sarthavaha were installing images in imitation of the features of their father and mother. And so their social position was almost equal to the king.

What appears from the foregoing discussion is that, though not in an explicit manner, these inscriptions offer important insights into the political culture of the kingdom of Champa during the rule of the dynasty of Indrapura. We are aware of the functioning of a monarchical polity centring in the Thu Bon Valley between fifth and eight centuries CE. During the time of the rulers of Indrapura, it further crystallized with bureaucratic machinery, which could be considered as an Indic borrowing. A clear evidence of hierarchy among officials is found in these inscriptions, albeit in a nebulous form. In spite of exalted titles taken by the king, the importance of nobility was recognized and the kings shared a complex relation of devotion, loyalty, and friendship with them. This was an influence of the early Indian political culture. The *Nitisara* indicates the great importance of the king's kinsfolk in the world of political power. Apart from their place in the royal household, the kinsfolk were allies too (*NS* 4.7.7.4). A similar situation is reflected when the king's kin are actually his ministers or subordinate rulers. Thus, it can be suggested that interaction with India helped in the formation of the idea of a reciprocal relation between the king and his courtiers.

Notes

1. Hermann Kulke, 'The Concept of Cultural Convergence Revisited, Reflections on India's Early Influence in Southeast Asia', in *Asian Encounters, Exploring Connected Histories,* ed. Upinder Singh and Parul

Pandya Dhar, Delhi: Oxford University Press, 2014, pp. 3–19. This recent essay gives us an idea of the different views related to 'Indianization'.

2. R.C. Majumdar, *Champa: History and Culture of an Indian Colonial Kingdom in the Far East 2nd to 16th centuries AD*, Delhi: Gyan, 2008; Phuong Tran Ky, *Vestiges of Champa Civilization*, Hanoi: The Gioi, 2004, p. 1.

3. William A. Southworth, 'The Coastal States of Champa', in *Southeast Asia from Prehistory to History*, ed. Ian Glover and Peter Bellwood, London: Routledge, 2004, p. 211.

4. Charles Higham, *Early Cultures of Mainland Southeast Asia*, Bangkok: Art Media Resources, 2002, p. 268.

5. Suchandra Ghosh, 'Champa: A Politico-Cultural Study', in *Ancient Indian Trade and Cultural Relations With South East Asia*, ed. Chittabrata Palit, Kolkata: Calcutta Chamber of Commerce and Maulana Abul Kalam Azad Institute of Asian Studies, 2013, pp. 88–101.

6. M. Vickery, 'Champa Revised', Working paper, Series No. 37, Asia Research Institute, National University of Singapore, 2005, p. 34.

7. For the Champa inscriptions, K.H. Golzio, ed., *Inscriptions of Champa*, Aachen: Shaker Verlag, 2004.

8. Vickery, 'Champa Revised'.

9. Daud Ali, *Courtly Culture and Political Life in Early Medieval India*, Cambridge: Cambridge University Press, 2004, p. 57.

10. K.H. Golzio, ed., 'Hoa-Que Stele Inscription of Bhadravarman (dated 909/910 CE)', in *Inscriptions of Champa*, Aachen: Shaker Verlag, 2004, pp. 97–106.

11. K.H. Golzio, ed., 'Nhan-Bieu Stele Inscription of Indravarman III (dated 911/12 CE)', in *Inscriptions of Champa*, Aachen: Shaker Verlag, 2004, pp. 107–14.

12. K.H. Golzio, ed., 'Lai-trung Stele Inscription of Indravarman II (dated 918/919 CE)', in *Inscriptions of Champa*, Aachen: Shaker Verlag, 2004, pp. 117–19.

13. Anne-Valérie Schwever, 'Le dynastie d'Indrapura (Quảng Nam, Viet Nam)', *Southeast Asian Archaeology 1998*, Proceedings of the 7th International Conference of the European Association of Southeast Asian Archaeologists, Berlin, 31 August–4 September 1998, Wibke Lobo and Stefanie Reimann Editors, Centre for Southeast Asian Studies, University of Hull, Special Issue & Ethnologisches Museum, Staatliche Museen zu Berlin, Stiftung Preussischer Kulturbesitz, pp. 205–17.

14. Golzio, 'Hoa-Que Stele Inscription of Bhadravarman (dated 909/910 CE)', p. 105.

15. Golzio, 'Nhan-Bieu Stele Inscription of Indravarman III (dated 911/12 CE)', p. 113.

16. Southworth, 'The Coastal States of Champa', pp. 209–33.

17. D.C. Sircar, *Indian Epigraphical Glossary*, Delhi: Motilal Banarsidass, 1966, p. 13.
18. K.H. Golzio, ed.,'Bakul Stele Inscription Dated 829/30 CE', in *Inscriptions of Champa,* Aachen: Shaker Verlag, 2004, pp. 55–6.
19. Sircar, *Indian Epigraphical Glossary*, p. 187.
20. Raja Rajendra Lal Mitra, ed., *The Nitisara by Kamandaki*, tr. Sisir Kumar Mitra, Kolkata: The Asiatic Society, 2008.
21. R.P. Kangle, *The Kautiliya Arthasastra*, pt I, Delhi: Motilal Banarsidass, 1986.
22. Upinder Singh, 'Politics, Violence and War in Kamandaka's Nitisara', in *Rethinking Early Medieval India*, New Delhi: Oxford University Press, 2011, p. 302.
23. Ibid., p. 112.
24. D.C. Sircar, 'Damodarpur Copper-Plate Inscription of the Time of Kumaragupta I-Gupta Year 124 (AD 444)', in *Select Inscriptions Bearing on Indian History and Civilization,* vol. I, Delhi: V.K. Publishing, 1993, p. 291.

2

The Search for the Soul of Bharat

Beyond Its Territorial Limits

Sarvani Gooptu

NATIONALISM SEEKS to rejuvenate and reinvent itself from time to time through different means, forms, and interpretations. The Indian national movement was no exception and till this day, we try to understand and analyse the different ideas and movements that were propounded by various individuals and groups. One of the many forms of nationalism that were being experimented within the second and third decades of the twentieth century was to look for a Bharat, historically and culturally, beyond the territorial boundaries of colonial India. It developed into a movement through the efforts of some of the leading intellectuals of Bengal, who tried to spread the idea of a Greater India in Asia, in the past and present, to the people.

The quest for a national identity through a historical understanding of the land and her people from ancient times has been reflected on the literary platform in various degrees. The complexes of the colonial subjectivity attempted an imaginary recovery through intellectual exercise in the study of history, for that remained the sole source of recognition for the nation and her people. During the previous decades, when the idea of the nation was being imagined, then too its proponents and visionaries looked beyond mere territorial constraints and let their imagination wander beyond seas and mountains to look for Bharat and its heroes. Bengali literature is full of such imaginative meanderings and travels. Through popular writings in books and journals, these proponents of nationalism tried to inspire high patriotism in their fellow countrymen by transforming a small and limited love for a locality and region into a larger love for the nation.

In the second decade of the twentieth century, during the years of lull in the aftermath of the aborted Non-cooperation Movement, an intellectual movement was being carried on by a group of historians and literary men to explore an arena where the glorious presence of Bharat remained intact and untrammelled by colonial arrogance. This arena was outside the territory of India in South East and East Asia where, as the Indo-French researches proved, India had spread her influence politically and culturally for many generations. This past was a time when narrow colonial interests had not been able to restrict the movement of Indian people, ideas, culture, and religion to its territorial boundaries; and India had taken a leading position in the Asian stage. These new discoveries of the explorations of the Indians outside India generated excitement and a hope for the present by which Indians could project the past into the present and create a new glorious future.

This search for a glorious India in Asia was on multiple levels, political and cultural, in the past and the present. The cultural pre-eminence that India had established in the other Asian countries in the past through religious, political, and culture explorations could be replicated even in the present, when the political element would be disregarded and cultural give and take would replace colonization. Thus, on this harmonious ground, a strong network of the countries of Asia would be created, connected by cultural ties and a common historical past. This was a movement in which the cultural leaders of the time would take lead and a mass base would be created by uniting the common people of all the countries of Asia. This united front would be formidable and yet would be free from chauvinism that plagued the nationalism.

Besides the essays and books in English and Bengali written in the 20s and 30s in the twentieth century, there was also an attempt to crystallize the various strands of thought into a united forum of intellectual activity through the founding of the Greater Indian Society. It is my aim to explore these various levels, through which a public opinion was being constructed for creation of a new facet of cultural nationalism, which broadened the Indian nationalism to an Asian one.

This ideological movement to look beyond the boundaries was both political and spiritual. On one hand, the idea was aimed at discrediting British scholarship which had created myths about India's isolation and limited her past achievements by looking at them through the prism of colonial mentality. On the other hand, creation of a strong public opinion through evoking images of a golden past when India sway politically and culturally over the Asian, together with an outlining of contemporary linkages would proclaim an advantage over the colonial powers through a show of cultural and historical solidarity between the nations of Asia. This linking of populations could become a powerful force against colonialism. But Rabindranath Tagore, one of the chief exponents of the movement, worried about the ease with which a country's nationalism could turn aggressive. The only way this danger could be minimized was through discovering a higher nationalism uncontaminated by political or economic greed. Only spiritual or cultural links could provide a long lasting bond, where exchanges were more important than influence. It was this philosophy of cultural and spiritual linkages that was stressed upon during the popularization of the mission through journals. As Tagore said in his essay 'Brihattara Bharat',[1] it should be the historical mission of all Indians to project the greatness of the nation to the world, and to discover the soul of the country in a wider arena because limited aspirations bring limited gains. Discovering the soul of Bharat outside the territorial limits would free Indian nationalism from the constraints that plagued it in his eyes. He expressed these ideas through popular articles in journals, books, and speeches within the country, as well as on his tours to other lands. In an interview, Tagore gave in Bombay soon after a tour in 1925, he was asked by the representative of the Free Press to explain the purpose and method of the mission of cultural unity. Tagore's reply was 'My idea is to establish contact with the whole world. In my view, India should not remain in utter obscurity. We should be able to take part in helping the world in her present situation and occupy an honoured place in the reconstruction of civilization.' To the question about how he proposed to achieve this, he replied, 'India should be linked both with east and west. . . . It is my belief that the recent visit to the Far East has helped to establish a cultural connection between India, China, and Japan.'[2]

He also experimented with cultural links at Visva-Bharati when he brought in teachers from different parts of Asia, and also incorporated the art and culture of the Asian countries into the curriculum. He took world tours and sent emissaries to acquire knowledge on the art and culture of the other countries, which he then applied in his university activities. Tagore and other intellectuals writing at this time spoke about a 'different and more long lasting colonization' which had been achieved by India, since her influence was not through arms but was spread through philosophic ideas and culture. This was something, no western colonial power had visualized. As proved by scholars and other people travelling to the countries of South East and East Asia, there was a warm acceptance of Indian civilization and culture for centuries there, and even in the second decade of the twentieth century, those ancient ties could be revived easily. This sense of pride in the achievement of the past was highlighted in the writing in these journals. There was an underlying hint that if the Indian mindset could be moved away from the Western orientation and an alternative focus of civilizational development discovered, British colonialism would be undermined and Indians would be empowered.

I must reiterate that all these ideas with their subtleties cannot be comprehensively dealt with in one paper and I am going to consider this as a pilot essay of a larger research. For this essay I have limited my discussion to articles in three journals—one English, *Modern Review* and two Bengali, *Prabashi* and *Bharatvarsha*, over the decade, from 1925 to 1935 approximately. I chose these two Bengali journals not simply because they were leading literary journals of the time, but also because they were led by two opposing camps of intellectuals: *Prabashi* was edited by Ramananda Chattopadhyay who was very close to Rabindranath Tagore; and *Bharatvarsha*, founded by Dwijendralal Roy, was edited by Jaladhar Sen belonging to the other end of the spectrum. Interestingly, both the journals have very similar essays and articles dealing with the ancient and present links between India and Asia. Every issue in both the journals during these years discussed findings and researches of Indian archaeologists and historians along with translations of the works of foreign scholars. Through travel writings and descriptive essays, there was a mission to educate the public about the different countries of Asia and their history and culture. In every article, a link was established between India and another Asian country whether in the past or present; political, religious, or cultural.

The nationalist agenda was fulfilled at many levels. An attempt was made to dissuade the public from believing in certain myths about India which had been popularized by the British scholars. As Kalidas Nag pointed out ironically,

... while it is possible for Mr Havell and Mr V.A. Smith to write elaborate histories of Indian art with only desultory allusions to Java or Cambodia, Coomaraswamy and his co-workers on the same field find it difficult not to devote a considerable part of their works to the detailed and intensive study of Far Eastern families of art and their Indian origins or affinities. It is no longer possible to discuss adequately the problems of Indian architecture, sculpture, or iconography without reference to their Asiatic context.[3]

Second, it was necessary to create an image of India which was not sullied by the present degradation under colonial rule. In the creation of this image, they had to find an India which was similar to the British yet totally dissimilar—in fact greater in moral achievement. The British Orientalists had created an image of India as a country in isolation who succumbed to British might. Now a new image of India was stressed upon, where she had been the colonizer in the past. It was a matter of pride but the nationalists shied away from being too British-like. So they spoke of a higher colonization, one which really benefited the colonized regions because there was no discrimination between the colonizers and the colonized, and therefore, was more acceptable and long lasting. India had established a wide '*Maha mandal* of friendship through a civilizational link of populations, represented through the exchange of pilgrims from and to China', as one of their spokesmen Nag called it. 'The main mantra of Greater India is service and friendship', he said.[4] Jadunath Sarkar talked about Further India, and did great service to the readers of *Modern Review* in collating and translating researches of French scholars in his article 'Hindu Influence on Further India'. He discussed how Indians from the sixth century BC 'impelled at first by the love of gain and later by the desire for religious propagation, crossed the sea at each instance to reach or settle themselves on the coasts of Indo China and of the Indian Archipelago.'[5]

The editorial view is sometimes expressed through choice of articles from other periodicals which, even when coming from the colonial viewpoint, may endorse their views. In the 'Foreign Periodicals' section of *Modern Review*, there is an article on the Asiatic League, where the *New York Herald* editorial has been quoted, 'the western policy of treating the Asiatic peoples as inferior with the exception of Japan and as incapable of wholly managing their own affairs—if long enough persisted in would naturally and inevitably have an unpleasant and dangerous result'. The author was complacent that

... there is no possibility for the people of Asia to outdo the Europeans in the manufacture of weapons used in modern warfare. Then again, the communal, tribal, national, or fanatical religious spirit will stand in the way of forming an Asiatic. We know that there are Indian patriots who hope for Asian independence through Asian cooperation. At the present stage of political awakening of Asia, the only kind of Asiatic League which will be of value is the League to promote cultural understanding among the peoples of Asia.[6]

Prabashi followed the visit of Tagore to East Asia in detail in the section 'Bibidha Prasanga'.[7] Some of Tagore's articles on his travels, as well as ideas about India's link with South East and East Asia, were published from time to time. In 1924, *Chin O Japaner Bhraman*

Bibaran (descriptions of travels in China and Japan) was published, where the poet wrote that his travels were not prompted by any desire for propaganda, but fulfilment of a long-time dream to understand the life force of an ancient civilization. Despite all the storms the country had faced from revolutions, invasions, and civil war for centuries; the inner strength of the huge population had remained undiminished. One should come to the country to pay homage to it in the same way one goes on a pilgrimage.[8]

At the same time, there are references to visitors from various Asian countries who came to pay homage to Tagore. Anath Nath Basu wrote about the welcome that Santiniketan gave to the Chinese poet and scholar Tsu Simo, a professor at Peking University, who was inspired by Tagore when the latter had visited China. According to Tsu, the ancient Sino-Indian cultural and spiritual contact had been revived by Tagore's visit. Most Chinese had been unaware of India, and Tagore's personality impressed everyone so much that they wanted to renew the contact between the two civilizations. To keep the memory of Tagore's visit fresh, a society had been set up in China called the Crescent Moon Society. Basu gave detailed descriptions of how Kala Bhavana was decorated for the visit of the Chinese scholar and how Tsu addressed the students after enjoying a cultural programme organized by Dinendra Nath Tagore.[9]

A large number of essays are travelogues in which places of tourist attraction are highlighted. The articles encourage visitors to travel to these places. To that end, the easiest travel routes are discussed in detail. Hemendralal Roy wrote about his travels to Thailand in *Prabashi* in 1924. He gave details about how to reach Thailand via Singapore and Kuala Lumpur, similarities between India and Thailand, descriptions of the settlers, and the Indian influence on architecture. He ends with a note of admiration that an Asian State so close to India was prospering on its own.[10] In *Bharatbarsha*, Ganesh Chandra Maitra published a pictorial journey of Burma called 'Brahma Prabasher Chitra'.[11] In *Bharatvarsha*, there is a descriptive essay on Korea where Bharat Kumar Basu lauds various aspects of life there, but laments the destruction of traditional handicrafts and customs with the Japanese occupation in 1904. However, he was happy to note that Korea had achieved something great—their women had been emancipated.[12] There is another essay by Gholam Mustafa on the Muslims of China where he points out that there is a bright future for the Muslims, 'As a Russian intellectual said at the end of nineteenth century (name not mentioned), in the near future

Islam will be the national religion of China, and the history of the East will be rewritten. The forecast has still not come about but there is hope that the East will be brightened by the rays of a new light.'[13] A travelogue *Japaner Pothe*, by the magician P.C. Sorcar was published serially in *Bharatbarsha*. He not only travelled all over Japan and visited all the tourist sites, his performance was deeply appreciated too—he was named Houdini of India and was given a giant card pack with the inscription that said, 'In appreciation of the great achievement you have made in the art of Indian conjuring'.[14] There is an interesting article in *Bharatbarsha* about a globetrotter on a bicycle tour through China. On his way to Outer Mongolia, Kshitish Chandra Bandopadhyay came upon by dacoits, his bicycle was hit by a bullet, and he was kidnapped. He fell unconscious and when he came to sense, he discovered that he was in a room surrounded by Chinese soldiers. Realizing that he was not among dacoits, he demanded to be taken to meet their leader. When he was taken to the captain's room, he noticed that behind the captain's desk were pictures of Lenin and Stalin. The captain asked his name and whether he was from India. He wanted to know the purpose of Bandopadhyay's visit and if he could prove that he was not a government spy. Bandopadhyay showed him his identity papers and a letter from Mahatma Gandhi appreciating his feat. The reaction was most gratifying since the captain immediately set him free, saying that he had deep respect for the Mahatma.[15]

The admiration of other States of Asia was another way to express a difference with the colonial West. Admiration for the rise of Japan as a strong power, yet maintaining her distinct identity seems to be the theme in many articles. Kalimohon Ghosh expressed admiration for how Japan met the Western powers on equal ground because she developed her inner strength and distinctive character, 'They have tried to incorporate the best qualities of world civilizations into their own national life to improve it'.[16] Tagore spoke about the great powers of concentration of the Japanese when he wrote about his visit there. He linked it to the influence of Buddhism. He claims to have been impressed by the discipline and patience of the people, not only during the lectures organized for him, but even in day-to-day life in various institutions, at the theatre, and even in parks.[17] Interest was also shown regarding China—her past traditions, as well as her present, new cultural movement or the neo-traditional ideas were admired. But to make it interesting for their Bengali readers, a link was always established with India or Bengal. Comparing modern China to Bengal,

Prafulla Chandra Roy praised the movement by the Peking students to eradicate national ignorance and illiteracy. They distributed pamphlets and copies of lectures in a language that would be comprehensible to the common people and established free schools. Roy then compared this endeavour to the attitude of students in Calcutta. The number of students in the city being so large, he pointed out that if they put their mind to it, they can educate large sections of the population. Roy wrote that Sir Ashutosh Mukherjee (Vice Chancellor of Calcutta University for five terms) had calculated that postgraduate students study only five months in a year. The rest of the time they spent in rest in their villages leading useless and wasteful lives, while their family toiled.[18] Roy concluded that each student of Presidency College requires ₹755 per year, of which ₹300 is paid by the government which comes not from the pockets of middle classes, but from that of the poor peasant. Therefore, these students have a duty towards the poor.[19]

The point that is reiterated is that Japan must be admired not only for her might but for her wise policies and cultural traditions. The education and culture in these Asian lands must be emulated in India. As Tagore wrote in his address to the Japanese people, reprinted in *Modern Review*.

... your people have produced something from their heart which is still burning in your society, giving out the bloom of beauty and your works of art bear testimony of your power of spirit and they are claimed by all men ... and for these, you can be proud and not for death dealing weapons, nor for wealth which is sure to vanish someday or other but for the immortal creations of spirit. I have come to claim them for humanity; I have come to praise them for the whole world.[20]

There is an underlying sense of fear in these essays that India does not appreciate nor understand the real strength of these nations so will never be able to emulate them. Benoy Kumar Sarkar wrote in *Modern Review* that the world is waiting to see if the modernization of China will be affected along Indian lines, i.e. through slavery to alien domination, or along Japanese lines of unhampered and independent development.[21] In a 1925 issue of *Modern Review*, there is a comparative analysis of the military expenditure of Japan and India where it is shown that

... India's expenditure on defence and offence absorbs a larger proportion of her revenue than Japan, but India has only an army and no navy making her dependent on England for protection from attacks by war vessels. Moreover

India's army has a standard of efficiency which did not deter even a small and backward Afghanistan from invading India some time ago. . . . Nor must we forget that India has no indigenous air force and it is manned entirely by foreigners and her artillery is also manned by non-Indians. . . . What Japan spends is paid to her own fighters and manufacturers of munitions and war vessels. On the contrary a very large fraction of India's expenditure goes to the pockets of foreigners.[22]

Recently, Nathoobhai D. Patel discusses Japan's achievement in medicine research and compares it to India in *Modern Review*. After a meticulous analysis of the research going on in Japan, he laments that despite the tradition of medicinal knowledge in India, there is no training given to the youth. He enumerated the causes of stagnation as follows:

1. Loss of freedom: Hindu medicine began to deteriorate after the coming of the Muslims. All attempts to synthesize Unani and Hindu medicine failed;
2. Existence of foreign medicine service deprives Indians of opportunity;
3. Allegiance of the Hindus to ancient Hindu medicine and innate conservatism of Hindus that prevents them from adopting new ideas;
4. False religious beliefs and vegetarianism contributed to the decay;
5. Defective system of medical education and unwise system of sending students abroad for study; and
6. Lack of state and private scholarships for study and research.[23]

This admiration was not mechanical and uncritical and was proved when Tagore raised his voice time and again in protest of any aggressive action by a country against another. Tagore in 'Unity of Chicago' expressed his horror and concern at the 'expedition to China' by British India in 1927:

The present expedition of the English against China is a crime against humanity and to our utter shame India is being used as a pawn in the game. . . . By fighting for a cause which is so disreputable, her sons cannot claim to be recognised as heroes, nor does it help her in the least to shake off the yoke of foreign domination that sits heavy upon her. That is why India is regarded by other Asiatic powers as a menace to their freedom. . . . It is she who has for ages supplied the spiritual nourishment to China and other Asiatic countries and sent out emissaries to preach the gospel of love and unity. But in the hour of China's perils, the fallen people of India now go there as the harbinger of political repression . . . can anything be more deplorable?[24]

Again in 1938, there is a note by Jaladhar Sen, the editor of *Bharatbarsha*, where he writes that famous Japanese poet Noguchi has written to Tagore justifying the Japanese attack on China but Tagore replied that Japan does not yet understand the inner strength of China. At the present moment, China has much greater moral strength than Japan and they should in the near future erase the painful memories and recreate a pure Asia.[25]

There was also an effort to bring to the knowledge of the Indian reading community: the details of the art and architecture, music, dance, and theatre of those regions. There are detailed descriptions of their art styles or forms of dance and theatre. These articles, along with the travelogue, make a very interesting read and must have been enjoyed by the readers much more than the more serious academic articles. Nandalal Bose in 'Chin Japaner Chithi'[26] discussed the different categories of painters of China—'artist craftsmen who were traditional, the mad artists who were cultured and aristocratic and did not need to worry about earning, the sane artists who were professionals and skilful and sometimes were patronized by the aristocracy and royalty, the thief artists who copied the work of others and the pottery artists. The first group are impossible to imitate and they are the path-breaking artists. The second and third groups may be copied and the fourth group specialized in doing that from the second and third group'. Nandalal was even trying to translate a paper by a Chinese artist. However, he felt that the Gurudev's vision of unity between India and China would not be possible because there, the people were only interested in meetings and lectures. He regretted that ornamentation in architecture was coming to an end in China. He believed that the people had lost their originality and were copying the West because they were embarrassed by their past traditions and were being trained by the 'civilized' artistes from England. Monindra Bhushan Gupta, on the other hand, talks of the similarity of Asian art and how different it is from Western art. But he believes that though China has been able to break the shackles of colonization and evolve her own nationalism, she needs to find her own art as well. Only then will her culture evolve.[27] Nag discussed the forms of drama in Java in an article curiously called 'Dwip Bharater Natyakala' (the Dramatic art of Island India). This article tries to trace similarities between the dramas of India and Java in different ways. He finds similarities between the Wayang Orang portrayal of the epics, the *Ramayana* and the *Mahabharata* and the yatra performances; as well as among the masked dance drama of Wayang Topeng of Bali, the Ramleela of North India, and the Kathakali of south India. He compared a puppet drama performance, he saw at a funeral service in Bali to the creation of *kush* (grass) puppets at a Hindu *shraadh* ceremony. The Wayang Golek puppets of midwestern Java are similar to Indian puppets according to Nag. The shadow play Wayang Purva is based on Indian epics, while the Wayang Gedok is based on local traditions and myths called Panji literature. He expressed hope at the end that there would be joint research on drama by Indian and Indonesian scholars.[28] Suniti Chattopadhyay provides detailed descriptions of Chinese theatre in Singapore in *Prabashi*—the costume and make-up of the artistes, and the very loud orchestra which sounds strange to Indian ears.[29] *Modern Review* provided a detailed description of the performance of a play *Sanyasi* by Tagore, at the Summer Theatre of China by Sansi Tayuanfu school of foreign languages. Twenty-six pictures were provided for the readers along with the story. Jadunath Sarkar in analysing the Indian influence on the art of Indochina reviews the research of Groslier and points out that the artists were in the service of an aristocrat who was half Indian and half native, whose sole preoccupation was to build temples and embankments to live in luxury, to use elegant and decorated utensils, to accumulate riches and religious merit. The influence of south India on Cambodia was local and accidental. There was both Chinese and Buddhist influence on art in Cambodia.[30] In the section 'Foreign Periodicals', a report from *Young East* has been quoted on Japan's debt to India in music, 'In fact it was a Champa priest who introduced Indian music to Japan and improved and developed Japanese musical art.'[31] Javanese dances have been discussed by J.V.H. Labberton, when a Javanese troupe arrived in Madras and a performance was organized at the Jubilee Convention of the Theosophical Society. He writes that

Wayang Wong is from the standpoint of art, a most beautiful expression of human soul dancing. These aristocratic dancers have an unimaginable grace. They dance a romance out of Mahabharata which is called the Bharata *yudha* in Java. A more delicate and refined dancing is allotted to the Pandavas each of whom, has his own dance. The Kaurava dance is more wild and aggressive, and the Danava dance is a savage dance. Accompanying Arjuna are three clowns who represent the powers of good.[32]

B.R. Chatterjee finds it interesting that 'in the Javanese puppet show known as Wayang, old Hindu tradition has been preserved even now when Java has been a Mohammedan country for more than five centuries.'[33] There is a descriptive essay on the Chinese art in *Bharatvarsha,* where the writer says with pride that the paintings may be incomprehensible to the Europeans, but to the Indians, they are familiar. Some aspects of Indian philosophy are reflected in the art. As he puts it, 'Oriental idealism is burning bright all over Asia'.[34] There are a number of essays that give details of adaptations of the *Ramayana* and the *Mahabharata* in the lands of South East Asia, and point out the differences with the Indian epics. Amulyacharan Bandopadhyay tells the story of *brata yudha* or the *Mahabharata* as told in the ancient language of Java called Kavi, completed in 791 shlokas.[35]

Tagore was so determined to undo the pride evoked in the memories of past colonization of Asia by India, that he decided that the only way to mitigate it was through an inverse colonization. Not being content with simply creating awareness, he devised a unique plan of cultural assimilation in his university curriculum. He invited scholars from various Asian countries to teach different subjects and languages at Visva-Bharati, Santiniketan. His large repertoire of songs which he set to tunes were influenced by world music; and in the dance dramas, he decided to experiment with various dance forms of Asia. An excellent description of this has been given by Santidev Ghosh who graduated from a student to a teacher around the 1930s. Since then, Ghosh was sent to different parts of India and Asia to learn some basic techniques of different dances. After learning Manipuri and Kathakali, Tagore sent him to Sri Lanka four times during 1936–8. There he was trained in the men's Kandi dance. In 1937, Ghosh went to Burma and learnt the hand movements of the Rampoye dance drama style from a veteran dancer. Then in 1939, he went to Java and learnt the royal dance at the invitation of the king and later spent a month in Bali learning the popular dances there. He quotes a letter from Tagore, which said that he should learn some distinctive steps of the various Asian dances but the implementation in Bengali dance dramas must be carefully done so that the Indian style is not swamped by the Asian. Ghosh learnt his lesson well. When he choreographed *Chitrangada*, he cast Maki, a Japanese No and Kabuki dancer, as Madan, who comes to give the boon of beauty to the princess. Madan's character possibly allowed the most innovation because Ghosh also cast alternatively a Western-style ballet dancer and a Vietnamese style dancer besides the Japanese. The dance of the *doiwala* (curd seller) in *Chandalika* was also set to the

Japanese dance style. There were a number of foreign students who knew different dance styles from Malaysia, Vietnam, and Java; and they were all associated in the dance movement of Tagore. Sometimes troupes from Visva-Bharati also travelled to other countries to perform dance dramas. Ghosh mentions performance of *Shaapmochon* in Sri Lanka in 1938 that was praised in the Ceylon Daily News.[36]

Not only through travelling, but learning about the art and culture of the countries of Asia also provides scope of linking the people through the Indian diaspora with those countries. In the articles there are frequent references to achievements by people of Indian origin who have settled there, professionals as well as ordinary people. *Modern Review*, in this decade, has a series on 'Indians abroad', where Banarasidas Chaturvedi has written extensively on the need to connect the people of India to the diaspora in Asia or 'Greater India' as he calls it.

Mr Andrews has been living in Greater India for the last 16 years and his mind has wandered from Borobudur in Java to the Khoja Jamat Kahna the great mosque at Nairobi. He realises that India had her cultural colonies in the distant past and she may have them again in the near future. Mr Andrews' Greater India will not belong to an imperial system, it will be definitely cultural. He knows that India has a message to give to the world and this message may be given by Greater India. What Mr Andrews sees in his imagination and what we cannot see is a Greater India of AD 2000.

Chaturvedi also points out that Indians do not realize the material and spiritual benefit that they can get from the 'people in the colonies', '. . . the Congress received not less than Rs 80,000 from Indians overseas in the Tilak Swarajjya fund and . . . if we have any ambition to spread our cultural ideas in the world, we cannot find better messengers than Indians overseas who link us up with the world.'[37] There are echoes of this in another article by Tarak Nath Das in the same year where he says that

. . . it should be noted that of all the peoples of Asia, the Japanese are doing some systematic work in the field of spreading their own culture. . . . It must be said India has done very little for cultural expansion during the last few centuries . . . the Indian people have not done their share to aid those Indians, mostly workers, who during the recent years ventured to foreign shores to make their living and at the same time, possibly unconsciously laid the foundation of a new and future Greater India.[38]

What strikes one most on reading these articles is the practicality of the ideology of a cultural Greater India or the Asiatic League which would create a powerful Asia. But even today, the people of Asia are no closer than they were in the 1930s. The dreams of finding the soul of Bharat outside her territorial limits were lost in the urgency to achieve independence and establish a new State. Nehru's ideas of 'Non Alignment' probably arose from a similar thought process and some international linkages were experimented with in those years. Unfortunately in some of the history writing of the sixties and the seventies of the twentieth century, despite the cautionary note by those propounding cultural linkages, political chauvinism was seen in the descriptions of the Indian colonization in the ancient and early medieval times in Greater India. These interpretations and histories extolling 'Hindu glory' became an embarrassment to the secular mainstream politics, and were gradually swept aside. If India wishes to look beyond her boundaries today and attempt to revive that civilizational link, then it would be wise to remember this ideological movement of the 1920s and 30s which tried to put a new perspective on the study of history, 'If history should stand, as it should stand, as the truly impartial record of Humanity, it must be purified from its disgraceful nationalistic bias and re-established on its only just and dignified basis—the basis of internationalism.'[39]

Notes

1. Rabindranath Tagore, 'Brihattara Bharat' (Greater India), in *Kalantor*, Calcutta: Visva-Bharati Granthana Vibhaga, 2002 (first published in 1937), pp. 300–9.
2. 'Notes', *Modern Review,* vol. XXXVII, no. 4, April 1925, p. 483.
3. Kalidas Nag, 'Art and Archaeology in the Far East: French Contribution', *Modern Review*, vol. XXXXVII, no. 1, January 1930, p. 63.
4. Kalidas Nag, 'Bharat Maitri Mahamandal' (India's Great Circle of Friendship), *Prabashi*, vol. 26, pt I, Baishakh 1320BY (1913), pp. 365–78.
5. Jadunath Sarkar, 'Hindu Influence on Further India', *Modern Review*, vol. XXXX, July 1926, pp. 4–7.
6. Notes, *Modern Review,* vol. XXXIX, January 1926, pp. 112–13.
7. 'Bibidha Prasanga' (Miscellaneous), *Prabashi,* vol. 28, pt I, Baishakh 1339BY (1932).
8. Rabindranath Tagore, 'Chin O Japaner Bhraman Bibaran' (Description of Travels in China and Japan), *Prabashi,* vol. 24, pt II, no. 1, Kartick 1331BY (1924), pp. 89–90.
9. Anath Nath Basu, 'Santiniketane Chainik Sudhi Su Simor Abhyarthana' (Welcoming the Noble Tsu Simo in Santiniketan), *Prabashi*, vol. 28, pt II, Chaitra 1335BY (1928), p. 386.

10. Hemendralal Roy, 'Shyamrajya' (The Kingdom of Shyam), *Prabashi,* vol. 24, pt II, no. 1, Kartik 1331BY (1924), pp. 64–73.

11. Ganesh Chandra Maitra, 'Brahma Prabasher Chitra' (Description of Life in Burma), *Bharatvarsha,* vol. 14, pt I, no. 3, 1334BY (1927), pp. 75–86.

12. Bharat Kumar Basu, 'Korea', *Bharatvarsha,* vol. 18, pt I, 1337BY (1930), p. 273.

13. Gholam Mustafa, 'Chine Musalman' (The Muslims of China), *Bharatvarsha,* vol. 18, pts 1, 2, 7, 8, 1337BY (1931), serially pp. 966, 55.

14. P.C. Sarkar, 'Japaner Pothe' (On the Way to Japan), *Bharatbarsha,* vol. 25, pt 2, 1344BY (1937), pp. 62–9.

15. Kshitish Chandra Bandopadhyay, 'China Doshyuder Haate' (In the Hands of Chinese Bandits), *Bharatbarsha,* vol. 26, pt I, no. 1, 1345BY (1938), pp. 261–5.

16. Kalimohon Ghosh, 'Japaner Grihadharmaneeti' (The Internal Policy of Japan), *Prabashi,* vol. 13, pt I, Baisakh 1320BY (1913), p. 33.

17. Rabindranath Tagore, 'Dhyani Japan' (Spiritualism in Japan), *Prabashi,* vol. 29, pt I, no. 5, 1336BY (1929), pp. 533–5.

18. Prafulla Chandra Roy, 'Nabya Chin O Bangala' (New China and Bengal), *Prabashi,* vol. 29, pt II, no. 1, 1336BY (1929), pp. 80–91.

19. Ibid., p. 86.

20. Rabindranath Tagore, 'To the People of Japan', *Modern Review,* vol. XXXVII, no. I, 1925, pp. 4–7.

21. Benoy Kumar Sarkar, 'The Eternal Chinese Question', *Modern Review,* vol. XXXVII, no. I, 1925, p. 180.

22. 'India and Japan's Military Expenditure' (Notes), *Modern Review,* vol. XXXVII, no. 4, 1925, p. 432.

23. Nathoobhai D. Patel, 'Medicine in Modern India and Japan', *Modern Review,* vol. XXXX, 1926, pp. 167–70.

24. Rabindranath Tagore, 'Unity of Chicago', quoted in Foreign Publications, *Modern Review,* vol. XXXXII, no.7, 1927, pp. 94–5.

25. Japan O Rabindranath, 'Samayiki', *Bharatvarsha,* vol. 26, pt I, 1345BY (1938), pp. 790–1.

26. Nandalal Bose, 'Chin Japaner Chithi' (Letters from China and Japan), *Prabashi,* vol. 28, pt I, no. I, 1339BY (1932), pp. 784–7.

27. Monindrabhusan Gupta, 'Chin Chitrakalar Itihash' (History of Chinese Painting), *Prabashi,* vol. 24, pt II, no. I, 1331BY (1924), pp. 81–9.

28. Kalidas Nag, 'Dwip Bharater Natyakala' (The Drama of Island Bharat), *Prabashi,* vol. 29, pt I, no. 6, 1336BY (1929), pp. 897–902.

29. Suniti Kumar Chattopadhyay, 'Javadwiper Pothe' (On the way to Island Java), *Prabashi,* vol. 28, pt I, no. 1, 1335BY (1928), pp. 142–5; no. 2. pp. 266–73; no. 3, pp. 480–7; no. 4, pp. 594–602.

30. Jadunath Sarkar, 'Indian Influence on the Art of Indo China', *Modern Review,* vol. XXXIX, no. I, 1926, p. 43.
31. Foreign periodicals, *Modern Review,* vol. XXXIX, no. I, 1926.
32. J.V.H. Labbeton, 'Javanese Dances, Gleanings', *Modern Review,* vol. XXXIX, no. I, 1926.
33. B.R. Chatterjee, 'Mahabharata and the Wayang in Java', *Modern Review*, vol. XXXXVI, no. 7, 1929, p. 658.
34. Jamini Kanta Sen, 'Chainik Chitrakalar Chhayapoth' (The Shadowy Path of Chinese Painting), *Bharatvarsha,* vol. 26, pt I, no. 5, p. 579.
35. Amulya Chandra Bandopadhyay, 'Javadwiper Mahabharata' (The Mahabharata of Java—a Story), *Bharatbarsha,* vol. 18, no. 2, 1337–8BY (1930–1), p. 601.
36. Santidev Ghosh, *Jiboner Dhrubatara* (Guiding star of Life), Calcutta: Ananda Publishers, 1996, pp. 141–3.
37. Banarasidas Chaturvedi, 'Three Letters on Greater India, Indians Abroad', *Modern Review*, vol. XXXXVII, nos. 1–6, 1930, pp. 136–9.
38. Tarak Nath Das, 'Value of Cultural Propaganda in International Relations', *Modern Review,* vol. XXXXVII, no. 3, 1930, pp. 287–91.
39. Kalidas Nag, *The Humanization of History, Memoirs, Vol. I (1891–1921)*, Kolkata: Writers Workshop Publishers, 1991, p. 8.

3

Indians in Colonial Burma

Aparajita Dhar

B RITISH ANNEXATION of Burma was accomplished in three clear-cut phases spread out over a little more than a century. The First Anglo-Burmese War of 1824–6 ended with Arakan and Tenassarim passing under the British rule. The Second Anglo-Burmese War of 1852 added the province of Pegu to the British possessions and finally, the Third Anglo Burmese War of 1885 led to the subjugation of the whole country and brought an end to the Burmese monarchy. For a few months after the fall of Mandalay, the British were undecided as to what they would do with their latest colonial acquisition; but by the beginning of 1886, the die was cast, 'Burma so radically different from India, by force of circumstances, became an appendage of the Indian Empire'.[1]

During the period 1874–82, the population of the city of Rangoon was not only increasing, it was changing in character too. The opportunities for trade and employment, which were then available, attracted a considerable Indian population. The census of 1872 shows that there were some 16,000 Indians, being 16 per cent of the whole population of the town of Rangoon. In 1881, there were about 66,000 Indians, being about 44 per cent of the whole. The Burmese population had actually undergone a slight decrease from 69,000, and had relatively declined considerably from nearly 70 per cent to 50 per cent. Of the total population in 1881, less than 49 per cent had been born in Rangoon. B.R. Pearn opines that thus was commencing the process that had made Rangoon an Indian rather than a Burmese city.[2] Following the annexation of Lower Burma as a British Indian territory; Indian men, money, and materials were needed in large quantities.[3]

Indian immigration was not a new phenomenon in Lower Burma, for there had been for centuries a close connection between Burma and the eastern coast of India. But it was not till the development of communications in the late 1860s and 70s (less passage-rates were consequent till then)—the establishment in 1873 of more frequent sailings between Rangoon and India, when India Steam Navigation company introduced fortnightly sailings between Rangoon and Madras in place of the previously monthly sailings—that such immigration became possible on a large scale. In 1880, the establishment of the Asiatic Steam Navigation Company in competition with the British line, led to a further reduction of rates and so accelerated immigration.[4]

The special correspondent of the *London Times* wrote on 15 January 1906

In this modern city where European and Burmese, Hindus and Chinese, jostle one another in a kaleidoscopic confusion of types and races, where the Burmese population has in fact been completely outnumbered by immigrants from Southern India and Bengal, where the ubiquitious Chinese asserts his superiority as a trader scarcely less irresistibly than the European his superiority as a ruler of men, it is difficult at first sight to tell which is the really prepondering element.[5]

The Burma Indian Chamber of Commerce, in the memorandum it submitted to the Baxter Commission, divided the Indians in Burma in the following ways:

There are those who are born and bred in Burma, have made Burma their permanent home and regard their future and the future of their families as bound up with its interests. There are those, who though not born in Burma, come to the country with the definite intention of settling there, and making it their future home; and there is another large body, who, even if they do not arrive with the intention formed of remaining permanently in Burma, do in fact devote the whole of their working lives to its service in trade, in commerce, in industry, in the transport services, and in many other directions. It can be truly said of this last class that the contribution which they make to the prosperity of the country is equal to that of any other community. Finally, there are those who come to Burma for periods, varying from a few months to several years, without perhaps any clear intention of settling in Burma, but who nevertheless perform essential tasks, in the absence of which the work of the country would be seriously prejudiced. In considering the problem of Indian immigration into Burma as a whole, regard should in the opinion of the chamber, be had to the different considerations, which should with justice apply to the several categories mentioned above for to treat them all on the same basis would be to ignore the essential facts of the problem. In passing, it is not out of place to mention that the bulk of the sea passenger traffic between India and Burma is not either by new immigrants or by persons intending to remain in Burma for short periods. It contains a large number of Indians who are settled in Burma as well as those, who though not settled here with their families, are moving to and from India between spells of active work.[6]

The above is corroborated by the inquiry of the Baxter Commission appointed by Resolution of 15 July 1939, to examine the question of Indian immigration into Burma. The Indian immigrants came in for three major purposes. First in importance, on account of the large numbers involved, were the Indian labourers who came in to do the heavy manual work for which Burman labour, because of the phenomenally rapid expansion of the area brought under cultivation, was not available and which was moreover uncongenial to them. Second, the Indian traders and businessmen who came to the country with access to capital and sought opportunities for the exercise of their commercial instincts; and third, the Indians with some degree of clerical or technical training who were introduced into public bodies such as the railways and commercial firms, before there were adequate numbers of educated and trained Burmans seeking similar employment.[7]

One must go back to the census of 1921 where it appears that 4 districts in Bengal, 7 in Madras, 3 each in Bihar and Orissa, and 4 in the United Provinces supplied 53 per cent of all Indian immigrants and probably, according to the census report, a considerable part of those for whom the district of birth could not be identified. Telegus came chiefly from the Gujarat, Godavari, and Vizagapatnam districts, Tamils from Ramnad and Tanjore, two-thirds of the Oriyas were from Ganjam, four-fifths of the Bengalis and Chittagongians from Chittagong, and the Hindustanis from Sultanpur and Fyzabad.

In 1931, the Indian population represented 6.90 per cent of the total population, and accounted for 10.90 per cent of the inhabitants of Lower Burma and 2.50 per cent of the inhabitants of Upper Burma. About 21.60 per cent of the Arakan population was Indian, the next highest percentage, namely 15.60 per cent was found in the Pegu division, while the population of the Irrawaddy and Tenassarim divisions were 4.80 and 6.40 per cent Indian, respectively.[8]

This essay seeks to address the question of the immigration of Indian labour to colonial Burma, and how they have played a crucial role in the development of the region from the nineteenth century onwards. The vast majority of Indians arrived in Burma as labourers and auxiliaries linked to the colonial enterprise which, in turn, constructed the framework upon which they functioned in those societies. This had repercussions on Indians in terms of their relationship within the land on which they laboured, and in the way they were perceived by other communities.

Immigration of Indian Labour
in Burma

How the question of the immigration of Indian labour into Burma is embedded in the development of the colonial economy can be seen from the following historical perspective. Burma's integration into world commodity and capital markets engendered an accelerated demand for their products, and coincided with the rapid expansion of agricultural and mineral production in the region. The particular way in which the export industries developed was determined by local conditions in these countries: the availability of natural resources and vast tracts of land, sparse and unevenly populated regions, and the response of various indigenous groups to the opportunities opened up by the growing market for export of tropical commodities. The colonial administration in Burma and Malaya consequently turned to India for their labour recruitment needs.[9]

Late nineteenth century labour migration was consistent with the international division of labour, and laid the framework for migrant labour diaspora in the region. It involved mass migration (both short and long distance journeys, the organization of travel arrangements, employment in the receiving countries, and an empire-wide sourcing of labour). It also involved two other groups in the migration process apart from the migrants. These were the private labour brokers and other intermediaries who organized travel arrangements and employments, and state officials. Particular labour regimes that relied on the use of sanctions to enforce wage labour agreements, or coercion through intermediaries, were also developed.[10]

The recruitment of Indian workers to Burma was also consistent with a rather elastic use of labour. The workers had many characteristics in common. They were young, predominantly unskilled adult males, who immigrated as individuals and had low dependency ratios. They also primarily comprised of illiterate peasants who had hardly spent any time away from their villages. They were mainly engaged in the production and processing of commodities, in factories, in the construction and maintenance of transport system, and in the ports. They remitted capital in the form of money to their places of origin. After periods of employment, they usually, but not always, returned to their countries of origin. The colonial authorities viewed them as sojourners to be repatriated when the demand for their services no longer existed.[11]

Three principles governed the colonial labour policy: the acquisition of a plentiful, diversified, and cheap supply of labour for colonial and capitalist enterprise; the limited assurance of the labourer's freedom of movement; and the provision of a limited amount of protection for workers.[12]

Owing to the existence of a strong and steadily rising demand for Burma's rice in Europe and other areas, the Irrawady Delta's economy expanded rapidly in the last half of the nineteenth century. Between the mid-1850s and 1900, additional 5 million acres of rice land were brought into production in Lower Burma, and the amount of rice exported annually from Burma rose from less than 2,00,000 tons to over 2 million tons. This growth was supported by a steady rise in the price of paddy from ₹45 to ₹95 per 100 baskets at Rangoon. Attracted by the profit and employment opportunities on the booming delta frontier, immigrants from Upper Burma and India, and to a lesser extent China, contributed to a sharp increase in the population of Lower Burma. Between the 1850s and 1900, the population of the region grew from approximately 1 to over 4 million. By the end of the nineteenth century, Lower Burma was the premier rice-exporting region in the world and one of the richest provinces of the British Empire. [13]

The growth of rice production and exports in Burma was a product of both political and economic factors. Politically, as the country was opened up to international trade, previous prohibitions on rice exports were lifted and the colonial authorities introduced measures to encourage rice cultivation and exports, partly as a revenue-raising measure. Equally significant was the fact that the imposition and more efficient collection of a variety of taxes that were levied in cash required peasants to seek cash incomes. The demand for rice tended to rise rapidly as the nineteenth century progressed. The demand for the export of Burmese rice came from India, Europe, and then increasingly from other South East Asian markets. The area under rice cultivation in Burma accorded a steady increase compared with the other two major rice producers in South East Asia, Thailand and Cochinchina. British land policy and the transformation of rice production into 'industrial agriculture' also led to a clear division between cultivation and processing activities and further specialization in the cultivation, financing, processing, and exporting of rice. Three main groups were involved: Burmese cultivators, who also processed some of the rice; Indian financiers, field workers, and rice mill workers; and European firms which dominated the processing of rice and its export.[14]

As Burmese labour became scarce, in cultivation, Burmese peasants turned to Indian labour to carry out such tasks as the construction and repair of bunds, ploughing, transplanting of seedlings, harvesting, and threshing. They also increasingly turned to either Burmese or Indian Chettiar money lenders to finance their activities. Indian rice-field workers' employment was seasonal and determined by the different phases of the rice season. The workers arrived in Burma between September and March to carry out a range of tasks associated with the cultivation and harvesting of rice. Between March and the following September, the workers either departed for India, or sought casual work in the towns in the rice mills or on the docks. The rice production cycle thus determined the seasonal character of most of the Indians' employment but not wholly. Although some of these workers made a return trip to India annually, they normally worked for a minimum of three years in Burma.[15]

In 1876, the Government of India enacted a Labour Act which provided for the appointment of an immigration agent and a medical inspector of immigrants to regulate the methods of recruitment, transport, and employment; and to safeguard the welfare of immigrants destined for Burma. Migration under this scheme proved to be unsuccessful, principally because mill owners found the conditions of the Labour Act onerous, and preferred to obtain their labour force through the agency of the labour contractors which enabled them to both manage and control workers. Consequently, Indian labour migration was entirely uncontrolled and there was no one responsible for the welfare or protection of the immigrants after they had actually landed in Burma. The labour migrants, comprising mainly Tamils and Telugus, hailed from the poverty-stricken areas of south India and did not have the means to move to Burma. Thus, they had to rely on two groups of intermediaries: the recruiting agent who acted on behalf of the labour contractor, and the labour contractor, known as *maistry* in the Telegu districts of south India. The recruiting agents went to the villages to recruit the workers who were then handed over to the labour contractors. The latter transported them to the immigration depot where they underwent official migration procedures and attested that they were migrating on their own free will. They were then taken to their place of employment in Burma and remained under the charge of the *maistry*. From these simple origins, the *maistry* system gradually evolved into a multi-tiered recruitment mechanism and authority system, and abuse and exploitation were enshrined at every level.[16] Indian workers were preferred for three main reasons. First, they were seen as a fluid labour supply, they were cheaper to hire and manage compared to Burmese workers, and their accommodation costs were also cheaper since they could be housed in substandard tenement housing. In comparison, Burmese workers were relatively immobile, they preferred employment in or near their home district, and required individual housing units. Second, the Burmese were primarily agriculturists and were not prepared to work the long hours in the mills, with very few rest days and holidays. Third, European firms in particular preferred to deal with a head *maistry* to hire and manage the workers rather than hire Burmese workers on individual contracts. Moreover, there were no Burmese head *maistrys* with capital who were in a position to make contracts with European firms or finance their own labour gangs.[17]

Housing the Rangoon Poor

The influx of Indian labour created problems of housing and sanitation.[18] The problem does not appear to have grown acute till the late 1870s, when uneasiness first began to be felt about the insanitary conditions under which the coolies lived. For reasons of economy, a number of men would club together to rent a single room, and owing to the absence of suitably designed buildings and lack of proper building and sanitary rules, gross overcrowding in the worst possible sanitary conditions occurred. It was in 1878–9 that the situation first began to raise concern. In that year, the Rangoon Municipality noted that the coolies were living in

. . . old pucka houses in a very dirty state, with few and small windows and doors which they are fond of keeping shut. The ground floors of most of these pucka buildings are damp and generally soaking with house slops and dirty water, together with other garbage. Many of these houses are very much overcrowded, and very little cubit space is allowed for each inmate. In one house in 29th street there were found in one room 23 inmates, the dimensions only being 18 by 14, and ventilation defective.

Many houses in the 27th and 28th Streets were overcrowded. But the Rangoon Municipality found that it was extremely difficult to take any effective measures towards the mitigation of these evils. It was the case that overcrowding was contrary to the law, but only a magistrate could pass orders for the reduction of the number of occupants of a house and could do so only after the health officer had inspected the premises and given evidence of overcrowding that would satisfy a court of law. Even if such evidence were secured, there was little likelihood that the magistrate would take adequate action, for the magistrates seemed to have been reluctant to enforce the law in municipal affairs. So while Rangoon was rapidly growing in prosperity, a large section of its population was housed under the worst possible conditions.[19]

In 1882–3, the health officer of Rangoon pointed out that 'the worst cases are about a hundred houses used as barracks; their occupants are Madras coolies'. It was, he considered, imperatively necessary that these barracks and the large number of dwelling houses used as lodging houses by a large floating population should be brought under proper supervision and control, the more so as these places were now being found in some of the best streets of the town, where they caused depreciation of property and were the foci of disease and filth of the neighborhood. He complained that the health of the city was at all times threatened by the arrival of thousands of coolies by the steamers from the Madras coast. On arrival, the coolies were crowded in places unsuited to their reception and should sickness break out, the consequences might be more disastrous. The condition of these unfortunate people was utterly miserable. They frequently arrived in Rangoon without the means of paying their passage money, when their services were virtually sold by auction to any person who would release them from their obligations. As the president of the Municipal Committee noted there was a suspicion that something resembling a slave trade was growing.[20]

British administrators thought that Indian immigrants constantly imported dangerous, infectious diseases into Burma. And there was a perception that the disease so introduced, spread rapidly among Indian immigrants in an overcrowded coolie barrack, and because of the fluidity of labourers, the disease became an epidemic in the wider area, which affected the Burmese population. This was the logic behind the perception that coolie barracks were 'the foci of the epidemic.'[21] The insanitary conditions in coolie barracks were attributed to an extent to Indian race, culture, and habits. The clearest expression of such thought was found in the Census Report 1911 which explained the cause of the overcrowding problem in Rangoon, 'The problem is very largely not one of space but of racial habits. The immigrant coolly from Southern India is accustomed to live in overcrowded barracks whatever may be the area of dwelling space available.'[22]

In a letter to the government dated 23 March 1899, H.L. Eales, the President of Rangoon Municipality emphasized the danger caused by the Hindu (probably labouring) classes from Madras Presidency and proposed the necessary measure. He wrote

Municipal Committee has been alive to the danger that Rangoon has been subject to for years from the presence in its midst, and the continued importation of a large unprotected class of Hindoos that is very subject to small pox, and the members of which from their habits and mode of life cannot help but foster and disseminate this fell disease throughout Rangoon. Their love of crowding together in their habitation and their practices of hiding cases of small pox, added to their unprotected state, make their presence in Rangoon the greatest factor in the propagation of small pox. I quite agree with the Municipal Health Officer and the Municipal Committee that nothing short of the compulsory vaccination of all unprotected coolies before being allowed to enter Rangoon will be of material effect in ridding Rangoon of recurring epidemics of small pox.[23]

In 1900, the Burma Vaccination Law Amendment Act was promulgated. It enabled the compulsory vaccination of inmates of coolie barracks, but the most important provision enforcing vaccination to immigrants at ports had been withdrawn before the enactment.[24] Finally, in 1909, the Act was amended again. Section 9 of this Act, for the first time, prescribed compulsory vaccination for unprotected immigrants at ports. Under this section, the port health officer of Rangoon was given the power to 'require any person who has travelled on board the vessel for the purpose of coming to Burma to work and as a labourer to be inspected, and if on inspection he is found to be unprotected, to be vaccinated'. This provision was intended for 'every person who when so requested fails to show by documentary or other evidence that he is not a labourer'.[25]

In August 1917, the government appointed a committee to consider the propriety of the measure. The committee consisting of six persons— the Commissioner of Pegu Division, the President of the Rangoon Municipal Committee, the Director of Pasteur Institute, the Chairman of the Burma Chamber of Commerce, and two representatives of Indian and Burmese communities—collected the related statistics and took evidence from witnesses. The committee reported that compared with other Indian provinces, Burma was unique in the point that the whole of the movement of the population took place through one port, Rangoon.

Mentioning that practically all immigrants were Indian, it stated that all but a small proportion of these immigrants were unprotected and belonged to the labouring class, whose habits were such as to make them peculiarly liable to smallpox infection. The committee added that the resident population of Rangoon was fairly well protected by vaccination and it followed, therefore, that the factors that kept the infection in existence were provided by unprotected immigrants.

The committee finally concluded that the danger to the health of Rangoon and incidentally to Burma from the annual influx of unprotected Indian immigrants was a real one, and although the arrangements at the wharf were far from ideal and ought to be improved, yet the inconvenience that they involved was small in comparison with the great dangers to health and life which the withdrawal of this precaution would entail. The government accordingly confirmed that the application of Section 9 of the 1909 Burma Vaccination Law Amendment Act was a necessary precaution to safeguard Burma from smallpox infection. Thereafter, the measure of the compulsory vaccination for immigrants of Rangoon port was regulated on a permanent basis.[26]

On the other hand, *The Report of the Deck Passengers' Committee* set forth with eloquent emphasis on the importance of the Indian labourers to the economic welfare of Burma and the largeness of their contribution to its progress and development. To the members of this committee, the Indian labourers had been presented in a somewhat different aspect and they were anxious to place some facts on record which indicated that there was another side to the question. To insist on the benefits derived by Burma from the Indian labourers while saying nothing of the advantages accruing to the labourers from their temporary sojourn in Burma was a one-sided way of looking at the matter. It was all very well to ask what would be the state of Burma but for the swarms of Indians who had poured in during the previous thirty years and had done so much of the work that was needed to bring the province to its present level of prosperity. Not to enter into a hypothetical question of how far the Burmans, if the Indians had stayed away, might have adapted themselves for what was necessary, it was still very pertinent to ask what would have been the economic position of the congested and poverty-stricken districts of the Presidency of Madras and the provinces of Bengal, Bihar, and Orissa, but for the relief afforded to their population and the opportunities of acquiring wealth presented by this fertile and undeveloped province. The advantages of the intercourse between Burma and the Indian labourers were mutual, a fact that should not be obscured by undue emphasis on the benefits derived by one party only. Another fact which this committee wished to place on record was that the advantages connected with the presence of the Indian labourers had been by no means unattended by serious evils. In intelligence and education, they were inferior to the indigenous inhabitant of the province and their standards of comfort and civilization were very much lower. Their habits were dirty and their presence in any numbers in a village rendered it difficult or impossible to enforce the simple but effective sanitary rules, whose efficiency in the prevention of disease had been proved by experience and which were imposed by the authority of Burmese public opinion. From their usefulness, therefore, must be deduced the fact that the Indian labourers were the centre and focus of disease whereever they had established themselves. It may be too much to credit them with the introduction of plague, cholera, and smallpox, to say that their presence had aggravated the difficulty of dealing with these scourges tenfold was a simple record of fact. It seemed to this committee, therefore, that it was the duty of the Government of Burma, while doing nothing, to lessen the benefits accruing from the presence of the Indian labourers, to enforce every safeguard against the dangers to the health and welfare of the permanent population of the province involved by labourers' residence among them. The committee considered that it had been proved that the free admission of immigrants from India, not protected by vaccination or a previous attack, was the real reason why the efforts of the authorities to suppress smallpox had been rendered futile. Too short a time had elapsed since the new measures of precaution were enforced to allow the committee to judge whether they would prove permanently effective or not. The committee had pointed out that they were theoretically imperfect in various ways. So far as they had gone, indications were promising and the committee therefore recommended that the new system should be continued with the modification suggested above, namely the provision of sufficient means of transport for passengers from ship to shore and of commodious accommodation for examination on shores and a modification of the law in order to render all passengers without distinction liable to examination. Should future experience show that these measures have failed wholly or partially, we are convinced that the remedy lies in stringency of examination and on the vaccination not only of all 'unprotected' persons as defined in the 1909 Act but of all persons who are unprotected from a scientific point of view.[27]

Repatriation of the Indians from Burma

Until the outbreak of the Second World War, Indian labourers greatly outnumbered Burmese. In 1941, the Burmese labour force in industries numbered 28,033 while the Indians were 74,516 or about 69 per cent of the total. Enumeration of the Indians according to their employment showed the great majority, about 66 per cent in unskilled or semi-skilled occupations. These included workers in manufacturing industry, public transport, public services like cleaning and public works, seasonal agriculture, and mining and the oil fields. About 10 per cent of the Indians were craftsmen and technicians of every kind, while about 16 per cent were traders and shop assistants. Around 4 per cent were clerks, many in the public offices, and another 4 per cent were professional people, landlords, and others with higher levels of income.[28]

The halcyon days of Indian immigration started to erode in the 1930s when the demand 'Burma for the Burmese' resounded in Burma.[29] It is no wonder that during the 1930s and 1940s, Burmese history witnessed a negative trend with respect to Indian immigration. The aspirant immigrants of India, who looked at the golden land with financial ambitions, realized that their days in Burma were numbered.[30]

According to an assessment, 70,000 to 80,000 Indians were evacuated to India by sea route and about 4,025 Indians were evacuated by air. It was estimated that by the end of March 1942, about 2 lakh evacuees had reached Chittagong by sea. Of these, a large number of Indians had been living in the western province of Burma, Arakan.[31]

The combined effect of the Burmanization and nationalization made the Indian business community in Burma feel as if their pinion was cut off. Above all, the disquieting political situation all over the world also contributed in pulling out of the Indians from Burma. The general economic depression of the 1930s also had its due impact on the Burmese economy. In the face of a cloud of a devastating war, it was only too obvious to foresee the gloomy fortune by the Indian business community in Burma. The latter also knew that Burma would become an abattoir once such a war broke out. They also closely watched Japan's growing involvement and relationships with Burma and the Burmese nationalist leaders. Moreover, the very revelation of the Indian capitalists that they are being looked as the representatives of the British interest in Burma made them extremely unnerved. In the end, due to the prevailing hostile political environment in Burma, the Indian business classes felt that it was too risky to get any more involved in any economic stake in Burma. The Indian landlords and moneylenders decided to transfer their capital to India. Data reveals that in the year 1937–8, ₹32,500,000 had been transferred to India from Burma by the postal money order channel. [32]

Although Burmese nationalist leaders also protested against the continued influx of large numbers of Indian labourers into Burma, they often singled out the Chettiars in their polemical assaults on the Indian community. The Chettiars' singular appearance and alien customs, and their wealth and social exclusiveness made them a likely scapegoat. They were blamed for many of Burma's economic woes. In the mid-1920s, Burmese agriculturists, prompted by nationalist leaders, formed *Sibwaye Athins* (development associations) whose purpose was to compel the Chettiars to reduce debts owed by Burmese cultivators and eventually to abandon their operations entirely. In the turbulent 1930s, their *pucca* agency dwellings with their ornate teak trim and iron-barred windows became major targets for wandering dacoits, agrarian rebels, and urban rioters. In the last years before the Japanese invasion in 1941–2, the Burma Legislative Council passed several agrarian relief measures aimed at reducing tenants' rental rates and reclaiming for the smallholder land that had been alienated to Chettiars and Burmese landlords. There were provisions for compensation, but these measures were cut short by the imposition of Japanese rule and the flight of the Chettiars and most of the Indian population from Burma.[33]

The Indian labour agitation in the 1920s was one of the factors responsible for initiating Burmese labour into the urban economy. In 1924, the Indian dockyard labourers struck in protest against the oppressive methods of coolie contractors. Soon their protests reverberated through other occupations, rickshaw pullers and handcarters went on a sympathetic strike. The employers engaged Burmese workers instead, but when the Indians capitulated, they discharged the Burmese and reinstated the Indians. The resentment of the Burmese was not vented upon the European employees, but upon the Indians. The rickshaw pullers were the first target and about 2,000 of their vehicles were destroyed by Burmese bullies. Some 7,000 Indians were scared out of their homes, and in June 1930, almost 33,000 Indians left Rangoon for their ancestral land.[34]

The riot of 1938 was the climax of the growing disenchantment between the two communities. The event that sparked off the riot was the publication of a book by a Muslim named Maung Shwe Hpi. Although the book was published much earlier in 1931, it did not have any impact in the years following its publication. However, in 1938, with the discovery of the most insulting passages in the book by an individual, some sort of hue and cry was raised. The polemics along the religious line started over the allegation that Buddhism has been attacked.[35] During the riot, quite a number of mosques were burnt and Indian houses attacked. [36]

After the terrible anti-Indian riots in 1938 in which many Indians lost their lives and others deported to India, the Burma Riot Enquiry

Committee confirmed the Burmese uneasiness and ill-feeling about the unrestricted Indian immigration. Thereafter in 1939, the government appointed a commission of inquiry to examine the question of Indian immigration into Burma. The commission was asked to report on the matters relating to the volume of Indian immigration, the extent to which it was seasonal and permanent, type of occupations Indians were mainly employed in and the extent to which they were unemployed or under-employed, whether in such employment Indians had either displaced Burmans or could be replaced by Burmans, and whether in the light of the statistics obtained and other relevant factors any system of equating the supply of Indian unskilled labour to Burman requirements was needed.[37]

The Baxter Commisssion made a thorough enquiry into the whole problem and observed that no accurate statistics were available on the volume of Indian immigration, it was impossible to say how many were permanent or temporary visitors, but the greater part of the visitors were unskilled labourers who came to Burma for temporary employment from two to three years. It was also stated by the commission that there had been a steady increase in the number of Indians born in Burma. About 40 per cent of the Indians in Burma in 1939 were born in the country and claimed to be regarded as domiciled in Burma. The Commission was of the view that there was no evidence that Indians had displaced Burmans from employment which they had previously obtained. The whole history of the development of Burma during the last four generation would suggest that there had been a general division of work between the two races and that Indian labour had been supplementary rather than alternative to Burman labour. It was further stated that there was no serious evidence of any serious excess of Indian labour over contemporary requirements except in Rangoon, particularly the Rangoon port.[38]

The commission strongly recommended the introduction of passports, registration, and other measures including an immigration agreement between India and Burma regulating the classification of Indian residents and future immigrants.[39]

This was the background of the negotiation of an immigration agreement between India and Burma in 1941 known as the Indo-Burmese Agreement. The Burmese ministers insisted on restricting new entries and imposed conditions upon existing Indian residents, including the power to deport anyone. A satisfactory compromise was in effect. But when the agreement was published in India, there was a storm of protest. Just at this moment the Japanese invaded Burma. The 1950s saw a steady movement of Indians from Burma to their homeland.[40]

Conclusion

India-Burma relations are rooted in shared historical, ethnic, and religious ties. Centuries old geographical, cultural, and strategic links between these two Asian neighbours, coupled with mutual economic interests and identical foreign policies made their relationship a notable example of friendship. India and Burma had many other common factors which played a vital role in determining the relations. These factors, besides colonial legacies, identical value systems, and personality orientation of post-independence leadership, were geographical situation, cultural links, economic activities, and foreign policy matters. Myanmar (formerly Burma) is the largest neighbour, touching India's east and acts as a buffer zone between its north-eastern region and the Chinese provinces. India has also recognized Myanmar as a crucial link between India and China. For maintaining peace in the north-east, it is in India's security interests to keep the momentum going in the right direction with Myanmar. India looks at the connectivity through Myanmar as being crucial for its Look East Policy, and for the development of stronger ties with the Association of South East Asian Nations (ASEAN) countries as an extended neighbourhood. In this context, it is important to examine the role of the Indian diaspora in achieving India's internal and external objectives; first that stabilizes its north-east border; and second, a stabilized north-east region will provide a much needed bridge for India's policy towards South East Asia.[41]

Notes

1. Aung San Suu Kyi, *Burma and India: Some Aspects of Intellectual Life under Colonialism*, Simla: Indian Institute of Advanced Study, 1990, pp. 1–3.
2. B.R. Pearn, *A History of Rangoon*, Rangoon: American Baptist Mission Press, 1939, pp. 233–6.
3. N.R. Chakravarti, *The Indian Minority in Burma: The Rise and Decline of an Immigrant Community*, London: Oxford University Press, 1971, p. 7.
4. Pearn, *A History of Rangoon*, pp. 233–6.
5. Aung San Suu Kyi, *Burma and India*, pp. 33–4.
6. James Baxter, *Report on Indian Immigration*, Rangoon: Office of the Superintendent, Government Printing and Stationery, Burma, 1941, p. 99.
7. Baxter, *Report on Indian Immigration*, p. 107.
8. Ibid, p. 17.

9. Amarjit Kaur, 'Indian Labour, Labour Standards, and Workers Health in Burma and Malaya, 1900–1940', *Modern Asian Studies*, vol. 40, no. 2, 2006, pp. 425–75.
10. Ibid., p. 427.
11. Ibid.
12. Ibid., pp. 428–9.
13. Michael Adas, 'Immigrant Asians and the Economic Impact of European Imperialism: The Role of the South Indian Chettiars in British Burma', *Journal of Asian Studies*, vol. 33, no. 3, 1974, pp. 385–401.
14. Kaur, *Indian Labour, Labour Standards*, pp. 432–3.
15. Ibid.
16. Ibid., pp. 434–5.
17. Ibid., p. 436.
18. W.S. Desai, *India and Burma: A Study*, Calcutta: Orient Longman, 1952, p. 27.
19. Pearn, *A History of Rangoon*, pp. 233–6.
20. Ibid., p. 257.
21. Noriyuki Osada, 'An Embryonic Border: Racial Discourses and Compulsory Vaccination for Indian Immigrants at Ports in Colonial Burma, 1870–1937', *Social Science Research on Southeast Asia*, vol. 17, 2011, pp. 145–64.
22. Ibid.
23. Ibid.
24. Ibid.
25. Ibid.
26. Ibid.
27. *Report of the Committee Appointed to Investigate the Alleged Hardships caused by the Compulsory Vaccination, under the Provision of Section 9 of the Burma Vaccination Law Amendment Act 1909 of Labourers Arriving in Rangoon by Sea*, Rangoon: Rangoon Office of the Superintendent, Burma, 1918, p. 11.
28. Hugh Tinker, *The Banyan Tree: Overseas Emigrants from India, Pakistan and Bangladesh,* London: Oxford University Press, 1977, p. 142.
29. Swapna Bhattacharya, *India Myanmar Relations 1886–1948*, Kolkata: K.P. Bagchi & Co., 2007, p. 91.
30. Ibid., p. 95.
31. Ibid., p. 100.
32. Ibid., p. 96.
33. Adas, 'Immigrant Asians and the Economic Impact of European Imperialism', p. 400.
34. Usha Mahajani, *The Role of the Indian Minorities in Burma and Malaya,* Bombay: Vora & Co., 1973, p. 12.
35. Bhattacharya, *India Myanmar Relations*, p. 78.
36. Ibid.

37. Baxter, *Report on Indian Immigration*, p. 107.
38. Ibid.
39. Tinker, *The Banyan Tree*, p. 144.
40. Ibid., p. 144.
41. Sarita Rai, 'The Role of Indian Diaspora in India-Myanmar Relations', M.Phil. dissertation, Sikkim University, Department of International Relations, 2015, p. 76.

4

Reflections on India's Relations
with ASEAN

From the Look East Policy to the
Act East Policy

Man Mohini Kaul

A PARADIGM SHIFT in India's policy towards Association of South East Asian Nations (ASEAN) took shape in the beginning of the 1990s as a result of the profound transformation that took place in the contemporary world after the end of the Cold War. Prime Minister Narsimha Rao, after he came to power in 1991, initiated the much needed economic reforms and the Look East Policy. The policy laid down the conceptual framework for engaging the ASEAN. The earlier constricted stance had become a major stumbling block in ASEAN's acceptance of India as a dialogue partner. The new strategy to promote

*This paper builds on some of the work published as chapters in books and articles in journals including the following: Man Mohini Kaul and Anushree Chakraborty, eds., 'From Look East to Act East: Evolution of India's Foreign Policy towards Southeast Asia and South Pacific', in *India's Look East to Act East Policy: Tracking the Opportunities and Challenges in the Indo-Pacific*, New Delhi: Pentagon Press, 2015, pp. 3–21; Fredric Grare and Amitabh Mattoo, eds., 'ASEAN-India Relations during the Cold War', in *India and ASEAN; The Politics of India's Look East Policy*, New Delhi: Manohar, 2001, pp. 41–66; V.R. Raghavan and Karl Fischer, eds., 'Indian Perspectives on Security Dimensions of India and Southeast Asia', in *Security Dimensions of India and Southeast Asia*, New Delhi: Tata McGraw-Hill, 2005, pp. 3–21; Y.Y. Yagama Reddy, 'India's Look East Policy: Posture and Reality', in *Emerging: India in Asia- Pacific*, New Delhi: New Century, 2007, pp. 240–59; and 'Regional Groupings: An Overview of BIMSTEC and MGS', *South Asian Survey*, vol. 13, no. 2, July–December 2006, pp. 313–22.

closer trade and security ties with South East Asia had immediate positive outcome with ASEAN accepting India as a sectoral dialogue partner in 1992 and a full dialogue partner in 1995. The relationship was elevated to an India-ASEAN Summit in 2002, bringing the engagement to a higher level, thereby indicating ASEAN's acceptance of India as a key player in the region. The Look East Policy was given a makeover and renamed the Act East Policy in November 2014. Although the policy was no different from the earlier one, the intent was to convey to the ASEAN countries that the Indian government attached great importance to the pursuit of active and result-oriented policy. The initiative stressed cooperation and building of constructive partnership with South East Asia in the new evolving strategic paradigm where China's role and militarization in the South China was becoming a threat to the existing regional order.

Since the commencement of the Act East Policy, many significant developments have taken place in world affairs that have considerable bearing on the geopolitics of the region. In the US, with President Donald Trump in power, it has become clear that many of the former President Barack Obama's foreign policy initiatives may be dropped. However, Trump's own foreign policy stance towards the Indo-Pacific is less clear and this is an evolving space to observe. China's assertion of sovereignty over the South China Sea is a major challenge that could lead to serious discord with grave consequences on the regional order.

This essay seeks to answer questions that are endemic to the relationship, such as how did ASEAN evolve as the hub of regional integration, what are the key determinants in India-ASEAN relations, and how relevant is India to ASEAN in view of China's influential role in South East Asia? Also, the evolution of India-ASEAN relations is reviewed in the context of the factors that finally led India to adopt a pragmatic and constructive policy towards ASEAN through the initiatives of the Look East Policy or the Act East Policy.

Introduction

For the ASEAN countries, Obama's 'rebalance' or 'pivot' to Asia was an assurance from the world's most powerful country that it would not abandon its allies to the machinations of China, especially in the South China Sea. India, as an important stakeholder, was also expected to adopt a more active policy in the region in partnership with the US, and this was taken forward eagerly. The personal bond between the two political leaders of India and the US also helped shape this new warmth in the India-US bilateral relationship, which underlined India's constructive and major role in this 'pivot'. China's 'One Belt One Road' (OBOR) initiative of 2017 renamed 'Belt and Road Initiative' (BRI) did receive an encouraging response even from unexpected quarters like the Philippines, Vietnam, and Japan (among the ASEAN countries, Vietnam is now openly expressing unease about China's lack of transparency in the region and its waters)—all three in the past have had verbal and military skirmishes with China.

The presence and support of ASEAN countries at the Belt and Road Forum (BRF) in Beijing in May 2017 was representative of the general mood of ASEAN to cooperate economically with China, the leading trade partner of most ASEAN countries. In the past, it was the Japanese FDI that helped the economic rise of the ASEAN countries but today, it is trade and investment from China that is seen as critical to the growth of their economies. Some conclude that the conciliatory approach towards China is due to the abandonment of the Trans Pacific Partnership (TPP) by Trump which has led to apprehension that this could also mean the end of the 'pivot to Asia'. However, an unanticipated development took place on 24 May 2017 which was seen by the allies as a positive sign from the Trump administration—a US Navy warship 'sailed within 12 nautical miles of an artificial island built up by China in the South China Sea . . . is the first such challenge to Beijing in the strategic waterway since U.S. President Donald Trump took office.'[1]

Evolution of India-ASEAN Relations

After Independence in 1947, India decided to pursue an independent and active nonaligned foreign policy attuned with its national interest. It placed itself outside all power blocs, declined to be drawn into military pacts sponsored by any of the superpowers, and consciously began to play an increasingly important role in Asian-African affairs. India's 'Non-Alignment' policy was primarily a rejection of bloc politics as 'Nehru was deeply suspicious of getting into entangling alliances that could limit India's strategic space, and his emphasis was on avoiding the limitations alliances imposed on nations.'[2]

While India was preoccupied with China and Pakistan, South East Asia was also going through turbulent times with many of its newly independent, pro-Western countries facing communist insurgencies.

Insecurity in these countries surfaced particularly in the 1960s with Britain's decision to withdraw from the bases in 'East of Suez' under Harold Wilson's Labour government followed by President Richard Nixon's Guam Doctrine of 1969, in which the US declared its expectation that allies would contribute significantly to their own defence, thus effectively distancing itself from future wars like the one being fought in Vietnam. The emergence of intra-regional conflicts, and the support from China to South East Asian communist insurgents, created further tension that was viewed by the ruling political elite as a serious threat to the stability of the new nations. The fall out of this was positive, with the initiators of ASEAN realizing that it was crucial for the well-being of the region to work towards building a common identity by establishing an organization for regional cooperation. Amitav Acharya explains, 'The founders of ASEAN had little conception of regional identity. But they clearly hoped to develop one through regional cooperation. ASEAN came to play a critical role not only in developing a sense of regional identity, but also laying down the boundaries of South East Asia region.'[3]

The Development of ASEAN

After many rounds of deliberations, and owing in great part to the improvement in Malaysia's relations with Indonesia and the Philippines, ASEAN was established on 8 August 1967 in Bangkok. President Suharto of Indonesia stated that ASEAN reflected the 'will and determination of its member nations to let the future of South East Asia be decided by the South East Asian nations themselves.'[4] In the Cold War era where South East Asia was grappling with the effects of the Vietnam War, reservations were expressed by some sceptics regarding the capability of this new organization to survive. Moreover, the 'special relations' of the Philippines and Thailand with the US which resulted in the presence of American bases in these countries and their membership of the US-sponsored South East Asia Treaty Organization (SEATO) shaped the attitude of countries like India towards ASEAN. Analysts agree that 'ASEAN was born as a reactive rather than a proactive organisation, a body with a stronger sense of what it was collectively against rather than what it was collectively for.'[5]

What is the magical formula that led to ASEAN's ultimate success? The proffered conclusion is that the 'agreement among its members on basic strategy and rules of the game, its subordination of bilateral disputes to the interests of regional peace and national economic development, and the avoidance by governments of interference in and even comment upon one another's domestic affairs.'[6] There is no doubt that the trigger for regional cooperation was the objective of containing communism; however, its founding leaders tried to moderate this impression by pointing out that the primary goal stated in the ASEAN Declaration of 1967 was to promote mutual cooperation. The Declaration clarified 'that all foreign bases are temporary and remain only with the expressed concurrence of the countries concerned and are not to be used directly or indirectly to subvert the national development.'[7]

The end of the Vietnam War in 1975 accelerated the process towards political cooperation which was demonstrated at the 1st ASEAN Summit in Bali on 24 February 1976, during which policy guidelines and directions were laid down. The heads of governments of ASEAN countries signed the Treaty of Amity and Cooperation in South East Asia (TAC) and the Declaration of ASEAN Concord, which were to guarantee regional stability and promote economic cooperation. The TAC established a framework for the ASEAN way whose fundamental principles are

mutual respect for the independence, sovereignty, equality, territorial integrity, and national identity of all nations; the right of every State to lead its national existence free from external interference, subversion or coercion; non-interference in the internal affairs of one another; settlement of differences or disputes by peaceful means; renunciation of the threat or use of force; and effective cooperation among themselves.[8]

The 2nd Summit was held in Kuala Lumpur in 1977, establishing the framework for ASEAN officials to meet and interact with dialogue partners. ASEAN achieved its first diplomatic success by overcoming differences among members over the Cambodian issue and cohesively dealing in isolating Vietnam internationally.[9] This led to a positive outcome, thereby enhancing ASEAN's reputation as a viable regional organization. In his autobiography, Lew Kuan Yew admits that it 'took 10 years before we developed cohesion and direction in our activities, time for the leaders and officials to get to know and take the measures of each other.'[10] These days it is difficult to keep track of ASEAN-organized meetings held at Track I and Track II levels—the interaction is taking place with regional and extra-regional powers. The principles of community building laid down at the 1st Summit continues to remain central to the 'ASEAN way'. However, there are analysts who believe that some of these very principles were a handicap in ASEAN's growth as an economic integration model 'wherein the key words are voluntary, consensus, and non-interference' and these are its weaknesses.[11] ASEAN has been now in existence for more than fifty years despite the occasional obituary by those who predicted its demise—the most memorable was during the Financial Crisis of 1997–8.

Divergence in Perceptions

The difference in perceptions of India and ASEAN members created road blocks in their relationship as well as India's approach towards ASEAN. Although, India did emphasize bilateral economic cooperation in the 1960s and 1970s by signing trade accords with several ASEAN countries (e.g., in 1966 with Indonesia; in 1968 separately with Malaysia, the Philippines, and Thailand), its capacity to play a consequential role in the region was marginalized again by its concern with domestic and border problems. This was exacerbated by India's closed economy which deterred several ASEAN countries from expecting a positive outcome from their economic engagement. The 1970s began on an ominous note with armed conflict between India and Pakistan on the issue of Bangladesh's independence.

In this crisis, the US supported its SEATO/Central Treaty Organization (CENTO), ally Pakistan, while India looked for reinforcement from its longstanding friend, the USSR. It was at this time that the Indo-Soviet Treaty of Peace, Friendship, and Cooperation was signed in 1971 which compromised India's policy of 'Non-Alignment' in the eyes of the ASEAN countries. The defeat of the US in Vietnam, the emergence of communist Vietnam in 1975, and Cambodia in close proximity to the USSR, all served to increase the anxiety arising from the involvement of superpower in the region. By 1976, it was quite apparent that ASEAN had survived against all odds and was emerging as a successful and sustainable regional organization. At last, India formally requested dialogue partnership status and diplomatic initiatives were taken towards creating links with ASEAN.

However, not much headway could be achieved due to serious disagreement on the Cambodian problem. The ASEAN countries had been alarmed by the Vietnamese invasion of Cambodia in 1978 and had wholeheartedly condemned this action, which led to the overthrow of the Pol Pot regime and setting up of a Vietnam-installed Heng Samrin administration in Phnom Penh. Contrarily, India was actively lobbying for Vietnam and sending emissaries, often camouflaged as private visits, to prevail upon ASEAN to change its negative stand.[12] India's attempts at pressurizing them to recognize the pro-Vietnam Cambodian regime upset the ASEAN countries and their misgivings about its intentions led to a postponement of granting dialogue status.

Throughout this time, some ASEAN countries (like Singapore and Malaysia) did want India to be part of the ASEAN process because they believed it could play an active and positive role in resolving tension in an increasingly complex South East Asia. Former diplomat Preet Malik remembers 'I had a discussion with the Tunku soon after I took over as High Commissioner to Malaysia in 1986 where he frankly expressed the view that both Nehru and Gandhi had failed to appreciate the goodwill that he and his country had for India'.[13] Singapore Prime Minister Lee Kuan Yew's keenness to involve India with ASEAN too met with failure when he visited India in December 1978. However, according to veteran journalist Sunanda K. Datta Ray, Lee Kuan Yew 'never wavered in his conviction that South East Asia needs India to cope with China'.[14]

While the ASEAN economies were expanding rapidly and steadily, India's ambiguous political stance prevented it from benefitting fully from the region's trade and commerce. However, the Indian private sector managed to achieve a fair amount of success despite considerable odds. All through this time, Indian academics and strategic analysts were calling for greater involvement of India with ASEAN, and pointing out the advantage of close historical and cultural links. On the other hand, a naïve and incorrect assessment of the Cambodian issue and its attempts at justifying its policy to the ASEAN states, were rebuffed by them, thus further marginalizing India's role in the fastest growing economies of the ASEAN countries.

From the trajectory of India's foreign policy before 1990, it becomes evident that Indian policymakers were unable to adopt a coherent policy towards the ASEAN. The exigencies of the Cold War, and political and security considerations at home—were key factors in India's negative approach towards regional cooperation in South East Asia. Moreover, the process to establish ASEAN was neither smooth nor above suspicion. Regional cooperation by non-communist, core members of South East Asia was seen by India through a simple set of interwoven security relationships that these countries had with the US.[15]

With the end of the Cold War, ASEAN's success as a regional organization received further boost when membership was expanded to Vietnam in 1995, Laos, and Myanmar in 1997, and Cambodia in

1999. Also, Prime Minister Mahathir of Malaysia, Prime Minister Lew Kuan Yew of Singapore, and President Suharto of Indonesia (despite the obvious flaws in their governance) did help in providing continuity and leadership to the ASEAN. Coherent strategies were laid down in a phased manner to achieve economic integration. For example, the Framework Agreement on Enhancing Economic Cooperation was adopted at the 4th ASEAN Summit in Singapore in 1992, and an ASEAN Free Trade Area (AFTA) was established to push economic integration further. The signatories were the original core members—Brunei, Indonesia, Malaysia, the Philippines, Singapore, and Thailand—and today AFTA includes all ten member countries.

The biggest challenge that ASEAN faced was the Financial Crisis of 1997–8. It seemed to prove the critics right that all was not well with the ASEAN model and the political economy of its member countries. In the face of the political instability that followed the Financial Crisis, it appeared that the espousing of 'Asian values' (which had annoyed the Western countries) were just empty words of authoritarian governments and like the domino theory, each country seemed to fall under the menacing spell of the crisis. However, ASEAN's strength was displayed in the way it was able to rise like a phoenix from the ashes with member states cooperating and strategizing for quick economic recovery. In 2003, learning from the financial crisis, the political elite decided to bolster the concept of an ASEAN Community ahead of an East Asia Community. It was agreed that the ASEAN Community would be based on three pillars: the ASEAN Political-Security Community, the ASEAN Economic Community, and the ASEAN Socio-Cultural Community.[16] With the establishment of the East Asia Summit (EAS) in 2005, ASEAN leaders felt the need to strengthen ASEAN in accordance with the Bali Concord II and the ASEAN Vision 2020. These measures were to keep pace with the process of globalization and widen the scope of ASEAN so that it would retain not only its position as the hub but also keep up its relevance in the new complex environment in the region.

In 2007, Singaporean Prime Minister articulated the need for closer integration within ASEAN.

To stay in the game, ASEAN must take decisive action. We must become a strong and effective grouping, able to partner China and India effectively. Many investors today see ASEAN as ten isolated, scattered national economies, too small to be worth paying attention to. If ASEAN's integration stagnates while the rest of Asia forges ahead, we will be left behind and become irrelevant.

The second reason for integration is an aspirational one—creating a united and coherent ASEAN organisation so that we are favourably positioned as the basis of the new regional architecture.[17]

However, this is not to suggest that there were no shortcomings in the regional organization, in fact in the late 1990s there was widespread consensus that ASEAN lacked 'a strong, capable engine for leading the integration process.'[18] Even so, ASEAN's strength has been that it has been able to overcome deficiencies by constantly reinventing itself to keep pace with the changing times resulting in the establishment of ASEAN Charter which led to institutionalization of the organization and strengthened the concept of the ASEAN Community, even though in recent years there are growing noticeable disagreements among them concerning China. Today, the time is opportune for India to promote closer bilateral relations with those ASEAN nations who share common concerns about China.

Working towards Closer Relationship

By the end of the 1980s, it was apparent that India had been left out from the process of regional cooperation in South East Asia, be it ASEAN or APEC. The Indian political elite had taken note of the drawbacks in the policy framework towards South East Asia and realized that a distinctive approach was needed to keep pace with economic and strategic developments in the region. Making amends for lost opportunities, India advocated a vigorous policy of engaging ASEAN by laying out the conceptual framework of the Look East Policy in 1992. The new strategy coupled with the initiation of much needed domestic economic reforms positively impacted India's interaction with ASEAN. Formal relations were established through a sectoral partnership and finally through a full dialogue partnership in December 1995.

India's change of policy towards South East Asia can be summarized as the end of the Cold War, economic and geopolitical significance of the region, India's recognition of ASEAN as a successful regional organization, China's rising influence in South East Asia, an improvement in India-US ties, and the growing awareness that economic growth would benefit by engaging with these vibrant economies. To find its place in the Indo-Pacific, India accepted the need to play a more vigorous role in the ASEAN if it was to be relevant in the ongoing process of regional cooperation.[19]

The dialogue partnership with ASEAN finally allowed India to considerably deepen its relationship with the member countries and this enhanced its profile in the region as a reliable political, strategic, and economic partner. India-ASEAN trade and investment relations started growing steadily, some recent figures show that bilateral trade increased from US$21 billion in 2005–6 to US$65 billion in 2015–16.[20] Also, by India signing the Comprehensive Economic Cooperation Agreement with some of the ASEAN countries helped the growth in investment as seen in the years 2016–17 when the 'Investment flows both ways' grew significantly with 'India's share of total exports and imports was around 11.2 per cent and 10.56 per cent, respectively'.[21]

At the Commemorative India-ASEAN Summit 2018 it was emphasized that both sides would 'further strengthen ASEAN-India economic relations, including through the full utilization and effective implementation of the ASEAN-India Free Trade Area, and intensify efforts in 2018 toward the swift conclusion of a modern, comprehensive, high quality, and mutually beneficial Regional Comprehensive Economic Partnership (RCEP)'.[22]

Comparison with China always looms high on India's head like a sceptre. No one can dispute the fact China that is economically miles ahead and has already expanded 'its economic clout in South East Asia through the Regional Comprehensive Economic Partnership (RCEP)'.[23] In comparison, India's external trade figures with ASEAN in 2016 were a paltry 2.60 per cent.[24]

India's rise and its integration with South East Asia in spite of the fault lines in its policy towards the region has not so far affected the general consensus in the ASEAN that India does have the potential to balance China's presence as an 'economic centre and competitor'.[25] Therefore, it was no surprise that India was elevated to a summit partner in the Phnom Penh Summit of 2002. The partnership was further institutionalized through the ASEAN-India multilateral dialogue at the highest level and expanding areas of cooperation at the Vientiane Summit of 2004 through the agreement on ASEAN-India Partnership for Peace, Progress, and Shared Prosperity.[26] The interaction has grown, resulting in various meetings at all levels including summits, ministerial, senior officials, and experts, as well as through dialogue and cooperation frameworks initiated by ASEAN such as the ASEAN Regional Forum (ARF), the Post Ministerial Conference (PMC) 10+1, the East Asia Summit (EAS), and the ASEAN Defence Ministerial Meeting Plus (ADMM Plus). It is officially acknowledged that in the 'last two decades of India-ASEAN dialogue has led to a deepening of cooperation across the three pillars of their relationship—politico-military, economic, and socio-cultural. The India-ASEAN dialogue currently has 26 inter-governmental mechanisms that cover a wide spectrum of areas'.[27] India is also actively cooperating with ASEAN in wider areas of common concern such as the management of Sea Lines of Communication (SLOC) and tackling issues of asymmetrical threats. At the Vientiane Summit, it was also agreed that India and ASEAN would cooperate in combating the menace of international terrorism and other transnational crimes.

To deepen the cooperation further, the leaders of ASEAN and India initiated the Plan of Action (POA) on 5 August 2015 in Kuala Lumpur to put the ASEAN-India Partnership for Peace, Progress, and Shared Prosperity (2016–20) into operation. It was stated that 'the POA 2016–2020 spells out and sets the course of joint actions, practical cooperation, and concrete projects and activities'.[28] Explaining further, the official statement stated that the 'POA 2016–2020 comprises three broad areas, namely political and security cooperation; economic cooperation; and socio-cultural cooperation. Projects and activities conducted under the POA 2016–2020 include annual meetings/visits, seminars/workshops, training courses, and exchange programmes'.[29] At the 13th ASEAN-India Summit held in Kuala Lumpur on 21 November 2015, 'the ASEAN Leaders welcomed India's initiative, namely the "Act East Policy" and "Make in India"; and noted that the initiatives could complement ASEAN's community building efforts. In that regard, the ASEAN Leaders encouraged India to work with ASEAN to realise the vision and goals outlined in the ASEAN 2025: Forging Ahead Together.'[30]

Evolving Security Dynamics
India and China

China became ASEAN's dialogue partner in 1996 and was the first of dialogue partners to accede to the TAC in 2003. ASEAN had welcomed China's firm and consistent support for its integration and community building process as well as for the organization's central role in East Asia cooperation in an evolving regional architecture.[31] ASEAN took a new economic initiative after the Financial Crisis of 1997–8 involving China, Japan, and Korea in recognition of the financial interdependence in East Asia. This process of increasing its cooperation with the three countries came to be known as the 'ASEAN Plus Three' process. After decades of cooperation it was acknowledged in a Joint Statement in 2007, 'that the ASEAN Plus Three process had brought about mutual benefits and closer linkages among the ASEAN Plus Three countries.'[32] This move towards economic integration with East Asia was no flash in the pan and it is the inclusion of +3 that gave shape to the East Asia Summit, which is seen by critics as a mirage. At the time of its establishment it was perceived to be a triumph for ASEAN that the three countries, with their acute differences had met at its behest and discussed long term cooperation.

The economic linkages between ASEAN and China have grown to momentous levels especially after the signing of the ASEAN-China Free Trade Area (ACFTA) in 2010. In the twenty-first century, China's economic enmeshment of the region has moved at an incredible speed with ASEAN showing equal keenness to build multifaceted links with China. Many joint initiatives and declarations like the 2003 'Joint Declaration on the ASEAN-China Strategic Partnership for Peace and Prosperity'. ASEAN officially acknowledged the constructive fallout of these initiatives stating 'for friendly relations, good neighbourliness, comprehensive and mutually beneficial cooperation between ASEAN and China.'[33] However, despite this growing closeness, China's brazenness and military posturing in the South China Sea irked the ASEAN nations and the standoff with Vietnam and the Philippines led the ASEAN foreign ministers to issue a strong statement on 19 May 2014, in which they reaffirmed freedom of navigation, maritime security in the South China Sea and ASEAN's Six-Point Principles on the South China Sea. They called on all parties to undertake full and effective implementation of the Declaration on the Conduct of Parties in the South China Sea (DOC), which they hold is important for creating mutual trust and confidence. The official statement also 'emphasized the need for expeditiously working towards an early conclusion of the Code of Conduct in the South China Sea (COC).[34]

In this unfolding security dynamics, India is a new entrant in the South China Sea imbroglio, and its involvement happened primarily due to the Oil and Natural Gas Corporation (ONGC) Videsh Limited engaging in oil and gas exploration projects in the blocks that are claimed by Vietnam. In July 2011, China warned India to 'leave Chinese waters' after an Indian naval ship made a goodwill visit to Vietnam.[35] India called this a violation of the 'freedom of navigation in international waters' including in the South China Sea.[36] At the East Asia Summit meet in Bali in November 2011, Manmohan Singh, the then Prime Minister of India, firmly rejected China's objections to India's presence in the South China Sea, and was quoted as having told the Chinese Prime Minister Wen Jiabao 'that Indian interests were "purely commercial" and sovereignty claims must be settled according to international law'.[37]

In the security domain, India and ASEAN are committed to support efforts to safeguard the freedom of commerce and navigation. Both are concerned about the maritime environment in the Indo-Pacific and are keen to prevent SLOCs from becoming the battleground for hostile powers. Any obstruction to free passage of ships through these waters would have major consequences for India's maritime interests. India has often stated that it has no 'extra-territorial ambitions' and its maritime interests are to safeguard its 'vital national interests' and maintain a 'secure environment'. The Indian political leader, on 14 November 2014, spoke of South China Sea at the the 9th East Asia Summit, when he clearly stated India's view, 'In a world of interdependence and globalisation, there is no option but to follow international laws and norms. This also applies to maritime security. For this reason, following international law and norms is important for peace and stability in South China Sea'.[38] In the joint statement issued during Obama's visit to India in 2015, South China Sea was mentioned once again.

Regional prosperity depends on security. We affirm the importance of safeguarding maritime security and ensuring freedom of navigation and over flight throughout the region, especially in the South China Sea. We call on all parties to avoid the threat or use of force and pursue resolution of territorial and maritime disputes through all peaceful means, in accordance with universally recognized principles of international law, including the United Nations Convention on the Law of the Sea.[39]

Significantly, in May 2017 a Framework Agreement between China and ASEAN was initiated which is expected to lead to the implementation of the Code of Conduct in the South China Sea. While some see it as 'a potentially significant step toward cooling tensions in the strategic waterway',[40] others like Huang Jing of Singapore's Lee Kuan Yew School of Public Policy see it as China's '. . . means to achieving its goal of keeping the U.S. and its allies from intervening in the matter in the name of freedom of navigation or maintaining regional stability'.[41] Thus, the challenge in the security domain is for India to strategise its policy towards South China Sea in a focused and integrated way in partnership with ASEAN.

India has signed strategic partnerships with several major countries in the region, though qualms have been expressed by observers that India has not played a discernible role in the Indian Ocean Region (IOR) or the South China Sea that is in consonance with its capability and size. India needs to rethink about its maritime policy which would translate words into action. This would definitely convey to all the concerned parties that India will not remain an innocent bystander while China continues with its military buildup in the South China Sea or in the Indian Ocean. Only then will the Delhi Declaration of January 2018 convey India's seriousness of purpose, where in a joint statement, it was stated 'the importance of maintaining and promoting peace, stability, maritime safety and security, freedom of navigation and overflight in the region, and other lawful uses of the seas and unimpeded lawful maritime commerce and to promote peaceful resolutions of disputes, in accordance with universally recognised principles of international law, including the 1982 United Nations Convention on the Law of the Sea (UNCLOS)'.[42] Frederic Grare in his recent book also agrees that India 'is often seen by its regional partners as a consumer rather than a provider of whatever regional security they may help generate. The same partners often complain of India's passivity'.[43]

In such testing circumstances, regional stakeholders have to contend with the ever changing power equations and groupings. These are illustrative of the contemporary geostrategic and geopolitical environment that may undermine the relevance of the East Asia Summit. Under such circumstances, where mutual suspicion seems to be gaining over the desire to forge a new regional architecture, there are challenges to ASEAN's cohesiveness especially due to the divisive tactics of China. This was apparent when for the first time since its formation, the 2012 meeting of ASEAN foreign ministers failed to issue a joint communiqué which was attributed to Cambodia's pro-China posture creating doubts on the role of the chair and future cohesion of the organization.[44] The cohesion issue rose again after the Philippines won the arbitration case in 2016 through the ruling of the International Permanent Court of Arbitration in The Hague, which rejected 'China's claims to most of the sea along with construction of artificial islands'.[45] The Philippines President Duterte in a volte-face refused to criticize China on South China Sea in a statement issued at the ASEAN's 50th anniversary meeting in Manila in April 2016.[46]

Since then, the relations have been getting closer and warmer. This bewildering change in the relationship is explained by the well-known academician from the Philippines, Ailleen S.P. Baviera, when she states that the

policy shift is being justified on several grounds, both short-term and strategic. Among the short-term goals are to attract Chinese investments and assistance (Manila secured $24 billion worth of deals during his October 2016 state visit alone) . . . strategic considerations involve the desire to preclude armed conflict with China given the Armed Forces of the Philippines' relative weakness in the face of multiple internal and external threats, as well as the lack of credible assurances of support from its US ally.[47]

A good deal of recent academic discussion has been dominated by China's unprecedented rise, its assertive behaviour, its intentions, its disregard for rule of law, and the consequences of its actions on the regional order. Some hold the view that this is an outcome of China's grand strategy and the developments in the South China Sea could lead to serious discord between the US and China.[48] Equally critical of China were those who viewed it as 'becoming giddy with success' and having 'become much more influential much more quickly than it expected'.[49] The debate has also revolved on China's contentious actions and views towards India. Well known expert on China, Mohan Malik writes

China has been concerned about India moving too close to the United States and Japan for Beijing's comfort. From Beijing's perspective, as long as India understands that China is the preeminent great power in Asia, and New Delhi keeps its subordinate place in the hierarchy, both will enjoy a mutually beneficial relationship. However, should India challenge or aspire to emerge as China's equal or peer competitor—and to do so with help from Japan and the United States—then the entire gamut of contentious bilateral issues are open for review and recasting.[50]

It is apparent that ASEAN nations on the whole do not want to lose their economic gains by openly antagonizing China. What is more, China is stealthily trying to create a division within the ASEAN-member countries that would perhaps help its claim in the South China Sea. China's compulsions are based on geostrategic considerations and dependence on Malacca Straits for passage of crucial resources; it does not want any restraint on its hegemonic ambitions. Considering the destabilizing influences working to create an internal rift, core members of ASEAN do not want their decades of hard work in crafting a viable regional organization with the target of an economic community to be jeopardized. How ASEAN will maintain its centrality in regional forums remains a question mark, however, it is up to them to find ways to remain cohesive and close—there is a need to further strengthen the relationship with India which has a benign and positive image. Earlier in 2005, India had been included as a member of East Asia Summit despite China's reluctance. The continued relevance of the East Asia Summit process for India (despite China's aggressive policies) is evident from Modi's speech at the East Asia Summit meet in November 2014 where he introduced his Act East Policy by stating 'Since entering office six months ago my government has moved with a great sense of priority and speed to turn our "Look East Policy" into "Act East Policy". The East Asia Summit is an important pillar of this policy'.[51]

Conclusion

The Act East Policy is based on the 1991 Look East Policy; what is new, is its emphasis on taking a hands-on approach in speeding up connectivity with the ASEAN region, based on initiatives taken by the Look East Policy. With little outcomes to show after nearly four years, the Act East Policy with its three Cs (Commerce, Culture, and Connectivity) gives the impression that it is caught in inertia and not really making an impact on the ground. The question arises when observed in the context of the strategic competition between the two countries (India and China)—how will the three Cs compare with China's much bigger and ambitious OBOR or BRI initiative from which India has kept its distance? Perhaps only time can tell, although admittedly, the government's affirmative approach and seemingly deft diplomacy has so far clearly received an encouraging response from the ASEAN countries, which have been waiting for twenty-five years for India to become proactive. Also, when compared to China, India has been cautious and slow in moving forward with the ASAEAN led RCEP.

The gaps in the policy towards South East Asia are becoming apparent. This could be due to India's preoccupation with the security challenges emanating from its immediate neighbourhood. India has been witnessing an increase in cross-border terrorism involving Pakistan and its attempts at destabilizing the country from within. Additional danger to India's territorial integrity comes from the growing nexus between China and Pakistan, especially through the China–Pakistan Economic Corridor (CPEC). Even though India is cooperating with China economically and to some extent strategically through multilateral forums and bilaterally, there is some complex political dynamics at play that is dictating this relationship. With the constantly evolving complexities and challenges in the neighbourhood, India will have to adopt innovative diplomacy and strategy in keeping with the fast-changing events; otherwise it will end up remaining a peripheral power lacking viability to contribute to the strategic trajectory in the region. In such an eventuality, as pointed out by analysts, ASEAN may soon start looking elsewhere for partners.

The Act East Policy is meant to be a roadmap towards the region that would respond to major paradigm shifts taking place in countries such as Myanmar, where there has been a transition towards democracy, although not completely. It was the earlier initiative of the Look East Policy that made India question the validity of ignoring a strategic neighbour like Myanmar (with whom it shares a border of 1,643 km. that includes the vital north-east states of Arunachal Pradesh, Manipur, Mizoram, and Nagaland). The Act East Policy must adjust to the new realities in its extended neighbourhood which demand wholehearted implementation of infrastructure projects with Myanmar through the sub-regional groupings like the Bay of Bengal Initiative for Multi-Sectoral Technical and Economic Cooperation (BIMSTEC) and the Mekong Ganga Cooperation (MGC).

Looking ahead, it is up to India to ensure that the momentum is maintained and the Act East Policy remains relevant in the coming years. In order to put the engagement with ASEAN on an even higher trajectory, an introspection of India's relationship with the region is key to both, consolidating the gains made so far and removing the obstacles that may hinder further progress. Regional integration, connectivity, and trade offer tremendous potential for economic growth and poverty reduction, as well as for peace and stability, and no amount of military posturing (by recalcitrant powers like China) can replace these innate goals.

Notes

1. 'U.S. Warship Sails Past South China Sea Islands in First Such Challenge to China under Trump', *Newsweek*, 25 May 2017, see https://uk.news.yahoo.com/u-warship-sails-past-south-072156038.html, accessed 2 July 2017.

2. C. Raja Mohan, *Crossing the Rubicon: The Shaping of India's New Foreign Policy*, New Delhi: Viking, 2003, p. 30.

3. Amitav Acharya, *Constructing a Security Community in Southeast Asia: ASEAN and the Problem of Regional Order,* London: Routledge, 2001, p. 28; Michael Leifer, *ASEAN and the Security of South-East Asia,* London: Routledge, 1989, p. 12.

4. 'President Suharto Speaks before Joint Session of Congress', Press Release, Manila, 14 February 1972.

5. David Wright-Neville, 'Southeast Asian security challenges', in *Strategy and Security in the Asia–Pacific,* ed. Robert Ayson and Desmond Ball, NSW: Allen and Unwin, 2007, p. 213.

6. David B.H. Denoon and Evelyn Colbert, 'Challenges for the Association of Southeast Asian Nations (ASEAN)', *Pacific Affairs,* vol. 71, no. 4, Winter 1998–9, pp. 505–6.

7. See http://asean.org/the-asean-declaration-bangkok-declaration-bangkok-8-august-1967/, accessed 2 March 2018.

8. See http://asean.org/treaty-amity-cooperation-southeast-asia-indonesia-24-february-1976/ accessed 2 March 2018.

9. See Amitav Acharya, *The Quest for Identity: International Relations of Southeast Asia,* Singapore: Oxford University Press, 2000; see also John Funston, ed., *Government and Politics in Southeast Asia,* Singapore: Institute of Southeast Asian Studies, 2001.

10. Lee Kuan Yew, *From Third World to First: The Singapore Story: 1965–2000,* New York: Harper Collins, 2000, p. 329; see also Anthony L. Smith, 'ASEAN's Ninth Summit: Solidifying Regional Cohesion, Advancing External Linkages', *Contemporary Southeast Asia,* vol. 26, no. 3, 2004, pp. 416–33.

11. Cao Sy Kiem, 'East Asian Economic Integration: Problems for Late-Entry Countries', in *East Asian Visions: Perspectives on Economic Development,* ed. Indermit Gill et al., Washington: World Bank and Institute of Policy Studies, 2007, p. 134.

12. *The Times,* London, 30 November 1979.

13. Preet Malik, 'India's Look East Policy: Genesis', in *Two Decades of India's Look East Policy: Partnership for Peace, Progress and Prosperity,* ed. Amar Nath Ram, New Delhi: Manohar, 2012, p. 29.

14. Sunanda K. Datta-Ray, *Looking East to Look West: Lee Kuan Yew's Mission India,* New Delhi: Penguin, 2009, p. 5.

15. Rajiv Sikri, *Challenge and Strategy: Rethinking India's Foreign Policy,* New Delhi: Sage, 2009, pp. 112–29.

16. See http://www.aseansec.org/15159.htm., accessed 14 May 2014.

17. See http://www.aseansec.org/20820.htm., accessed 14 May 2014.

18. Sy Kiem, 'East Asian Economic Integration', p. 136.

19. Mukul Asher and Rahul Sen, 'India; An integral Part of New Asia', Version 2, unpublished, 2005.

20. See http://www.assocham.org/upload/docs/ASEAN-STUDY.pdf, accessed 5 March 2017.

21. See https://www.thestatesman.com/business/india-asean-trade-on-the-rise-business-may-touch-200-billion-by-2022-1502576960.html, accessed 5 March 2018.

22. See http://www.thehindu.com/todays-paper/tp-business/india-asean-target-swift-deal-on-rcep/article22531737.ece, accessed 5 March 2018.

23. See https://thediplomat.com/2018/02/indias-role-and-chinas-roads-in-the-indo-pacific/, accessed 5 March 2018.

24. Ibid.

25. C. Raja Mohan, 'India and the Balance of Power', *Foreign Affairs*, July/August 2006, see http://www.cfr.org/india/india-balance-power/p10948, accessed 7 May 2014.

26. 'ASEAN-India Partnership for Peace, Progress and Shared Prosperity', 30 November 2004, see http://asean.org/?static_post=asean-india-partnership-for-peace-progress-and-shared-prosperity-2, accessed 7 May 2014.

27. See http://www.asean.org/news/item/overview-of-asean-india-dialogue-relations, accessed 2 October 2015.

28. Ibid.

29. Ibid.

30. Ibid.

31. Ibid.

32. 'Second Joint Statement on East Asia Cooperation Building on the Foundations of ASEAN Plus Three Cooperation', 20 November 2007, see http://www.asean.org/news/item/second-joint-statement-on-east-asia-cooperation-building-on-the-foundations-of-asean-plus-three-cooperation, accessed 25 September 2015.

33. 'Statement of the 14th ASEAN-China Summit to Commemorate the 20th Anniversary of Dialogue Relations', 18 November 2011, see http://www.asean.org/news/asean-statement-communiques/item/joint-statement-of-the-14th-asean-china-summit-to-commemorate-the-20th-anniversary-of-dialogue-relations, accessed 25 September 2015.

34. 'ASEAN Foreign Ministers' Statement on the Current Developments in the South China Sea', see http://www.asean.org/news/asean-statement-communiques/item/asean-foreign-ministers-statement-on-the-current-developments-in-the-south-china-sea, accessed 2 October 2015.

35. Liu Sheng, 'India makes Waves with South China Sea Oil and Gas Exploration', *Global Times*, 17 September 2011, see http://www.globaltimes.cn/NEWS/tabid/99/ID/675647/India-makes-waves-with-South-China-Sea-oil-and-gas-exploration.aspx., accessed 7 May 2014.

36. Ibid.

37. Indrani Bagchi, 'Prime Minister Manmohan Singh to China's Wen Jiabao: Back off on South China Sea', *The Times of India*, 19 November 2011, see http://timesofindia.indiatimes.com/india/PM-Manmohan-Singh-to-Chinas-Wen-Jiabao-Back-off-on-South-China-Sea/articleshow/10786454.cms, accessed 3 May 2014.

38. 'Modi Aims Subtle Barbs at Neighbour over South China Sea', *Business Standard*, 14 November 2014, see http://www.business-standard.com/article/economy-policy/modi-aims-subtle-barbs-at-neighbour-over-south-china-sea-114111400007_1.html, accessed 30 November 2014.

39. 'U.S.-India Joint Strategic Vision for the Asia-Pacific and Indian Ocean Region', 25 January 2015, see https://www.whitehouse.gov/the-press-office/2015/01/25/us-india-joint-strategic-vision-asia-pacific-and-indian-ocean-region, accessed 2 October 2015.

40. 'Draft a Sign of Progress on South China Sea Code of Conduct', see https://www.washingtonpost.com/world/asia_pacific/china-reports-progress-on-south-china-sea-code-of-conduct/2017/05/18/4b538176-3c3f-11e7-a59b-26e0451a96fd_story.html?utm_term=.24a8f21d7086, accessed 29 May 2017.

41. Ibid.

42. See http://asean.org/storage/2018/01/Delhi-Declaration_Adopted-25-Jan-2018.pdf, accessed 28 February 2018.

43. Frederic Garare, *India Turns East: International Engagement and US-China Rivalry*, Gurgaon: Penguin, 2017, p. 216.

44. See https://www.voacambodia.com/a/cambodian-minister-urges-closer-asean-ties-with-china/1734770.html, accessed 2 October 2015.

45. June Teufel Dreyer, 'ASEAN Summit's China Tilt Portends a New World Order', 16 May 2017, see http://yaleglobal.yale.edu/content/asean-summits-china-tilt-portends-new-world-order, accessed 29 May 2017.

46. Ibid.

47. See http://www.maritimeissues.com/politics/dutertes-evolving-south-china-sea-policy.html, accessed 5 March 2018.

48. Charles Scanlon, 'South China Sea Tensions Rattle China's Neighbours', *BBC News*, 4 November 2011, see http://www.bbc.co.uk/news/world-asia-pacific-15578083, accessed 15 September 2015; see also Thomas J. Christensen, 'The Advantage of an assertive China: Responding to Beijing's Abrasive Diplomacy', *Foreign Affairs*, vol. 90, no. 2, 2011, p. 55.

49. Scanlon, 'South China Sea Tensions'.

50. See https://thediplomat.com/2017/09/china-and-india-the-roots-of-hostility/, accessed 5 March 2018.

51. See http://www.narendramodi.in/english-rendering-of-prime-minister-shri-narendra-modis-remarks-at-the-east-asia-summit-nay-pyi-taw-6881, accessed 2 October 2015.

5

India's 'Look East' Policy in the New Global Promenade

The Effective-Ineffective Stock Taking and the Boulevard ahead

Tridib Chakraborti

T HE HISTORY of India's foreign policy has always been characterized more by continuity rather than change, and has propelled to develop its own concepts for international relations according to the existing global scenario. Broadly, the Indian foreign policy has remained the same for nearly three decades and the shifts that have occurred are not sudden and have rarely, if ever, been political or practical. Hence, India's policy of new regionalism towards the South East Asian countries and later on towards East Asia arose in response to the prevailing international environment at the end of the Cold War. The sudden collapse of the former Soviet Union in 1991 prompted the emergence of a new global political and economic scenario that led to the shift in India's strategic world view from its non-aligned posture, reliance on Soviet military hardware, bilateral treaty commitments to an autonomous global view, and proactiveness. To cope with this new international milieu in July 1991, New Delhi, under the leadership of P.V. Narasimha Rao, announced its New Economic Policy (NEP) which was guided more by economic imperative and judiciousness, and less by political rhetoric.

The Singapore Lecture in 1994 by the then Indian Prime Minister Rao, on India's Look East Policy further augmented India's close interaction with the countries of South East Asia. This paradigm shift in India's overall economic reforms and market liberalization policy, followed by a new outlook in foreign policy, naturally attracted many countries of South East Asia to develop better economic linkages with the former. The Association of South East Asian Nations (ASEAN) members also realized the growing importance of the role of economic diplomacy in relations between nations, and were convinced of the seriousness of India in her liberalization policy. These new economic dynamics and the reorientation of foreign policy promoted India from a 'Sectoral dialogue' partner of ASEAN in 1992 to a Summit level partner in 2002. However, the major achievement of this policy was India's promotion as a partner of the East Asia Summit (EAS) in 2005. This presence of India in the East Asian orbit has been, no doubt, a good beginning in its ultimate integration with the East Asian region, and can be seen as a stepping stone in fulfilling its potential to play a major role in global affairs in the twenty-first century. Thus, in the Indian foreign policy domain, New Delhi's Look East Policy has been, no doubt, a major initiative taken by our policymakers in the post-Cold War years towards a region with which it has past historical and cultural linkages.

Presently, India's Look East Policy has been in effect for more than two decades. During this span of time, India has gained several economic, strategic, and political advantages in the Asia Pacific region by executing this policy. However, when compared to China, India's position in the region has not been very prominent. There are certain obstacles, both within the formulation of India's Look East Policy, and emanating from regional and extra-regional powers. In this backdrop, the purpose of this essay is to highlight the dynamics of India's Look East Policy in the last two decades and outline the contours of achievements and hindrances in the implementation of this policy.

From down to up the Memory Lane

Indian Prime Minister Manmohan Singh stated at the 7th India-ASEAN Summit and the 4th EAS held in Hua Hin, Thailand on 25 October 2009:

I am extremely satisfied with the outcome of the India-ASEAN Summit. I found a strong desire among the ASEAN countries to substantially strengthen their links with India in all areas. This includes not only economic cooperation and trade, but also science and technology, human resource development, protection of the environment, and deeper political and security cooperation . . . and therefore the sky is the limit for our engagement with this region.[1]

Manmohan Singh also called for an Asian regional trade agreement as a pivotal step towards the integration of the region into a broader 'Asian Economic Community'. This statement has been quite strategically vital for New Delhi in the context of its Look East Policy, under the second tenure of the United Progressive Alliance (UPA) government established in 2009. Although the process of India's Look East Policy has been effectively accelerated after Rao's Singapore speech of 1994, the manner in which India has played an effective role during this period of nearly two decades in formulating this policy will be the main subject matter of study of this essay. ASEAN was formed on 8 August 1967 in Bangkok, by five members—Indonesia, Malaysia, Singapore, Thailand, and the Philippines. The objectives were to promote the economic, social, and cultural development of the region through cooperative programmes; to safeguard the political and economic stability of the region against big power rivalry; and to serve as a forum for the resolution of intra-regional differences. Gradually, over time, it increased its membership to 10 with the joinings of Brunei in 1984, Vietnam in 1995, Laos and Myanmar in 1997, and Cambodia in 1999. After more than forty-five years of operation, it came to be recognized as one of the most successful examples of economic and trade cooperation in Third World regionalism for attracting many countries outside the region to develop better linkages with it. However, in spite of its economic achievements during the Cold War years, India and ASEAN remained 'awkward strangers' and their relationship lacked economic and political substance.[2] New Delhi was not among those, who enthusiastically welcomed the formation of ASEAN in 1967. Its attitude was rather diffident. India's lack of warmth in political relations and weak economic linkages (due to closed and regulated economy) with ASEAN were caused due to their differences in perception and actions in security, and other related issues of great power activities in the South East Asian region. India's insidious association with the former Soviet Union and its inclination towards Vietnam and Cambodia displeased many South East Asian countries as well. Its recognition of the Heng Samrin government in Cambodia in July 1980 was a further obstruction in the development of better ties with ASEAN members. In fact, New Delhi, at this time, did not risk surrendering its close ties with Hanoi and Moscow because it valued its warm relations with these countries to be much more strategically important than its standing among the ASEAN countries.[3]

In early 1990s, the global and regional politics underwent qualitative changes. With the collapse of the Soviet Union at the end of the Cold

War and with the onset of globalization, nations were beginning to realize that the means to make wealth is by securing international trade and encouragement of foreign investments. The 1990s was a phase which witnessed rapid economic development and growth of Asian countries, especially in South East Asia. In the context of the new world order, India recognized the economies of the neighbourhood and emerged as a willing partner in the process of regional economic integration. The new policy under the leadership of Rao had embarked on a substantive and wide-ranging programme of economic reforms, restructuring, and liberalization. It brought the Indian economy in line with the economies of the ASEAN countries. India's decision to give a special policy thrust to its relations with the ASEAN and 'desired improved relations with individual countries in the ASEAN region and with ASEAN as a collective entity' virtually obliterated its hitherto indifferent outlook to this regional organization.[4] India, under the Prime Minister Rao, announced its Look East Policy, which was very well calculated and thought-out, buttressed by its conscious attempt to engage East Asia. Rao perceived that the end of the Cold War had given India an opportunity to broaden its relations with and focus on countries which were traditional friends and long-standing partners and were of special importance, but with whom relations were compromised due to the imperatives of Cold War politics. Therefore, India's Look East Policy was a product of both the force of liberalization and the desire to replicate the East Asian growth miracle.

For ASEAN, India's size, population, educated middle class, industrial base, military strength, technical capability, ancient cultural history, and presence of overseas Indians were factors in its favour. Moreover, ASEAN's perception of New Delhi as an emerging regional power and China as a source of security threat, coupled with the grim situation in the South China Sea because of conflicting claims over the Spratly Islands; the stand-off in the Taiwan Straits and the Korean Peninsula; and the troubled ties among the US, Japan, and China had convinced ASEAN of the need for a paradigm shift in India-ASEAN ties. It was also felt by the ASEAN members that India's image and peaceful rise as a benign power accrued significant strategic benefits for them to play a more effective role in the region. Thus, mutual needs affected their convergence. New Delhi's Look East Policy, therefore, coincided with ASEAN's 'Look West' line. This new-found regionalization drive ultimately led to an overall normalization of relations between India and ASEAN. This favourable environment resulted in ASEAN governments responding to Indian overtures in 1992; and between 1992 and 1996, New Delhi first became a 'sectoral dialogue' partner of the grouping and thereafter a 'full dialogue' partner. India also joined the security entity of the ASEAN, the ASEAN Regional Forum (ARF), in 1996. This allowed it entry into multilateral security deliberations outside the aegis of the United Nations for the first time. In the same year, at New Delhi, the ASEAN-India Joint Cooperation Committee held its first meeting and the two sides started a political dialogue and consultations at the senior officials' level in 1998. In addition to an ASEAN-India Business Council, the two sides agreed to set up three ASEAN-India working groups dealing with development cooperation, science and technology, and trade and investment respectively. Thus, with these reciprocal interactions, ASEAN's closer ties with India began to take shape in world politics. However, in the initial years, the Look East Policy generated impetus towards the economically developed members of ASEAN, while neglecting the economically backward countries of South East Asia.

India's Look East Policy towards the economically feeble countries of South East Asia (i.e. Vietnam, Cambodia, Laos, and Myanmar) gathered its momentum after Vietnam joined in 1995, Myanmar and Laos in 1997, and Cambodia in 1999 within the ASEAN orbit. All these countries have a history of acute internal suffering, vulnerable economies, drug trafficking, and low intensity conflicts. Therefore, induction of these countries within the ASEAN circuit took New Delhi's Look East Policy to a new height. The entry of Myanmar has provided India a long boundary to go along with its extensive maritime border with the ASEAN region and has dilated New Delhi's economic, security-specific, and political opportunities with the countries of South East Asia. The signing of the Mekong-Ganga Cooperation (MGC) on 10 November 2000 in Vientiane among five neighbouring countries—Myanmar, Thailand, Cambodia, Laos, and Vietnam—further accelerated the development of bilateral ties between India and the less developed countries of South East Asia. One major goal of this subregional initiative was to enhance the transport links that span India, Myanmar, Thailand, Cambodia, and Vietnam. A major vision of this programme is to establish a Delhi–Hanoi road and railway link in the near future, and also to develop transportation networks including the East–West Corridor project and the Trans-Asian Highway. These important initiatives would ease the cross-border movement of goods and services across these nations and in the process will facilitate the operation of the ASEAN-India FTA. Further, the linkages between India and these countries of the

Indochina region might give New Delhi an opportunity to expedite economic development of its north-east region. Therefore, though clogged, India's Look East Policy towards the less developed countries of South East Asia clearly exhibited an upward mobility of bilateral relations. It is to be noted here that before the formation of MGC in June 1997 under the aegis of India and Thailand, BIST-EC (Bangladesh, India, Sri Lanka, Thailand-Economic Cooperation) was formally launched—later known as BIMSTEC—with the primary goal of acting as a vehicle for promoting trade and tourism in the Bay of Bengal region and offered New Delhi an opportunity to strengthen its ties with the eastern neighbourhood, much in conformity with the core of its Look East Policy.

India's 'Look East' diplomacy reached its height when the ASEAN leaders at their 7th Summit held in Brunei in November 2001 agreed to convene the ASEAN-India Summit. The decision for a separate ASEAN-India Summit clearly demonstrated that New Delhi was not treated at par with the countries of East Asia (i.e. Japan, China, and Korea), but it provided an opportunity to India to prove its economic influence and dynamics in the region. This promotion of India as a new actor in the orbit of ASEAN's economic, political, and strategic process was a product of history of more than a decade. In this summit, the then Prime Minister Atal Behari Vajpayee represented India and had the distinction of being the first leader not only of India, but also from the entire South Asia to address the ASEAN Summit. Prime Minister of Cambodia Hun Sen inaugurated this summit and launched 'The Phnom Penh Agenda: Promoting Shared Prosperity and Peace Across ASEAN'. This included a four-point agenda comprising of enhanced cooperation in the Greater Mekong Subregion (GMS), complementary to the implementation of Initiative for ASEAN Integration (IAI), promotion of ASEAN Tourism, special ASEAN focus on fighting terrorism and promoting sustainable environment, including the ratification of the Kyoto Protocol. Apart from participation at the summit, Vajpayee proposed to create an ASEAN-India FTA by the year 2012, which, covering about 1.5 billion consumers with a combined GNP of US$1.7 trillion, would gradually eliminate the trade barriers between the member countries of ASEAN and India. Vajpayee also agreed to offer greater tariff concessions to less developed members of ASEAN: Laos, Cambodia, Vietnam, and Myanmar. At the end of ASEAN-India Summit in Phnom Penh, Vajpayee, in a press conference said that 'our intention is with each of the ASEAN countries to enhance our level of dialogue, our economic interaction and political interaction and to have credible and respectable portfolio of activities that are going on with them.'[5] Thus, this India-ASEAN Summit was, no doubt, a watershed event in the history of bilateral relations between India and South East Asia since the fall of the former Soviet Union. Having reached greater heights, it is now imperative to implement India's long-drawn Look East Policy not only in theory, but also in practice.

Footsteps of Accomplishments in India's Look East Policy

India, through its protracted political, economic, and strategic relations with the countries of South East Asia, has been able to prove its genuine interests towards the region. Through its Look East Policy, New Delhi clearly put up a satisfactory performance in its development of relations with some economically advanced countries of South East Asia, though this could not be repeated with others who were economically vulnerable. Singapore is now investing more in selected areas in India. Singaporean companies have been active in information technology, communications, construction, and ports. Malaysia's relation with India, which were based for a long time on palm oil exports and counter trade, have now taken on new dimensions with Malaysian companies' involvement in the power and road building sectors in India. In the other direction, Indian companies have invested in Thailand, Malaysia, and Indonesia in pharmaceuticals, textiles, paper and pulp manufacture, and palm oil refining. Besides this, New Delhi also developed better economic ties with Thailand, Indonesia, and the Philippines. But it lacked attention towards Brunei, another developed country within South East Asia, whose per capita Gross Domestic Product (GDP) remains second only to Singapore due to unknown reasons. In spite of the growing economic ties, India's bilateral relations with the economically advanced countries of South East Asia have not yet evolved into a meaningful partnership. ASEAN trade and investments in India by these countries (i.e. Singapore, Malaysia, Thailand, Indonesia, and the Philippines), after an initial spurt, have stagnated in part because of ASEAN's own preoccupation with the financial crisis in the region, but also largely due to its disillusionment with New Delhi's daunting procedures, requirements, and an unresponsive bureaucracy. However, currently there has been a forward momentum in the India-South East Asia economic and political ties.

India and ASEAN as regional trade partners, offer a huge and attractive, interconnected, and geographically contiguous market of more than 1.5 billion people. Growth in India's exports to ASEAN countries in the recent past has been much higher in comparison to other important destinations, though in case of imports, those from other regions have achieved faster growth than ASEAN's imports into India. Trade ties between them over the years have clearly exhibited a sharp increase in India's exports to this area. ASEAN accounted for 3.60 per cent of India's exports to the world in 1980 which by 1992 increased to 6 per cent. In terms of value, India's export to ASEAN countries had more than quadrupled in 1992. And, in the later years, India's trade in terms of both exports and imports with ASEAN increased very rapidly. In fact, India's exports to ASEAN have more than doubled in the last five years and India's imports from ASEAN countries have nearly doubled. The merchandise exports in 2012–13 stood at over US$301 billion and this offers a very realistic picture of the export target in the region. India's trade with the South East Asian countries, during 2014–15 was US$76,527.35 million, twenty times more than in 1992–3. However, the balance of trade, except for 1993–4, has always tilted in favour of the South East Asian countries (Table 5.1). Compared to other regional groupings, ASEAN is the fifth most important market in the world in terms of Indian exports and fourth in terms of imports. This region has great importance in the Look East Policy of India and accounts for about 12 per cent of India's trade with the world. The four major trading partners from the ASEAN are Singapore, Indonesia, Malaysia, and Thailand for India; and accounts for more than 85 per cent trade with ASEAN. Trade with Cambodia has been the least in value terms (as per 2014–15 trade statistics). The top ten items of export to ASEAN region in 2014–15 were petroleum and petroleum products, transport equipment, machinery and instruments, meat and their preparations, gems and jewellery, dyes, cereals, drugs, pharmaceuticals and fine chemicals, primary and semi-finished iron and steel, and oil meals. The region has great potential for export of most of the Indian products due to the proximity and cultural bonding. Besides this, there are a lot of trade promotion activities in the South East Asian region. India has an ASEAN India Business Council (AIBC) and Joint Business Councils (JBC) with Singapore, Malaysia, Myanmar, Indonesia, Thailand, Vietnam, and the Philippines. Since 1999, there has been a recovery and trade flow once again started its normal long-term trend. In fact, growth in India's exports to South East Asian countries in recent

TABLE 5.1: India's Trade with South East Asia

(in million $)

Year (April–March)	Exports	Imports	Total Trade	Balance of Trade
1990–1	748	1,474	2,222	–726
1991–2	1,022.30	1,274.60	2,296.90	–252.30
1992–3	1,508.25	2,230.24	3,738.49	–721.99
1993–4	1,981.71	1,950	3,931.71	+31.71
1994–5	2,326.27	3,059.50	5,385.76	–733.23
1995–6	3,177.77	3,881.88	7,059.65	–704.11
1996–7	3,353.46	4,492.58	7,846.04	–1,139.12
1997–8	2,987.21	5,177.91	8,165.12	–2,190.70
1998–9	2,090.35	5,865.13	7,955.48	–3,774.78
1999–2000	2,721.05	6,281.73	9,002.78	–3,560.68
2000–1	3,362.20	5,210.49	8,572.69	–1,846.31
2001–2	3,945.86	5,767.12	9,712.98	–1,821.26
2002–3	5,219.16	6,565.61	11,784.77	–1,346.45
2003–4	6,494.35	10,058.46	16,552.81	–3,564.11
2004–5	8,425.89	9,114.66	17,540.55	–718.77
2005–6	10,411.30	10,883.68	21,294.98	–472.38
2006–7	12,607.43	18,108.48	30,715.19	–5,501.05
2007–8	16,413.52	22,674.81	39,088.33	–6,261.29
2008–9	19,140.63	26,202.96	45,343.59	–7,062.33
2009–10	18,113.71	25,797.96	43,911.67	–7,684.25
2010–11	25,627.89	30,607.96	56,235.85	–4,980.07
2011–12	36,744.35	42,158.84	78,903.19	–5,414.49
2012–13	33,008.21	42,866.36	75,874.57	–9,858.15
2013–14	33,133.55	41,278.09	74,411.64	–8,144.49
2014–15	31,812.58	44,714.77	76,527.35	–12,902.19

Source: Prepared by the author from various tables and pages based on *Ministry of Commerce Annual Reports*, Government of India, New Delhi, from April–March 1990–1 to April–March 2014–15.

years has been much higher vis-à-vis other important destinations. Moreover, as committed by the Government of India earlier, on 13 August 2009, the India-ASEAN FTA in goods was signed in Bangkok and came into effect from 1 January 2010 with Malaysia, Thailand, and Singapore. It was also stated that this agreement would reach full circle with other ASEAN members by 2016 which would collectively cover a market of nearly 1.8 billion people, whose economy is comparable to that of China, Japan, and South Korea, and it proposes to gradually slash tariffs for over 4,000 product lines.[6] This FTA was signed at the 7th ASEAN Economic Ministers (AEM)-India meeting, held in conjunction with the 41st AEM meeting from 13 to 16 August and marks ASEAN's fifth such agreement after the ASEAN-Japan, the

ASEAN-China, the ASEAN-Korea, and the ASEAN-Australia and New Zealand FTAs. Under this agreement, ASEAN and India would lift import tariffs on more than 80 per cent of traded products during 2013–16. Tariffs on sensitive goods would be reduced to 5 per cent in 2016 and up to 489 very sensitive products would be maintained.[7] Following this FTA in goods, the bilateral trade figure between India and ASEAN increased and improved very rapidly and as a result, the trade between them reached nearly US$76 billion in 2012–13 and both the sides have aimed at increasing it to US$100 billion by 2015.

Besides this, with economic liberalization, businessmen in ASEAN are increasingly undertaking Foreign Direct Investment (FDI) in India in crucial infrastructure sectors, such as telecommunications, heavy industry, fuels, hotel and tourism services, chemicals, fertilizers, textiles, paper and pulp, and food processing. Among South East Asian countries Malaysia, Thailand, and Singapore have become the major sources of FDI in India. From a negligible amount in 1991, cumulatively approved FDI from ASEAN has so far reached more than US$5 billion. Although flows to India have increased significantly in recent years, the level of FDI is still considered low in comparison to its GDP, and it has been felt by the policymakers that lifting restrictions on foreign equity ownership in many sectors, in particular the service industries, can boost investor sentiment.

New Delhi has also set up joint working groups with Malaysia, Indonesia, etc., for working towards Comprehensive Economic Cooperation Agreement (CECA). The Comprehensive Framework Agreement was signed by the leaders of India and ASEAN at the Bali Summit in 2003, and laid a strong base for the eventual establishment of an ASEAN-India Regional Trade and Investment Area (RITA) which includes FTA in goods, services, and investment. However, on 13 August 2009 at Bangkok, after six years of negotiations, the India-ASEAN FTA, as part of the CECA was finally signed and came into effect from 1 January 2010. The agreement was only for trade-in goods and did not include software and information technology. This FTA in goods would integrate the two globally important economic blocks for mutually beneficial economic gains. Under the ASEAN-India FTA, the ASEAN member countries and India would eliminate tariffs for about 4,000 products (which include electronics, chemicals, machinery, and textiles), out of which, duties for 3,200 products were to be reduced by December 2013, while duties on the remaining 800 products was to be brought down to zero or near-zero levels by December 2016. Though New Delhi has been campaigning for multilateralism and acting as a responsible member of the World Trade Organization (WTO), regionalism as a reaction to the multilateral process has gained its ground in its foreign policy agenda in the twenty-first century and this FTA is a major step of India's Look East Policy in reducing its dependence on trade with the US and the EU, and turning towards South East Asia will strengthen its regional dynamics and also reduce ASEAN dependence on China.

The second major achievement of India's Look East Policy involves security cooperation and expansion of its area of influence in the South East Asian region, with a view to becoming a major player in the emerging balance of power in Asia. This security cooperation involves joint operations to protect sea lanes and pooling resources in the war against terrorism. The Indian Navy has been playing an effective role in combating piracy in the Malacca Straits, and has offered to cooperate with the littoral states in the implementation of the 'Eyes in the Sky' programme for patrolling the piracy-infested Malacca Straits. The terrorism menace, both from within and across borders as faced by both India and the countries of South East Asia, has been tackled by both of them through close monitoring, coordination, and with joint efforts. Among other areas where India and the ASEAN members are jointly harmonizing their efforts are the problems of piracy, insurgency, trafficking of small arms and drugs, illegal migration, environmental pollution, narcotics traffic, and other security-related issues including the safety of the Sea Lines of Communication (SLOC) that have been indispensable for the development of economic richness of the region. Furthermore, India's recent growing naval activities in the Indian Ocean region, based on the Indian Maritime Doctrine of 2004, and its 'Look East' security thrust involving the ASEAN and the 'rim land' states farther afield—Japan and South Korea—has been no doubt a successful exercise in its naval diplomacy. New Delhi has also quietly begun to put in place arrangements for regular access to ports in South East Asia. India's defence contacts have widened to include Japan, South Korea, and China, which hitherto were never engaged by India in such a multi-directional diplomatic endeavour.

Furthermore, the expansion of the Indian Navy, establishment of Indian Far Eastern Naval Command (FENC) mainly in Andaman and Nicobar Islands, and its warming relations with the ASEAN members indicate that New Delhi desires to balance China and act as a balancer, in the Indian Ocean or Pacific regions, with the collaboration of the US in the South East Asian region and beyond. The bilateral naval exercises were a manifestation of a more pragmatic and vision-based Look East Policy. Since 2000, joint naval exercises and patrols as well as regular port calls by their respective navies have become a regular feature. Indian Navy sent warships, tankers, and submarines to Japan, South Korea, Thailand, Malaysia, Indonesia, Singapore, Cambodia, and Vietnam for bilateral exercises. There were several objectives of these joint naval exercises with the South East Asian countries. For instance, since 1998 Indian naval ships have visited various Vietnamese ports regularly and thereby tested the future viability and strategic cooperation in the naval domain with Vietnam.[8] From 2000, until September 2012, various Indian ships have visited multiple ports of Vietnam more than sixteen times as a goodwill visit. The objective of the expedition is to enhance people-to-people and naval links between India and the ASEAN and it remains one of the major flagship events being undertaken by ASEAN and India together to mark this important stage of bilateral relations.[9]

In fact, this has been also pragmatically realized by the Indian policymakers that its Look East Policy domain should not be confined only to trade, but also extended to the new military-security power projection in the South East Asian region, particularly through naval deployments and maritime diplomacy. The deepening dependence on Gulf oil and gas raises important security issues. The oil and gas from the Persian Gulf area pass through several vulnerable maritime choke points, such as the Hormuz Strait, the Gulf of Aden, the Suez Canal, and the Malacca Straits. Problems of gun running, drug trafficking, piracy, and terrorism constitute major threats to maritime security in this region.[10] As a gesture of goodwill, through regional confidence-building and cooperation mechanisms like the ARF, the Regional Cooperation Agreement on Combating Piracy, Armed Robbery against Ships in Asia (ReCAAP), and the MILAN exercises India tries to keep its presence in the region. As a gesture of firm commitment of New Delhi's joint exercise with Vietnam, on 24 May 2013, four Indian Navy ships—INS Rana, INS Shakti, INS Shivalik, and Kurmak—toured across the South China Sea on their way to Shanghai, where they arrived for a goodwill visit for a couple of weeks.[11] Furthermore, in the wake of the Tsunami disaster in December 2004, Indian ships were immediately sent to Sri Lanka, Maldives, Thailand, and Indonesia, which was widely acclaimed by all the countries of South East Asia. Thus, India's growing naval strength and its maritime security diplomacy gave many South East Asian countries security relief and brought them closer to each other.

The third achievement of India's Look East Policy is its growing defence cooperation with various countries of South East Asia and beyond. India's de facto nuclear weapons power status since 1998 is another factor that has earned it grudging recognition as a major player in international relations. In military terms, India has embarked upon an immense military growth programme. Much of this military maturity is focused upon projecting power throughout the Asian region, starting from the Indian Ocean to the South China Sea. Its latest inclusion of a sea-based nuclear power posture, substantial air force development (including combat aircraft, Il-78 tanker aircraft for in-air refuelling, and AWACS systems), and major investment in the expansion of its types of missiles and surface and submarine naval capacities have resulted in sharing defence experience, know-how, and material between India and the ASEAN States. This resulted in both India and the ASEAN states showing identical curiosity in sharing defence experience, know-how, and material. As an outcome, in more than one decade, India has signed a number of bilateral defence pacts with most of the South East Asian states by providing various defence technologies, training personnel, and joint military exercises with a motive of two prime factors: reuniting US military pre-eminence in the Asia Pacific and matching China's growing dominance in the region. The major defence cooperation agreements that took place over the years are the Defence Cooperation Agreement signed by India and Singapore in October 2003;[12] a strategic dialogue between India and Singapore modelled after the Indo-US strategic dialogue, held in 2007; the Bilateral Agreement on Cooperative Activities in the Field of Defence signed by India and Indonesia in 2001;[13] a joint declaration establishing a new strategic partnership and a plan to hold annual strategic dialogues, signed with Indonesia in November 2005 during the visit of Indonesian President Susilo Bambang Yudhogona;[14] the Protocol on Defence Cooperation signed with the Vietnamese Defence Minister in 2000 by the Indian Defence minister;[15] a Joint Declaration on Framework of Comprehensive Cooperation and an agreement to raise bilateral relations to the level of a broad-based strategic partnership, signed by India and Vietnam in 2003;[16] and a joint declaration on establishing a strategic partnership signed by the Indian and the Vietnamese prime ministers in July 2007.[17] Therefore, the growing defence-understanding between India and some countries of South East Asia can be interpreted as a major dividend of India's Look East Policy initiative.

The fourth achievement of India's Look East Policy has been its engagement with South East and East Asia. The 1st EAS, which was held in December 2005 in Kuala Lumpur and consisted of sixteen countries (ASEAN, China, Japan, Korea, India, Australia, and New Zealand) has remained a historic event in emerging global politics. In this meeting of EAS, five issues of 'financial stability, energy security, economic integration, growth, and trade and investment expansion, narrowing down of the developmental gap and eradication of poverty, and good governance' were given special emphasis. This new space in the East Asian region has marked a return of India's active dialogue and participation in the politico-economic processes at work in the larger Asia Pacific region. The process has also brought together leaders from the ten ASEAN members with their counterparts from the north-eastern Asian States of China, Japan, and South Korea. The EAS is more than a near and next extension of the ASEAN Plus, its formation can be termed as the first step for establishing an East Asian community on the lines of the European Economic Community. It aims to create a forum for dialogue on broader strategic, political, and economic issues of common interest with the aim of promoting peace, stability, and economic prosperity in East Asia.

India, being an Asian nation, has participated in the 1st EAS held at Kuala Lumpur on 14 December 2005. Prime Minister Manmohan Singh, after attending it, clearly said that it was important for India to be in a group that had the 'potential to play a major role in global affairs. Its composition, its evolving agenda, and format give it the potential to play a major role in global affairs. India's presence in this group from its very outset is an opportunity we value.' In fact, rapid integration with East Asia as part of India's Look East Policy, Phase II has made the region India's largest trade partner, ahead of the EU and the US. India is evolving a complete FTA with ASEAN, and is presently studying FTAs with Japan, China, and South Korea; and trying to integrate as a part of the growing larger web of FTAs in the region. The participation of India in the 4th EAS, held in Hua Hin, Thailand in October 2009, has once again clearly exhibited New Delhi's growing importance in the Asia Pacific region and recognized the impact of India's socio-economic transformation on the reshaping of the global economic order, and the opportunities this has for accelerating Asia's own growth. In this meeting, there was agreement related to issues of terrorism and nontraditional threats. The EAS leaders endorsed the establishment of Nalanda University as a centre of excellence in education and international understanding as proposed by India. Therefore, the increasing relevance of India in the East Asian framework has contributed to its rising interaction with ASEAN.

The fifth achievement of India's Look East Policy has been its active participation in the IAI programme which has been a regional framework, aimed at narrowing the developmental gap within ASEAN and enhancing regional integration. The IAI aimed to narrow developmental division between ASEAN's old and new members, to promote equitable economic development, and to help alleviate poverty within the new members. India being a responsible dialogue partner of ASEAN had actively played a very constructive role in this initiative. India has successfully completed the Railway Training Programmes for 48 trainers from (Cambodia, Lao PDR, Myanmar, and Vietnam) CLMV countries in India. In addition, India is presently implementing a project, India-Singapore Joint Training Programme for CLMV in English language Training. New Delhi is also involved in an entrepreneurial development project in each of the CLMV countries. The objective of this project is to provide technical and advisory services to CLMV for the establishment of entrepreneurial development institutes in each of these countries as part of the efforts to train entrepreneurs and prepare small enterprises that face the challenge of globalization. So far, New Delhi has already established such centres in Cambodia, Laos, and Vietnam, and in Myanmar it will be set up soon. This active focus of New Delhi on the IAI has been looked upon by ASEAN countries as a sign of India's commitment to ASEAN and its forward-looking processes. Therefore, India's ASEAN policy in the twenty-first century has become truly multidimensional and multi-pronged in character.

Sixth, through India's Look East Policy, New Delhi has at least created an image of an emerging power in the Asian region. Its close understanding with the US, Japan, South Korea, and Australia brought her the status of a more effectual power in the emerging security architecture of the Asia Pacific region. Some of the members of ASEAN consider India to act as a balancer in the growing power struggle in the south-eastern region and beyond, against China. In fact, the growing Indo-US strategic understanding would make it easier for India to establish security links with the American allies in Asia and the Pacific, i.e. Australia, South Korea, and Japan. During his address to the Indian Parliament on 8 November 2010, US President Barack Obama said, 'More broadly, India and the United States can partner in Asia. . . . Like your neighbours in South East Asia, we want India to not only "look East," we want India to "engage East"—because it will increase the security and prosperity of all our nations.'[18] Similar views were expressed by US Secretary of State Hillary Clinton, in her last foreign policy speech at the Council on Foreign Relations (CFR) at Washington. To quote Clinton, 'America supports New Delhi's move to weave it into the fabric of Asia Pacific region. We've encouraged India's Look East policy as a way to weave another big democracy into the fabric of the Asia-Pacific.'[19] Therefore, these growing relations have increased India's diplomatic leverage in international politics.

Seventh, India's defence capabilities are formidable (its navy is the largest in the Indian Ocean littoral) and its economy is one of the fastest growing. Therefore, it is the only country in the region that can match China in terms of size and military power in the region.

Eighth, there is a domestic political and public consensus on India's Look East Policy. No party has ever questioned the desirability of closer engagement with South East Asia and beyond. This is no doubt the prime achievement of India's Look East Policy.

Finally, New Delhi participated in a number of ARF activities relating to confidence-building measures (CBMs), maritime search and rescue, peacekeeping, nonproliferation, preventive diplomacy, and disaster management. These activities proved productive and useful for the facilitation of the introduction of appropriate CBMs among the participants. This participation of India through its Look East Policy has ensured it a unique role to play in the Asia Pacific balance of power equation.

Major Impediment of India's Effective Look East Policy

India's Look East Policy during its two decades of performance has failed to display the expected result, unlike China's attempts during the same period.

First, China remains an important hurdle to India's Look East Policy. China does not favour a strong Indian presence and influence in South East Asia. Traditionally, China has been very dismissive of India, treating it as a mere South Asian player. However, over the last decade or so, the Chinese have been somewhat intrigued by the steady rate of India's economic growth and its political stability. So, they have no option but to consider India more seriously in the regional calculus. China has applied diverse strategies at multilateral and bilateral levels in the South East Asian region through assistance to the ASEAN countries during the East Asian financial crisis and the global meltdown in 2008, thereby earning an enormous confidence from the ASEANs' end, which India missed.

China has provided military support to most of India's neighbours and significant assistance to Pakistan for its nuclear programme, thus becoming a serious destabilizing factor for India. Unlike China, which enjoys a number of economic and military advantages over India in tangible and quantitative terms, India cannot rely on FDI as a springboard for achieving a well-developed economy thriving on service sectors and tertiary industries.

Second, New Delhi failed to take a sufficient strategic perspective on its relationship with Myanmar. Myanmar borders a region of India that unfortunately does not have much political weight in New Delhi's mindset, resulting in a tendency to sideline it. Though India's trade with countries bordering the north-east has been visualized as the most dramatic expansion, this expansion has had little or no impact on north-eastern economy as most of this trade expansion is through seaports. In spite of huge potential, the Indo-Myanmar trade remained insignificant, when comparing with China and others. There is no rigorous effort on the part of the government to develop the border regions and increase tradable items.

The third obstacle remains the north-eastern region. In the north-east, there are four Indian states—Arunachal Pradesh, Mizoram, Manipur, and Nagaland—that have borders with Bangladesh and Myanmar, and are strategically important on account of a number of reasons.

1. It is important to develop better linkages with these countries in order to prevent the promotion of cross-border anti-national activities.
2. Improvement of the economic condition of north-eastern region will be essential since this region solely determines the connectivity from north-east to Myanmar and beyond.
3. India's energy demands and its connectivity policy would be essential for cross-border communication networks including air, roads, railways, and waterways promoting free trade and transit facilities as well as development of transnational oil and energy-transmitting pipelines.

However, the major hurdles with reference to this region are the weak communication links between the central government and the north-eastern states, which resulted in the existence of lack of the 'we' feeling. Besides this, there are important hurdles such as difficult regional geography (mountains, jungles, waterways, etc.); lack of harmonization of railway networks; lack of standardization of all-weather paved roads; inefficient and underdeveloped land border custom-stations; absence of enabling software such as smooth transit procedures; inadequate use of security personnel; cumbersome trade-documentation requirements; illegal immigration tensions among India, Bangladesh, and Myanmar; poor health policy and weak health infrastructure; rules of law and anti-corruption; other nontraditional security threats—human, narcotics, and arms trafficking, food insecurity, etc. So, improved governance, increased trade with neighbours, increased agricultural productivity and improved infrastructure are much needed in this region. In order to gather the benefits of this policy and from FTAs with the economies of the east, the key variables are transit arrangements, proliferation of trade routes and custom-check post, and easy visa regime making it possible for traders, businesspersons, and transport operators to move in and out of the region. Therefore, it requires massive investments in infrastructure: construction of roads, railways, air transport, and communication facilities, which are largely absent.[20] Unfortunately, the current political and security environment cannot draw private investors and for that the central government should craft a safe environment by initiating dialogue with radical elements to bring peace and stability in this conflict-ridden region. Otherwise, the region would just be a passage between mainland India and South East Asia.

The fourth obstacle, which remains indirectly connected with India's Look East Policy, is the development of better ties between India and some of its South Asian neighbours (mainly Bhutan, Nepal, and Bangladesh). India's policy of strengthening its ties with its eastern neighbours has been inadequate to counter insurgency penetration as seen in Bhutan and Myanmar. The Look East Policy is used as a means to persuade the neighbouring countries to halt the various insurgents groups which are operating in these countries. Sincere and political dialogues and militaristic moves to contain insurgency activities would not bear a durable result, and for that regular dialogues and consultation could be essential. While highlighting the importance of India's Look East Policy, Ambassador Rajiv Sikri, in an interview to the Institute of Peace and Conflict Studies, New Delhi, October 2009, said

India should invest more money in Bangladesh and Myanmar. If India can give US$1.2 billion to Afghanistan, which isn't even one of our immediate neighbours, Myanmar and Bangladesh, which are much larger countries, should each get at least the same amount. There is a need to cooperate with both countries on water, energy, transport, drug trafficking, illegal migration and infrastructure. Regional economic integration is also necessary. In fact, the North-east Region, Bangladesh and Myanmar form an integrated whole. . . . There needs to be more Indian investment in projects in Bangladesh and Myanmar, but this investment should be in projects that are seen as bringing primarily local benefits; if a project is seen as benefiting India, without obvious benefits to the host country, this would arouse political controversy and opposition.[21]

He further emphasized on connectivity with special focus on the Bay of Bengal Initiative for BIMSTEC as a good framework for regional integration.

Connectivity must be pursued far more vigorously by New Delhi. Good infrastructure beyond our borders, for example, on both sides of the India-Bangladesh border, would lead to better ties between the two countries. The Bay of Bengal Initiative for Multi-Sectoral Technical and Economic Cooperation (BIMSTEC) is a good framework for regional integration.[22]

Interestingly enough, the recent people-to-people contacts through border 'haats' which were obliterated more than four decades ago, was reactivated on account of the micro connection with reference to India's Look East Policy. Moreover, the border communication between some north-eastern states of India and Bangladesh was lost on account of two important factors—the sudden deterioration of Indo-Bangladesh relations since the mid-1970s, and severe political uncertainty which evolved in the north-eastern region. However, the reactivation of this 'haat' concept in recent years by New Delhi may be interpreted as a new communicative diplomacy, in order to regenerate the lost era of communication between India and Bangladesh. The revival of more 'haats' along the Indo-Bangladesh border, akin to those in operation along the Indo-Myanmar border, will not only naturally enhance the mode of communication and economic and cultural exchanges of India's land-locked north-eastern states with Bangladesh but also with the further east, albeit with Dhaka and Yangon as the successive geographical and strategic centres of gravity. This may be termed as 'India's North-east-Bangladesh Arc (INBA) Project'. It is to be noted here, that this 'haat' initiative should not be allowed to be held hostage to the incidence of transnational crimes and the mushrooming of cross-border terrorist outfits, unlike the past.[23] Thus, the role of north-eastern states in the Look East Policy is trifling till date. So far, it is interpreted by many analysts that it is a one-track policy of the central government and the response on the side is a bit indistinct and diffident. This partial lack of coordinative mindset must be withered away and for tightening the overall Look East Policy, both the central and north-eastern state governments must evolve a proactive and responsive outlook towards each other, in order to make this policy an effective one. Taking a cue from China, New Delhi should rely on the execution of soft power. The major components of India's Look East Policy would be culture, education (human resource development), tourism, civil society, information technology, experience of nation-building and democracy, Indian diaspora, etc., in this context. If India wants to make its Look East Policy an effective one, New Delhi must use the north-eastern region as a connecting point. It is an absolute priority for New Delhi to bring Myanmar and Bangladesh into the core of its 'Look East' checklist even more expeditiously, in order to balance the north-eastern region. After all, the development and prosperity of its north-eastern region—situated at the doorstep of these two countries— is fundamentally connected to the overall effectiveness and judicious implementation of the 'Look East' journey of India.

Fifth, India's Look East Policy of engagement with the region has not been sensible. New Delhi has failed to spell out its interests, concerns, and strategic ventures rationally, which often results in substantial bewilderment, especially in the South East Asian region and beyond.

Finally, a new phenomenon that the policymakers of India are facing is the emergence of coalition politics. For instance, Dravida Munnetra Kazhagam's (DMK's) stand on Indian Tamils in Malaysia in 2007, the Teesta agreement between India and Bangladesh, etc., are important issues, which occasionally created some strains in implementing our Look East Policy.

The Way ahead

In the outlook of ASEAN, India has exhibited itself as an emerging power in Asia and is keen to develop relations with it that would be beneficial not only with these countries within ASEAN, but to the region as a whole. It realizes that India possesses significant strategic capabilities and can be a strong stabilizing force in the region. Economically, India, with its burgeoning middle class, can be a huge market for ASEAN manufactures and consequently, an important source of welfare for the region. Similarly, it is in its interest to establish beneficial linkages with the countries to benefit from their past experience and current standing. India should play a more pragmatic, practical, and effective role through its Look East Policy in order to establish itself as a stable and strong powerhouse in the Asian region. Its Look East Policy needs to be nursed more without deviating its focus and objectives. In fact, India has given far more preference to Europe and the US, where its best diplomatic energies are currently concentrated. Consequently, an average outlook has been exhibited vis-à-vis the South East and East Asian region. This is the time to rethink and make India's Look East Policy an effective one. Towards this end, incumbent on the foreign policymakers of India was to follow a more pragmatic, practical, and vision-oriented Look East Policy; to minimize the space which it has lost during this short span of time. While keeping this in mind, External Affairs Minister of India Sushma Swaraj, during her official visits to South East Asian countries, redefined this policy as 'Act East' instead of simply 'Look East'. While addressing a gathering of the Indian community soon after her three-day visit to Vietnam, Swaraj stated on 14 August 2014 that India had adopted a 'Look East Policy' under the Vajpayee government and 'now it is time to not just look but act. Under the Narendra Modi government, we will have an Act East Policy'.[24] Her statement was further endorsed by the External Affairs Ministry spokesperson Syed Akbaruddin, who said Swaraj's three days' visit to Vietnam was part of the Act East Policy. She said, 'It is not enough to Look East but Act East. This is Act East in action. We began with the focus on neighbourhood and this has now moved on with the focus on ASEAN. Our Prime Minister is going to Japan, so it further moves eastwards. India is keen to boost its ties in the region especially with ASEAN'.[25] This statement clearly reflects government's foreign policy towards the South East Asia and beyond with three main mantras: strength, proactivity, and sensitivity. For the Indian government, the Look East Policy is a long road for future economic destiny of India and to reach that opulence, 'Act East' incorporates greater action and dynamism.

In the present scenario, India holds for the future of Asia and other countries of the globe, a template for democracy, interfaith coexistence, secularism, gender equality; and a dynamic, expanding middle-path economy that can become a model for a large number of nations to follow. Right now, it is a key player in the ongoing multilateral negotiations on major global issues, namely trade, climate change, energy security, and global security issues, particularly international terrorism and proliferation of weapons of mass destruction. Today, with no political uncertainty on account of acquiring a massive mandate to rule, the government has acquired a safe mode role to reactivate its current 'Act East' policy more dynamically than the past governments and it is generally expected that by creating an image of a responsible major power, a benign power of consequence, systematic and comprehensive engagement with the region, it could play a more vibrant international role in the emerging global order, commensurate with its power and strength as reflected through this policy.[26]

Notes

1. See http://pmindia.gov.in/speech-details.php?nodeid=806, accessed 15 October 2015.
2. Tridib Chakraborti, 'Disparate Priorities: Explaining the Penumbra of India's Look East Policy', in *India and ASEAN: Foreign Policy Dimensions for the 21st Century*, ed. K. Raja Reddy, New Delhi: New Century, 2005, p. 52.
3. Ibid., p. 58; for a detailed analysis of India's stand on the recognition of Heng Samrin Government of Kampuchea, see Tridib Chakraborti, *India and Kampuchea: A Phase in their Relations, 1978–81*, Calcutta: Minerva, 1985.
4. Chakraborti, 'Disparate Priorities', p. 53.
5. See http://www.mea.gov.in/outoging-visit-detail.htm?20159/ Prime+Minister#1, accessed 15 October 2015.
6. See http://www.deloitte.com/assets/Dcom-India/Local%20Assets/ Documents/India_ASEAN_FTA.pdf, accessed 13 October 2015.
7. Sri Wahyuni, 'ASEAN-India FTA signed in Bangkok', *The Jakarta Post,* 14 August 2009.
8. *Annual Report: 2000–1*, Policy Planning and Research Division, Ministry of External Affairs, Government of India, New Delhi, 2001, p. 25.
9. See http://www.aseanindia.com/press-release-ins-sudarshini/, accessed 13 October 2015.
10. W. Anderson, 'A Growing Congruence of Interests with Korea', in *India's Foreign Policy: Retrospect and Prospect*, ed. S. Ganguly, New Delhi: Oxford University Press, 2010, pp. 175–205.
11. Indrani Bagchi, 'Four Navy Ships in South China Sea to Mark Indian Presence', *The Times of India*, 24 May 2012.
12. *Annual Report: January 2003 to March 2004*, Policy Planning and Research Division, Ministry of External Affairs, Government of India, New Delhi, 2004, p. 43.
13. *Annual Report: 2003–4*, Policy Planning and Research Division, Ministry of External Affairs, Government of India, New Delhi, 2004, p. 19.

14. *Annual Report: 2005–6*, Policy Planning and Research Division, Ministry of External Affairs, Government of India, New Delhi, 2006, p. 22.

15. *Annual Report: 2003–4*, Policy Planning and Research Division, Ministry of External Affairs, Government of India, New Delhi, 2004, p. 25.

16. Ibid., p. 45.

17. *Annual Report: 2007–8*, Policy Planning and Research Division, Ministry of External Affairs, Government of India, New Delhi, 2008, pp. 28–9.

18. See http://www.ndtv.com/article/india/full-text-obama-s-address-to-parliament-65093, accessed 16 October 2015.

19. *The Hindu*, '"Look East" Policy Brings India into Asia Pacific: Clinton', 1 February 2013.

20. 'Transforming the Northeast: Tackling Backlogs in Basic Minimum Services and Infrastructural Needs', *High Level Commission Report to the Prime Minister*, New Delhi: Planning Commission, Government of India, 7 March 1997, see http://planningcommission.gov.in/reports/genrep/ne_exe.pdf, accessed 16 October 2015.

21. An interview with Ambassador Rajiv Sikri, 'India's Look East Policy: A Critical Assessment', *IPCS Special Report*, October 2009, p. 5, see http://www.ipcs.org/pdf_file/issue/SR85-SEARPInterview-Sikri1.pdf, accessed 13 October 2015.

22. Ibid.

23. See Mohor Chakraborty, 'India's "Look East" Policy: The Foreign Policy Dynamics from ASEAN Orientation to "Move East"', unpublished Ph.D. thesis, Department of International Relations, Jadavpur University, Kolkata, 2013, p. 485.

24. Tridib Chakraborti, 'India-Vietnam Relations: Transcendence from 'Gaze' to Action', *World Focus*, vol. 35, no. 12, December 2014, p. 51.

25. Ibid.

26. Tridib Chakraborti, 'Modi's "Act East" Policy: Its Blueprint and the Future Promenade', in *Modi's Foreign Policy: Challenges and Opportunities*, ed. N.N. Jha and Sudhir Singh, New Delhi: Pentagon Press, 2016, p. 319.

6

Trade Relationship between Thailand and the North-Eastern Region of India with Special Reference to the Look West Policy of Thailand and the Look East Policy of India

Jatindra Nath Saikia

Background

INDIA HAS CLOSE proximity to South East Asia geographically, and it shares maritime and land borders with it. No other country has influenced the region as much as India, by way of religion, language, culture, and civilization. It can be further stated that in the first-half of the twentieth century, the common colonial past was a strong feature, which united India and the South East Asia. India's freedom struggle for Independence was a great source of inspiration for the freedom movement in the South East Asian nations. The Asian Relations Conference that was held in New Delhi in 1947 encouraged the Asian nations to be united against colonialism. That could be regarded as a move to end the colonialism which brought India and South East Asia together. The Bandung Conference of 1955 held in Indonesia laid down the principle of peaceful coexistence and showed a new direction towards mutual cooperation.

*I am indebted to the Indian Council of Social Science Research (ICSSR), New Delhi for sponsoring my visit to Thailand under ICSSR-NRCT Bilateral Exchange of Scholar Programme, 2013, which facilitated me to collect necessary information from different departments of Thailand.

Post the Second World War, global politics and international relations were completely dominated by the Cold War power block politics and the military alliance system which inversely affected India's relationship with South East Asian nations. As a newly emerged country, India preferred to remain outside the alliance system and tried to project herself as one of the initiators of the 'Non Alignment' movement. Indonesia became a founding member of this movement.[1] But the Cold War power politics was not as simple. The end of the Cold War had reminded each and every country of the world to develop their own economy and to integrate it with the rest of the world. So India adopted the Look East Policy and Thailand adopted Look West Policy in order to integrate their economy with the vast market of the world.

North-Eastern Region of India
and Thailand: Connectivity

Both Thailand and the north-eastern region of India are very important and integral regions of the Look West Policy of Thailand and the Look East Policy of India. The north-eastern region of India has been identified by Thailand as an important destination for investment, and a potential subregional market centre since the region is the land bridge connecting Thailand with the vast market of India.

It is noteworthy that the Prime Minister of India Manmohan Singh and Myanmar's President U Thein Sein signed an agreement on 28 May 2012, where India agreed to upgrade an extensive network of road and bridges in Myanmar that would effectively connect the north-eastern region of India (also the entire India) to Thailand by 2016. Both sides are also exploring the possibilities of setting up train routes in order to improve the connectivity.

The Look West Policy of Thailand entered the second phase in 2004 and since then, the Royal Government of Thailand has been adopting new strategies in order to make the policy a reality. Vibhansu Shekhar has mentioned that three important developments can be highlighted in this regard.[2] The first and the most important development is the growth in the bilateral trade, and the emergence of India as an important market. Calling for further strengthening of the India-Thailand partnership in various sectors such as infrastructure, food products, tourism, and entertainment; the Chairman, Board of Trade of Thailand Pramon Sutivong attributed the growth in bilateral trade to the complementary character of India's Look East Policy and Thailand's Look West Policy. Second, there has been a concerted effort to develop physical connectivity between the two countries. Various programmes developing physical connectivity between India and Thailand via the north-eastern states of India further reinforced these considerations. Finally, during the last few years, the Government of India has launched a special drive for bringing the north-eastern region of India into the central focus of the Look East Policy.

One of the most important aspects to be taken into consideration while discussing the trade relationship between the north-eastern region and Thailand is the physical similarity between the people of the north-eastern states and Thailand. Most of the indigenous people of the north-eastern region are of Mongoloid origin. The Tai-Ahoms, who ruled Assam for nearly 600 years, migrated from Yunnan Province of China just like the Thais had migrated from the same province to Thailand. When the Thai Princess Mahachari Srinindhorn visited Assam,[3] she was surprised by the similarity between the indigenous people of Assam and Thai people. She stated

This is an exploratory visit for me. I am moved by the similarity of these people with our people. I am impressed how they have been maintaining their identity for so long, I have come here to get a feel of the people who are so much like us and learn more about them. There is nothing official about my visit. I have come here just for an interaction and I am very pleased to find the people here so enthusiastic.[4]

The north-eastern region of India is blessed with a vast biodiversity, hydro-potential, and resources like oil and gas, coal, limestone, and forests. The soil of the region is very fertile and suitable for a wide range of plantation crops, spices, fruits and vegetables, flowers, medicinal and aromatic plants, etc. Assam, one of the major states of the region, is famous for tea and the golden Muga Silk.

Thailand is South East Asia's second largest economy, with a Gross Domestic Product (GDP) of around US$300 billion.[5] With a free market economy, the kingdom has a strong domestic market and a growing middle class with the private sector being the main engine of growth. The Thai economy is well integrated into the global marketplace with exports accounting for over 70 per cent of the kingdom's GDP. Thailand also has a strong industrial sector (40 per cent of GDP) and a robust and growing services sector (50 per cent of GDP) centred on the tourism and financial services industries.[6] Thailand is a key player in the Association of South East Asian Nations (ASEAN), enjoying a strategic location that provides easy access to a larger market of nearly 600 million people which is expected to gain even more strength when the ASEAN vision of 'One Community' materializes in future, making it a community of connectivity, a single market, and a production base.

Prior to the formulation of the Look East Policy of India, north-east India was not given much importance by the central government, even though the region had immense potential to grow owing to its natural and human resources. Since the Government of India has been paying special attention to develop the region at present, there is immense opportunity for the region to develop and grow with the help of the Look East Policy of India and Look West Policy of Thailand. The policy initiatives to develop connectivity between the north-eastern region and Thailand via Myanmar would definitely increase the trade volume of both the regions. However, no comprehensive study has been done on the trade relationship between Thailand and India's north-eastern region in the light of the Look East Policy and Look West Policy.

It is also a fact that trade relationship between India's north-eastern states and Thailand cannot be studied without taking into account the aspects discussed. Similarly, in order to study the possibilities and challenges of the trade relationship between the two regions, we have to know how India's north-eastern region is positioned in the Look West Policy of Thailand. This essay has tried to encompass all these following aspects:

1. Study the latest strategies that have been adopted by the Royal Government of Thailand in case of the Look West Policy.
2. Study the position of India's north-eastern region in the Look West Policy of Thailand.
3. Study the potential sectors of the north-eastern region of India where Thai businessmen would be interested to invest.
4. Identify different thrust areas of the north-eastern region of India where businessmen of India and Thailand can jointly work or cooperate with each other.

Methodology

This essay has incorporated both primary and secondary data. Primary information has been collected from the Department of Trade Promotion, Ministry of Commerce, the Royal Government of Thailand; Department of Trade Negotiations, Ministry of Commerce, the Royal Government of Thailand; Ministry of Foreign Affairs, The Royal Government of Thailand; The Tourism Authority of India; Thailand-India Chambers of Commerce; and Indian diaspora in Thailand by canvassing questionnaires. Apart from the filled in questionnaires, the views of officials in these responsible positions have also been incorporated in preparing this essay. An in-depth interview has been conducted with a number of social science university professors and personnel from a few corporate houses. Secondary data has been collected from different books, papers presented in international and national seminars, and relevant websites.

The data so collected are analysed in a logical and descriptive way. Thus, the research endeavour in this regard is logical, analytical, and descriptive.

Root of India's Look East Policy

The post-Cold War period created a congenial environment for India to establish relationships with South East Asian countries. Accordingly, the ASEAN countries also started realizing India's potential in shaping the future political and security environment in Asia. These countries found many positive aspects in India's sustainable democratic system and stable political institutions. Moreover, the economic liberalization initiated by the then Prime Minister P.V. Narashima Rao paved the way for adopting a new economic diplomacy. This new encouraging environment gave birth to the Look East Policy of India to facilitate closer economic ties with its South and South East Asian neighbours with emphasis on renewing political and economic contacts. India became a full dialogue partner of the ASEAN in the 5th summit at Bangkok in December 1995. In July 1996, India became a member of ASEAN Regional Forum (ARF), which deals with strategic and political issues in the Asia Pacific region. The 1st ASEAN-India summit of November 2002 was held in Phnom Penh, Cambodia 'to mark a major milestone in integrating India into South East Asia. The 5th India-ASEAN Summit was held in Cebu, Philippines, in January 2007 which resolved to implement free trade agreements and is considered a significant breakthrough for the Look East Policy.'[7]

All these events indicate that times have changed and all countries need to respond accordingly. The movement of capital and labour across international borders has become very important for the economic development of each and every country of the world, particularly for a developing country like India. In response to the changing scenario, India has adopted some policies which have helped to restore its historical connections and integrate its economy with the global economy. This new environment gave birth to the Look East Policy, which can be regarded as the political and economic convergence with the East and South East Asian Pacific region. So, 'the Look East is a part of India's grand strategy—a strategic shift in India's vision of Asia and India's place in the evolving global economy.'[8]

Over the past two decades, India's Look East Policy has been complemented by the Thailand's Look West Policy in bringing the two countries closer. India and Thailand celebrated sixty-five years of their diplomatic relations in 2012. In recent years, political contacts have intensified as reflected in a series of high-level visits by leaders of the two countries. Trade and economic linkages and tourist traffic between the two countries continues to grow steadily.

Both the countries are important regional partners linking South and South East Asia. They cooperate closely in the ASEAN, East Asia Summit (EAS), Bay of Bengal Initiative for Multi-Sectoral Technical and Economic Cooperation (BIMSTEC) groupings, Mekong-Ganga Cooperation (MGC), and Asia Cooperation Dialogue (ACD). The implementation of the India-ASEAN Agreement on Trade in Goods (IAATG) from January 2010 is the latest important milestone of this partnership.

Economic and Commercial Partnerships

Economic and commercial linkages form an important aspect of India's partnership with Thailand. The past few years have shown a rapid growth in this area.

In November 2001, the Prime Minister of Thailand Thaksin Shinawatra and the then Prime Minister of India had agreed to set up a Joint Working Group (JWG) to undertake a feasibility study of a Free Trade Agreement (FTA) between India and Thailand. The JWG had observed that the policy regimes in both the countries were conducive to more intensive bilateral economic integration and an FTA could prove to be a building block for other subregional, regional, and global economic integration processes, of which both countries are a part. Having observed the rich potential of trade expansion, the JWG concluded that the proposed FTA between India and Thailand is feasible, desirable, and mutually beneficial. Accordingly, a Joint Negotiating

Group (JNG) was set up to draft the framework agreement on India-Thailand FTA.

During the visit of the Indian Prime Minister to Thailand, a framework agreement for establishing the free trade between India and Thailand was signed by the commerce ministers of the two sides on 9 October 2003 in Bangkok, Thailand. The framework agreement covers FTA in goods, services, and investments, as well as in other areas of economic cooperation. It also provided an Early Harvest Scheme (EHS) for elimination of tariff on a fast track basis on eighty-two items of export interest to the sides.

The tariff concessions on these items of EHS list began from 1 September 2004 and had become zero for both sides from 1 September 2006.

The India-Thailand Trade Negotiating Committee (ITTNC) has been constituted to negotiate a comprehensive FTA, covering trade in goods, services, investment, rules of origin, dispute settlement mechanism, etc. So far, a good number of meetings of the TNC have been held.

Bilateral Trade has multiplied eight times since 2000 to reach US$7.72 billion in 2016 (see Table 6.1). The global economic and financial crises impacted the bilateral trade during 2009. The trade figure for 2009 was US$4.9 billion, declining by 17 per cent (Indian exports were US$1.7 billion, down by 34 per cent, while Thai exports were US$3.2 billion, declining by 3.60 per cent). However, trade data for January–June 2010 showed bilateral trade at US$3.23 billion, an increase of 53 per cent over the corresponding figure of the previous year.[9] Bilateral trade in 2016 totalled US$7.72 billion, with about US$5.15 billion in Thai exports to India and US$2.57 billion in Indian exports to Thailand.

TABLE 6.1: Thailand-India Bilateral Trade Relations

(in million $)

Year	Thailand's Export	Thailand's Import	Thailand's Total Trade with India
2012	8.87	5.47	3.40
2013	8.69	5.19	3.50
2014	8.66	5.62	3.04
2015	7.92	5.29	2.63
2016	7.72	5.15	2.57

Source: 'India Thailand Economic and Commercial Relations', Embassy of India, Bangkok, 26 March 2018, see http://www.indianembassy.in.th/pages.php?id=174.

Investments by Indian and Thai companies into each other's countries have been growing. Indian investment in Thailand was around US$33.44 million in 2016. Thailand has invested over US$68.87 million in India in 2016. Thus, Thai investment in India is higher.[11]

The Major Indian Groups Doing Business in Thailand

Indian corporate groups like TATA (automobiles, steel, software), Aditya Birla (chemicals, textiles), Indo Rama (chemicals), Ranbaxy, Dabur, Lupin (pharmaceuticals), Bharti Airtel, NIIT, etc., reflect the diverse sectors that have established business interests in Thailand.

Leading Thai companies in the fields of agro-processing infrastructure, automotive engineering, banking, housing, and hospitality have active and growing business presence in India. Major Thai companies are active in India, such as C.P. Aquaculture (India) Ltd., Italian Thai Development PLC, Krung Thai Bank Pcl, Charoen Pokphand (India) Private Limited, Stanley Electric Engineering India Pvt. Ltd, Thai Summit Neel Auto Pvt. Ltd., Thai Airways International Pcl, Precious Shipping (PSL) of Thailand, Pruksa Real Estates, and Dusit and Amari Group of Hotels.

The IAATG was signed in Bangkok on 13 August 2009. The Services and Investment chapters of the India-ASEAN FTA were concluded in December 2012 and signed in September 2014.

India and ASEAN, on 25 March 2018, agreed for a swift conclusion of the comprehensive and mutually beneficial Regional Comprehensive Economic Partnership (RCEP). An EHS under the proposed India-Thailand FTA is in place since September 2004 covering eighty-four products.

The Ministry of Commerce, Government of Thailand, informed that the 27th meeting of the ITTNC held during 10–12 July 2013 in Bangkok discussed the issues on trade in goods, services, investments, Sanitary and Phytosanitary (SPS Agreement), and Technical Barrier to Trade (TBT Agreement). Though both sides show flexibility in order to reach the completion of FTA negotiations within 2013, there were still some pending issues. However, both the countries have realized that the important goal of FTA is to strengthen bilateral economics and to expand trade and investment between Thailand and India.

The Department of Trade Negotiations, Ministry of Commerce,

Royal Government of Thailand, stated that the BIMSTEC was initiated with the goal to combine the Look West Policy of Thailand and ASEAN with the Look East Policy of India and South Asia. So it can be assumed that BIMSTEC is a link between ASEAN and South Asian Association for Regional Cooperation (SAARC). BIMSTEC covers thirteen priority sectors led by seven member countries in a voluntary manner, namely trade and investment, technology, energy, transport and communication, tourism, fisheries, agriculture, cultural cooperation, environment and disaster management, public health, people to people contact, poverty alleviation counterterrorism, and transnational crimes.[12]

North-Eastern Region of India
Gateway to the East

Manmohan Singh characterized Assam, the premier state of the north-east India, as a 'Gateway to the East' in November 2004. The north-eastern region of India comprises of eight states, viz., Assam, Arunachal Pradesh, Manipur, Mizoram, Meghalaya, Nagaland, Tripura, and Sikkim. The geographical location of the north-eastern region of India is very suitable to integrate India with South East Asia. The north-eastern region of India represents 7.90 per cent of India's total geographical area and shares 3.80 per cent of India's total population.[13] Then Minister of External Affairs, Pranab Mukherjee said in a seminar on Look East Policy held in Shillong,

Arunachal Pradesh, Manipur, Mizoram, and Nagaland share a 1643 km long border with Myanmar. Assam, Meghalaya, Tripura, and Mizoram share an 1880 km border Bangladesh. Arunachal Pradesh, Assam, and Sikkim share a 468 km border with Bhutan. Arunachal Pradesh and Sikkim share a 1325 km border with the Tibet Autonomous Region of the People Republic of China.[14]

The enormity of shared international borders of the north-eastern region with other countries proves its value and worth in creating and maintaining a prosperous cultural, economic, and political relations.

The north-eastern region of India is rich in biodiversity, hydropotential, oil and gas, coal, limestone, and forest resources. Dilip Gogoi mentioned that the north-eastern region of India is ideally suited for the whole range of plantation crops, spices, fruits, vegetables, flowers, and herbs; much of which could be processed and exported to neighbouring countries.[15] The north-eastern region of India has 38 per cent of the country's hydropower potential. The region has natural gas reserves of 190 billion cu. m., coal reserves of 909 million ton, hydroelectric potential estimated at 49,000 megawatt, oil reserves of 513 million ton, and a forest cover accounting for 25 per cent of the country's forest area which is the highest forest protection record in the country.[16] B. Bhattacharya and Prabir De stated the potentials of the north-eastern region of India as

. . . a market of 800 million people combining the strength of countries like Bangladesh, Nepal, Bhutan, Southwest China, and ASEAN, its strategic location and natural resources makes it a potential for India's next powerhouse; Brahmaputra Valley provides fertile soil for cultivating horticultural products, plantation crops, vegetables, spices, rare herbs, and medicinal plants; fuelling a vibrant agro-export processing zone which could also be a green tourism destination with rare flora and fauna, natural scenic beauty; unique performing arts and varied cuisine and handicrafts, market proximity to South West China and South East Asia makes the north-east a strategic base for foreign/ domestic investors to tap the world's largest market consisting of South Asian Association of Regional Cooperation (SAARC), Bay of Initiative for Multi-Sectoral Technical and Economic Cooperation, and ASEAN; and it has also an excellent intra-regional distribution capacity with internal waterway linkages connecting Bangladesh and Myanmar, giving across to the parts of Chittagong (Bangladesh), Kolkata, and Haldia.[17]

People to People Cooperation between the North-Eastern Region of India and Thailand

One of the most significant aspects is the view of the learned people about the north-eastern region of India. In different seminars, it is always opined that there must be trade and investment linkages between the north-eastern region of India and Thailand. A seminar was organized by the Indian Chambers of Commerce (ICC) and the Ministry of External Affairs, Government of India, in January 2013 at Bangkok in order to discuss the business relationship between India and Thailand. The ICC invited Dr Nalinee Taveesin, the permanent representative of the prime minister's office, the Royal Thai Government, and she visited the north-eastern region of India to enhance the bilateral and trade relations between Thailand and the north-eastern region of India.

Taveesin, Thailand's former trade representative and currently a cabinet member in Thailand's prime minister's office, along with the Royal Thai Government trade delegation, interacted with the industry and government in Guwahati, hosted by ICC.[18] Some positive outcome can be expected from the visit relating to the trade relationship between the north-eastern region of India and Thailand when both the prime ministers (India and Thailand) expect that the Trilateral Asian Highway will be completed in 2019.

In terms of investment, Thailand ranks thirty-sixth among the largest investors in India with a cumulative FDI outflow of US$94.8 million or about 0.06 per cent of India's total FDI, mostly in machinery, feed and livestock products, and construction.

Taveesin highlighted the Thai government's efforts to increase trade ties with the north-eastern states and said that there is a wide open door for closer cooperation in numerous fields such as agriculture, forestry, mining, energy, hydropower, and ecotourism.

There is no denial of the fact that India's land connection with South East Asia is through its north-eastern region—the strategic area of India which has long been neglected by New Delhi mainly due to the region's relatively weak representation in the parliament. Without a reasonable level of economic development and stability in the north-eastern part of India, as well as better infrastructure on its borders, the fruit of the India's Look East Policy can never be harvested.

Of late, the north-eastern region of India has been made visible on New Delhi's radar because of the Look East Policy of the Government of India, as India cannot enter the South East Asian market without the development of the infrastructure of the north-eastern states.

However, the development of infrastructure on the border between the Indian states and its neighbours is insignificant, e.g., construction of roads and bridges for the Imphal–Mandalay bus service which was proposed during Singh's visit to Myanmar. The Myanmar Government had started construction of two bridges in 2016. The Indian cabinet has also sanctioned ₹371.58 crore (US$55 million) for constructing the remaining 69 bridges. So far as the progress of other projects are concerned, such as the Kaladan Multi-Modal Transit Transport Project which seeks to connect Kolkata with Sittwe Port in Myanmar by sea, is not satisfactory and has been delayed due to excessive bureaucratic red tape.

Important Projects for Creating
Infrastructure to Link North-Eastern
India with South East Asia

Moreh–Tamu–Kalewa Road

This is the first infrastructural project taken up to create connectivity between the north-eastern region of India and South East Asia. India's Foreign Secretary J.N. Dixit, while visiting Myanmar in 1993, gave a serious thought to this project. In 1995, when India's then Minister of State for Commerce P. Chidambaram signed an agreement with Myanmar's counterpart, it intensified the road project to some extent. The project took shape when a 165 km. long Tamu–Kalaymyo–Kalewa Road in Myanmar's Sagaing Division was constructed in 2001 by the Border Road Organization of India, with a budget of ₹1,000 million.

The Tamu–Alaymyo–Kalewa Road is also known as India–Myanmar Friendship Road and is further connected to Moreh in Manipur, which is the ending point of NH 39 of India. This small project has given birth to a new trilateral highway connecting India–Myanmar and Thailand. But it is observed that the border trade volume has not increased after opening the Moreh–Tamu–Kalewa Road.[19]

Moreh–Bagan–Mae Sot Trilateral Highway

After completing the Moreh–Tamu–Kalewa Road, the Government of India started paying special attention to improve the physical connectivity with South East Asia as a part of India's Look East Policy. Consequently, talks to implement a trilateral highway project where India, Myanmar, and Thailand are the parties, has been started. The project got some impetus when the India-Myanmar-Thailand Ministerial Meeting was held in 2002 in Myanmar. Apart from constructing a highway from Moreh in India to Mae Sot in Thailand through Bagan in Myanmar, the project also includes the development of a highway from Kanchanaburi in Thailand to Dewei deep-sea port in Myanmar, and shipping links to the sea ports in India.[20]

An ambitious project to develop a 3,200 km. highway linking India, Myanmar, and Thailand was an important item on the agenda of Manmohan Singh, during his visit in Thailand. He and his Thai counterpart Yingluck Shinawatra expressed the hope that the highway would be ready by 2019. India has already given Myanmar US$500 million in loan, a part of which will be used to fund the project.

Apart from these, there are a good number of projects proposed by the two countries to connect India with the South East Asian countries.

It is a fact that both the Look West Policy of Thailand and the Look East Policy of India are mutually beneficial policies. The convergence of Thailand's policy since 1996 and India's policy of 1993 has resulted in mutually beneficial cooperation covering diverse dimensions ranging from trade and investment, science and technology, defence, agriculture, connectivity, and tourism; to culture and education. But the concerned bodies have opined that there should definitely be some ways to engage the north-eastern region in strengthening people-to-people linkages between India and Thailand. Frequent seminars should be organized to find ways to link people of the north-eastern region of India and Thailand. Some result-oriented decisions have to be taken to identify the opportunities of both the sides. A SWOT analysis of both the sides has been suggested by the authorities of Thailand. Moreover, Thailand has specifically informed that the north-eastern region of India is one of the most important regions for Thailand to reap the benefit of the Look West Policy of Thailand.

Suggestions and Recommendations to Improve the Trade Relationship between North-Eastern Region of India and Thailand

The Government of India should change its approach to the north-eastern region of India and it should adopt a strong policy that would help in a comprehensive development of the region. The people of these states should be made stakeholders of the decision-making process at all stages. In this regard, New Delhi should not consider the strength of the representation in the parliament from the region but should consider the fact that the north-eastern region of India is the gateway to the east, and the Indian economy needs to be integrated with the fastest growing economies of the South East Asian countries. If it is done in real spirit, keeping aside all political gains, the north-eastern states will feel integrated with the rest of India; and India as well as the north-east of the country would benefit from the economic integration with South East Asia, including Thailand.

As is known to the world, China targets the big and has completed the infrastructure in their border provinces. Development in the Chinese province of Yunnan which shares a border with Myanmar, is an example of Chinese move towards establishing better ties with its neighbours, via her border regions. India should create necessary infrastructure in the north-east without wasting time to reap the benefits of the integration. If India sits idle or goes slow, China will overtake India very easily.

The Government of India should adopt a specific policy to create a strong service sector in the north-eastern region of India. The north-eastern states of India have got immense potential for ecotourism/green tourism. Steps must be taken to develop the service of power supply. At present, the north-eastern region of India has been struggling with erratic power supply.

The Government of India should also take necessary steps to improve the communication network in the north-eastern region of India since in most of the places, which are regarded as strategic from the security point of view, there is no communication network. It is the demand of time to transform this geographically isolated area into a potential economic corridor between India and the nations of the South East Asia.

It has been observed that in different seminars, conferences, and discussions of several fora, the issue of the cultural relations of the people of the north-eastern region of India in general, and of Assam in particular, with the people of Thailand get priority. If such relations are utilized or exploited properly, new opportunities in the current context of Look East Policy will surely appear. As has already been mentioned, most of the ethnic groups of north-east India are not Indo-Aryan by origin, but primarily consist of peoples of Mongoloid origin who have migrated long time ago from Thailand, Myanmar, Cambodia, China, etc. As is known to all, Ahoms are an offshoot of the Tai people, who are known as Shan in Myanmar, Thai in Thailand, Lao in Laos, and Tay-Thai in Vietnam. This sort of relationship should be tapped by the people of the region as well as the governments. The government should focus on developing its soft power regionally. For instance, there should be greater investment in sports and sports infrastructure and the Government of India should consider establishing sports tournaments between the north-eastern states and Myanmar, and at some stage even other countries in South East Asia, including Vietnam and Thailand. This would enhance people-to-people contact and has the potential to increase the influence and to spread of India's soft power.

The Government of India should consider the views of state governments in the north-eastern region in both economic and foreign policy issues. This is particularly important in the context of trade with Myanmar and Bangladesh, as well as infrastructure projects where any of the states of the north-east is involved. A successful Look East Policy will only be possible if New Delhi invests not just economically but also politically in India's north-eastern region.

In order to understand the needs, priorities, and potentialities of the north-eastern region of India and Thailand, a 'Trade and Investment Promotion Forum' between Thailand and the north-eastern region of India should be set up without further delay. In such a forum, businessmen and academicians should also be included and frequent discussions should be held among the members.

The north-eastern region of India and Thailand can jointly work for the development of tourism in the north-eastern region of India. It is believed that the oldest Buddha Temple of Asia is situated in Assam. This aspect can be capitalized in promoting tourism in this region. Since Thailand is one of the most popular tourist destinations of the world and has expertise in this sector, a joint effort to promote tourism in the north-eastern region of India will surely pave the way for many opportunities. In this regard, The Tourism Ministry of India should tie-up with the Tourism Authority of Thailand. The stunning scenic beauty, wonderful and diverse culture, rich biodiversity, wonderful wild life, unique and varied cuisine, and with the wonderful people of the region; would surely make the region a most coveted place for the tourists of the world.

Thailand has expertise in food processing. The climate and soil of the north-eastern region of India is also favourable for growing fruits and vegetables. Businessmen of the north-eastern region of India can work jointly in this profitable sector.

The north-eastern region of India does not have sufficient technical and management institutions. The Government of India as well as state governments should set up a good number of technical institutes and management schools, apart from supporting the institutes imparting liberal arts education. Similarly, Thailand should also try to prepare her people, particularly the young generation, with English language skills.

The north-eastern region of India and Thailand can jointly work on silk garments. Assam is famous for its unique muga silk which is endemic to the region and Assam produces 95 per cent of the world's total muga silk. Assamese people have expertise in weaving. Similarly, Thailand is also famous for silk. So there is scope to work together.

In order to work together, firm-to-firm relationship between the north-eastern region of India and Thailand has to be built up. Both the parties (firms from both sides) should do SWOT analysis before joining hands together.

Management of knowledge is very important; particularly, the north-eastern states of India must pay special attention to this aspect. Knowledge industries of the north-eastern region of India have to strive to be innovative at all times. If required, transfer of knowledge should also be materialized between the firms of the two countries.

Conclusion

The Trade relationship between the north-eastern region of India and Thailand would be fruitful when the infrastructural facilities in the north-eastern Region are properly created. North-eastern India is a vast area with the potential to be a business hub in South East Asia. But the Government of India and the different state governments of the region have to adopt a comprehensive policy to develop the region without further delay. Merely organizing seminars or cross-border visits between India and Thailand is not enough. The people of the north-eastern region of India must understand about the Look East Policy of the government and the benefits that can be enjoyed by the people of the region. The Government of India should pay special attention to provide proper security to the people who will work on different projects relating to the Look East Policy of the government. India also needs to explore more meaningful engagement in the cultural line and promote cross-border economic activities by fully exploiting north-east India's history and culture. The people of the north-eastern region of India should acquire knowledge and skills relating to trade and commerce regularly. If the Look East Policy becomes successful, both the countries, i.e. India and Thailand would be benefitted and their economies would be stronger than earlier.

Underdevelopment gives birth to resentment, and long-time resentment due to long-time negligence gives birth to extremism. The people of the north-east of India have been experiencing this since long. Thus, it is high time to take action on economic development, welfare of people, and sustainability and growth of the region by the central and state governments and the people of this region.

Notes

1. Dilip Gogoi, 'East through Northeast: India and Southeast Asia in the new Asia', in *Beyond Borders: Look East Policy and North East India*, Guwahati: DVS Publishers, 2010, p. 35.

2. Vibhansu Shekhar, 'Thailand's Look West Policy: Opportunities and Challenges for India's Northeast', in *Beyond Borders: Look East Policy and North East India*, ed. Dilip Gogoi, Guwahati: DVS Publishers, 2010, p. 171.

3. Thai Prince Maha Chakri Sirindhorn visited a village of Dibrugarh District, Assam on 2 February 2009 to observe the culture and customs of the people of the village named Nam Phake or Tai Phake. The residents of Nam Phake village of Assam have very close affinity with the Thai people living in Thailand. With near about 150 odd families living in the village, it is the largest village of Tai Phake people of Assam. It is also one of the oldest and most respected Buddhist monastery of Assam, India. The village folk speak a dialect similar to the language in Thailand and still follow the traditional customs and dress code of the great Tai race; *The Telegraph*, Tuesday, 3 February 2009, Kolkata, see www.telegraphindia.com/1090203/jsp/northeast/story-1047528.jps, accessed 28 February 2013.

4. Thai Princes Mahachari Srinidhorn, after reaching the Tai Phake or Nam Phake village on 2 February 2009 by a special helicopter from Mohanbari Airport, Dibrugarh, Assam with an official Thai delegation, mesmerised the people of the villagers with her emotional lecture. While delivering the lecture in the village she stated the objectives of her visit to the place; see www.telegraphindia.com/1090203/jsp/northeast/story-1047528.jps, accessed 2 January 2013.

5. See www.acd-dialogue.org, accessed 5 September 2013.

6. Ibid.

7. Dilip Gogoi, ed., *Beyond Borders: Look East Policy and North East India*, Guwahati: DVS Publishers, 2010, p. 40.

8. Ibid., p. 41.

9. *Thai-India Directory, 2011–12*, Bangkok: Thailand-India Chambers of Commerce. Data collected from the Thailand-India Chambers of Commerce, Bangkok; and Thailand directly; when the author visited the country from 17 November to 7 December 2013 under the India-Thailand Bilateral Scholar Exchange Programme, 2013.

10. Ibid.

11. An in-depth interview was conducted with Ms Orathai Leksakulchai, Head, Department of International Trade Promotion, Asia and Oceania Region, Ministry of Commerce, Royal Government of Thailand in November 2013. During the interactive session, a good amount of information was noted down including the information incorporated here. Interaction with high-level officials of the Department of International Trade Promotion, Ministry of Commerce, Royal Government of Thailand was one of the objectives of the author at the time of visiting the country as one of the Indian scholars under the India-Thailand Bilateral Scholar Exchange Programme, 2013.

12. See www.databank.nedfi.com, accessed 10 September 2013.

13. The then Minister of External Affairs Pranab Mukherjee, Government of India, speaking in a seminar held in Shillong on 16 June 2007 on India's

Look East Policy expressed his observation. Mukherjee summed up the qualificatory importance of the northeastern region geographically in terms of India's Look East Policy, see carnegieendowment.org/newsletters/SAP/pdf/july07/speech_east_policy.pdf, accessed 17 July 2013.

14. Gogoi, *Beyond Borders*, p. 45
15. Ibid.
16. B. Bhattacharya and Prabir De, 'Promotion of Trade & Investment between People's Republic of China and India: Toward a Regional Perspective', *Asian Development Review*, vol. 22, no. 1, 2005, pp. 53–4.
17. Dr Nalinee Taveesin, formerly Thailand's trade representative and currently a cabinet member in Thailand's prime minister's office along with Royal Thai Government Trade Delegation interacted with industry and government in Guwahati hosted by the Indian Chambers of Commerce in March 2013, see www.assamtimes.org/node/8046, accessed 13 September 2013.
18. 'A Road to S-E Asia', *Hindu Businessline*, 10 April 2002; see http//www.thehindubusinessline.com/2002/04/10/stories/2002041000030800html, accessed 2 January 2013.
19. 'Myanmar, Thailand to Build Deep Seaport', *Xinhua News Agency*, 12 January 2004, Research Service, Washington DC, Library of Congress, see www.highbeam.com/doc/1G1-112071220,html, accessed 12 September 2013.
20. At the invitation of the then Prime Minister of the Kingdom of Thailand Yingluck Shinawatra, the then Prime Minister of the Republic of India Manmohan Singh paid an official visit to Thailand on 30–31 May 2013. The official talks between both the leaders were held on 30 May 2013. Both the leaders reaffirmed the importance of the India-Myanmar-Thailand Trilateral Highway project. They also noted that the Joint Task Force Meeting on the trilateral highway, held in New Delhi in September 2012 agreed to make all efforts to complete the trilateral road connectivity by 2016.

7

Thailand's Economic Integration with Neighbouring Countries

Implications for India and Its North-East Region

Suthiphand Chirathivat
Kornkarun Cheewatrakoolpong

Introduction

AMIDST AN uncertain global economic environment, regional cooperation and integration continue to set an unprecedented trend worldwide, and also in South East Asia.[1] To a certain extent, the ten South East Asian countries' regional grouping embarks on its own regional integration, by stepping up through the establishment of the Association of South East Asian Nations (ASEAN) Community by the beginning of 2016. At the core of this concept of achieving the ASEAN Community, is one of its three pillars, the ASEAN Economic Community (AEC), aiming at creating a single market and production base within the region. Similarly, the regional grouping has been able to advance further on the master plan of ASEAN connectivity in order to further enhance its regional integration process.[2]

Thailand has been an active member of the ASEAN from the very beginning. With the recent transformation of ASEAN, particularly for

*The authors would like to thank Christoph Odermatt and Kaniknun Na Suwan for their kind assistance in the preparation of this essay. This version is largely drawn from the ADBI Working Paper Series, no. 520, 'Thailand's Economic Integration with Neighboring Countries and Possible Connectivity with South Asia', April 2015.

the Mainland of South East Asia including the latest change in Myanmar, Thailand has a naturally strong advantage in regional community building. In contrast to the Cold War period, Thailand's geographical location now faces pressure in the opposite direction in its strategic role in linking its neighbouring countries in the Greater Mekong Subregion (GMS) and beyond.[3] These unique opportunities are clear and tangible, with projects on physical connectivity which aim to facilitate trade and investment through new transport and other infrastructural developments, thus fostering Thailand's linkages with the region.

This essay aims to discuss Thailand's economic integration and cooperation with South East Asia and South Asia. As the country is undergoing tremendous change in its economic structure, particularly the extension of manufacturing activities and the emergence of a new middle class in different regions beyond Bangkok, it is interesting to see how improving connectivity, both hard and soft infrastructures in Thailand, within ASEAN and between the two regions, could support Thailand's future growth.[4] If successfully developed, these concrete projects and programs could be a strong addition to the country's ASEAN community-building efforts for better connections with India and possibly north-east India.[5]

Economic Structure, Macroeconomic Performance, and External Orientation

Thailand has gone through several shocks both from within and outside, ranging from political transformation, major flooding of 2011, and the global financial crisis (2007–8). On the other hand, Thailand has not been growing very fast since the recovery of the Asian financial crisis of 1997–8, with an average growth of only 4.20 per cent per year in the past decade. In 2012, Thailand's Gross Domestic Product (GDP) growth recovered from the major flooding of 2011 by only 0.10 per cent to stand at 6.40 per cent, with per capita income at US$5.473, placing the country in the middle-income level. However, there is still concern over the size of public debt that has recently slightly increased due to the populist policies of the former PM Yingluck's government. Thailand's public deficit in 2012 stands at 9.30 per cent or around 43.50 per cent of the GDP (Table 7.1).

Despite these setbacks, the country is looking forward to progressing, internally and externally, with a strong-based middle class demand, a large industrial base, strong supply chains, and a new path of more connections with regional economies. Since 2007, it is interesting to observe a major transformation that has taken place in the regional GDP structure of Thailand, with Bangkok growing at the lowest level (33 per cent) against the three highest regions; northern (50.20 per cent), north-eastern (58.30 per cent), and southern (57.20 per cent) (Fig. 7.1). As a result, Bangkok and its vicinity's share of GDP has been reduced to stand around 44 per cent in 2011, while the rest takes the share as follows: eastern, 18 per cent; southern, 10 per cent; north-eastern, 10 per cent; and northern, 8 per cent. Given these recent changes of regional economies of Thailand, the key question is likely to be—what kind of economic performance and external orientation will drive Thailand's economic development as a whole?

Thailand is considered an open economy with more trade and investment exposure than a number of its Asian counterparts, except Hong Kong, Malaysia, and Singapore. For quite some time, and in particular, since the last Asian financial crisis of 1997–8, trade has always been an important engine of growth, as well as the foreign exchange earnings that have helped to replenish the reserve surplus. However, export performance has been quite weak lately, particularly since the global financial crisis, which has contributed to unusual up and down trends, unlike an annual average of 12 per cent a decade earlier. As a result, trade surplus has been narrowed down since 2011 till date (Table 7.1). This is not to say that Thailand has lost its trade advantages of the past. On the contrary, like many Asian countries that have been suffering from their own export-oriented economy, Thailand is struggling to find its own way of adjusting the external sector to the new 'normal' reality of the global economy, given the impact of the global financial crisis which has lasted longer than expected.

Taking a closer look at Thailand's trade structure, it is observed that much has changed in its trade orientation and integration, like movement towards emerging economies like ASEAN, China, and to a certain extent, India; in addition to traditional trade partners like Japan, the EU, and the US. As a result of its increasing links to regional supply chains, Thailand supplies intermediate inputs and raw materials to regional economies, which help them to produce final goods for the global economy. Thailand has also benefitted from this to produce its own final goods to supply the regional and global economies. Thailand is making deeper changes in trade structure, rather than simply trading in goods.

(in US$)

TABLE 7.1: Thailand's Macroeconomic Performance

	2000	2001	2002	2003	2004	2005	2006	2007	2008	2009	2010	2011	2012	2013
GDP (billion)	122.73	115.54	126.88	142.64	161.34	176.35	207.09	246.98	272.58	263.71	318.91	345.67	366.00	387.30
Real GDP growth (%)	4.75	2.17	5.32	7.14	6.34	4.60	5.09	5.04	2.48	-2.33	7.81	0.08	6.50	2.90
GDP per capita	1,968.54	1,831.90	1,988.73	2,211.87	2,478.82	2,689.95	3,143.24	3,737.72	4,118.40	3,978.91	4,802.66	5,192.12	5,479.76	5778.98
Exports (billion)	67.90	63.10	66.10	78.10	94.90	109.40	127.90	151.30	175.20	150.70	191.60	219.10	225.90	225.40
Imports (billion)	56.20	54.50	57.00	66.90	84.20	106.00	114.30	124.60	157.90	118.10	161.90	202.10	219.90	218.70
Trade balance (billion)	11.70	8.60	9.10	11.20	10.70	3.40	13.60	26.70	17.30	32.60	29.70	17.00	6.00	6.70
Current account balance (billion)	9.30	5.10	4.70	4.80	2.80	-7.60	2.30	15.70	2.20	21.90	10.00	4.10	-1.50	-2.50
Current account balance to GDP (%)	7.60	5.40	5.50	5.00	1.70	-4.30	1.10	6.30	0.80	8.30	3.80	1.20	-0.40	-0.60
Population (million people)	61.88	62.31	62.80	63.08	61.97	62.42	62.83	63.04	63.39	63.53	63.88	64.08	64.46	64.79
CPI inflation (%)	1.60	1.60	0.70	1.80	2.70	4.50	4.70	2.30	5.50	-0.90	3.30	3.81	3.02	2.18

Table 7.1

	2000	2001	2002	2003	2004	2005	2006	2007	2008	2009	2010	2011	2012	2013
Exchange Rate, US$1 (TH฿)	40.16	44.48	43.00	41.53	40.27	40.27	37.93	34.56	33.36	34.34	31.73	30.49	31.08	30.73
Deficit (billion) (positive is surplus)	−2.90	−2.43	−2.76	0.83	0.43	0.42	0.12	−2.74	−0.72	−12.15	−6.26	−6.58	−9.23	−6.80
Deficit per GDP (%) (positive is surplus)	−2.40	−2.10	−2.20	0.60	0.30	0.20	0.10	−1.10	−0.30	−4.70	−2.00	−1.90	−2.60	−1.80
Debt (billion)	69.83	65.97	68.44	70.55	77.64	81.39	85.24	91.97	102.16	116.54	133.33	145.89	160.66	176.72
Debt per GDP (%)	56.90	57.10	53.94	49.46	48.12	46.15	41.16	37.24	37.48	44.19	41.81	42.21	43.45	41.34

Source: Bank of Thailand, Statistics Section; Ministry of Foreign Affairs, Thailand's Economic Fact Sheet; World Bank.

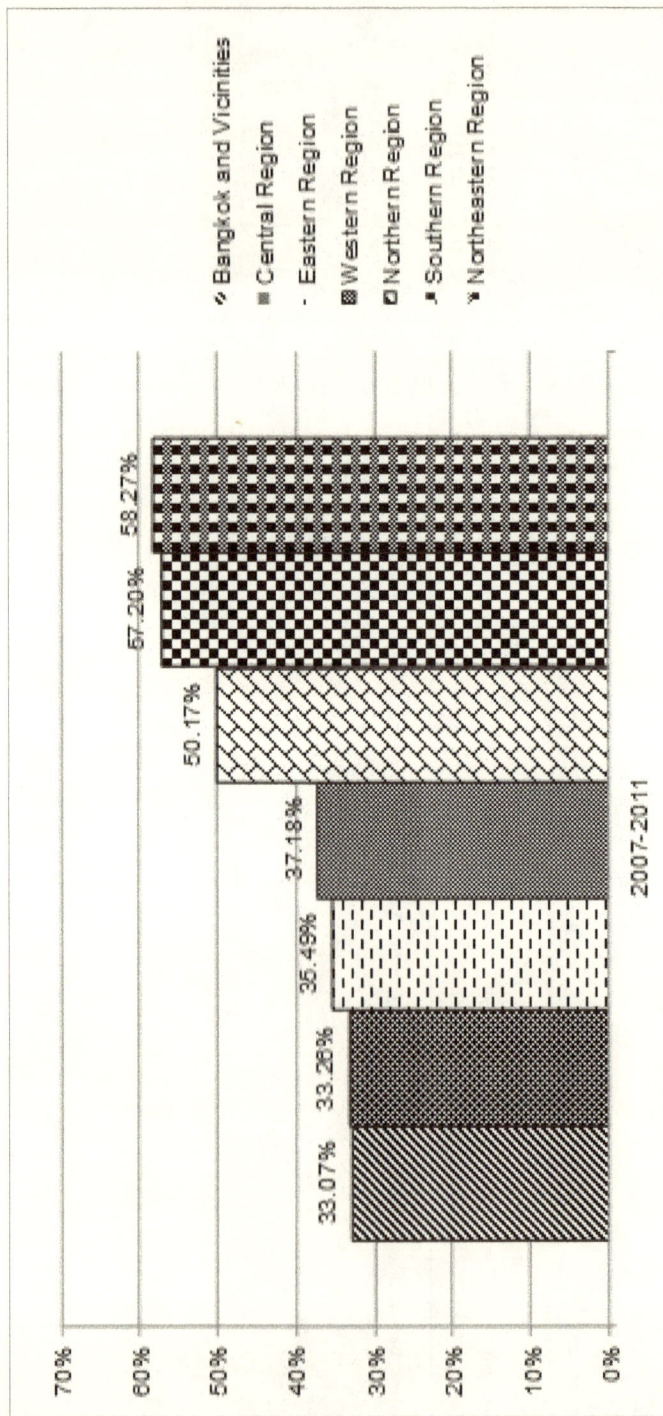

FIG. 7.1: Regional GDP Growth from 2007 to 2011

Source: Statistical yearbook of Thailand, National Statistical Office of Thailand.

Recent Trends of Trade with Its
Mainland South East Asian Neighbours
and South Asia

As far as Thailand's trade with its immediate neighbours is concerned, it is interesting to observe quite an impressive growth and pattern of this border trade; with a surge from a total of less than US$10 billion in 2003 to around US$30 billion in 2012, representing an increase of 3.2 times compared to an increase of 2.3 times of Thailand's total trade. As a result, the share of border trade to Thailand's total trade has also increased from 4.40 per cent in 2003 to stand now at more than 60 per cent (Table 7.2).

Among the four neighboring countries, Malaysia has for long been responsible for more than 60 per cent of Thailand's border trade. But for the first time, this share dipped below 60 per cent in 2012 to stand around 56 per cent. This can be explained by the share increase in the same year of the three other neighboring countries, which has increased their role in order of their importance, with Myanmar accounting for 19.8 per cent, Lao PDR 14.50 per cent, and Cambodia 9 per cent (Fig. 7.2). The 2012 figures show Thailand's share of border trade to country's total trade for four countries—Cambodia 65.90 per cent, Lao PDR 88.30 per cent, Malaysia 65 per cent, and Myanmar 85.40 per cent (Fig. 7.3).

When taken into consideration, the export and import figures with the four neighbours (Fig. 7.4) clearly show that trade balance has always been favourable for Thailand, with border exports contributing around 8 per cent to Thailand's total trade, and border imports around 4 per cent of the same. The surplus position has been quite large for any single trading partner, like Cambodia, Lao PDR, and Malaysia. Myanmar is the only exception, because of Thailand's huge import of natural gas of around US$3.5 billion or more than 95 per cent of total imports. Without this huge trade in natural gas with Myanmar, Thailand would have a very large surplus with Myanmar.

An interesting pattern can be observed with China and Vietnam. Although they do not share a border with Thailand, border exports from Thailand to China and Vietnam have increased very rapidly to stand at more than 10.10 billion ฿ and 25.20 billion ฿ in 2012, respectively, or more than 3 per cent of Thai exports to China and 10.80 per cent of Thai exports to Vietnam in recent years (Fig. 7.5). On the other hand,

TABLE 7.2: Share and Growth of Four Neighbouring Countries

	2003	2004	2005	2006	2007	2008	2009	2010	2011	2012
Thailand total trade (world)	6,466.60	7,755.70	9,185.00	9,811.00	10,106.50	11,797.00	9,795.00	12,016.10	13,690.60	14,895.40
Total border trade 4	285.92	377.46	441.61	532.33	551.80	708.38	633.80	770.11	890.67	910.50
Total border trade 4 + V	285.92	377.46	441.61	532.33	551.80	708.38	636.88	775.77	898.55	922.18
% border 4/total trade	4.42	4.87	4.81	5.43	5.46	6.00	6.47	6.41	6.51	6.11
% border 4 + V/total trade	4.42	4.87	4.81	5.43	5.46	6.00	6.50	6.46	6.56	6.19
% change total trade	–	19.94	18.43	6.82	3.01	16.73	–16.97	22.68	13.93	8.80
% change border 4	–	32.02	17.00	20.54	3.66	28.38	–10.53	21.51	15.65	2.23
% change border 4 + V	–	32.02	17.00	20.54	3.66	28.38	–10.09	21.81	15.83	2.63
Growth rate total trade	100	119.94	142.04	151.72	156.29	182.43	151.47	185.82	211.71	230.35
Growth rate border 4	100	132.02	154.45	186.18	192.99	247.75	221.67	269.35	311.51	318.45
Growth rate border 4 + V	100	132.02	154.45	186.18	192.99	247.75	222.75	271.32	314.27	322.53

Source: 'Cross-border and Trans-border Trade Statistics', Border Trade Service Center, Ministry of Commerce.

Note: Four neighbouring countries are Cambodia, the Lao People's Democratic Republic, Malaysia, and Myanmar. V = Vietnam.

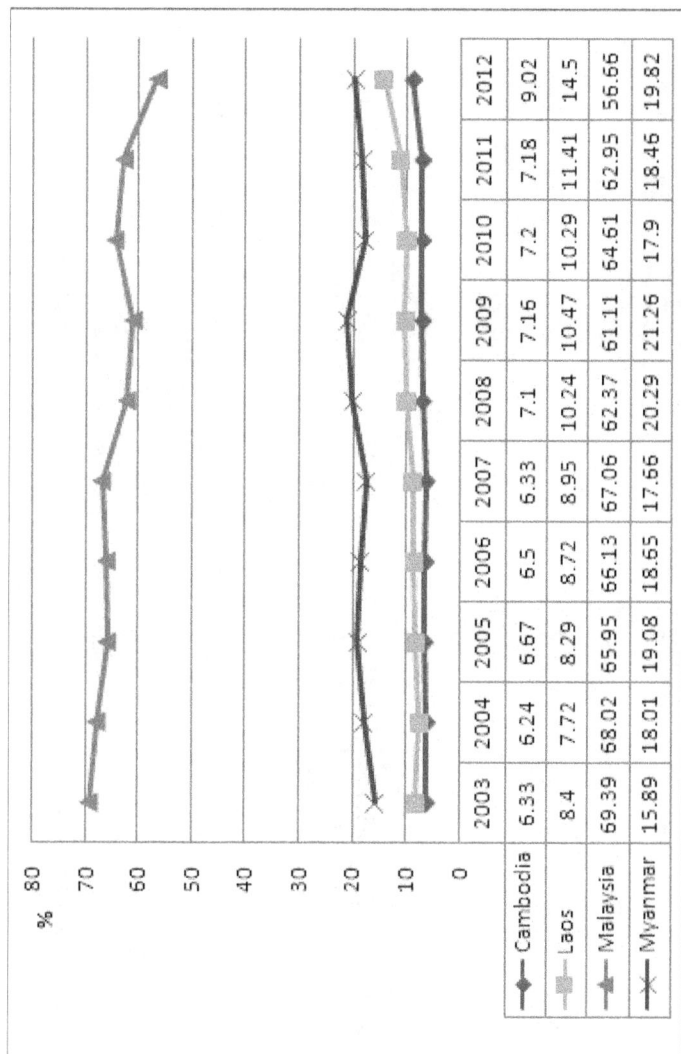

	2003	2004	2005	2006	2007	2008	2009	2010	2011	2012
Cambodia	6.33	6.24	6.67	6.5	6.33	7.1	7.16	7.2	7.18	9.02
Laos	8.4	7.72	8.29	8.72	8.95	10.24	10.47	10.29	11.41	14.5
Malaysia	69.39	68.02	65.95	66.13	67.06	62.37	61.11	64.61	62.95	56.66
Myanmar	15.89	18.01	19.08	18.65	17.66	20.29	21.26	17.9	18.46	19.82

FIG. 7.2: Share of Border Trade among the Four Countries

Source: Division of Information Technology, Department of Foreign Trade with the Cooperation of the Department of Customs.

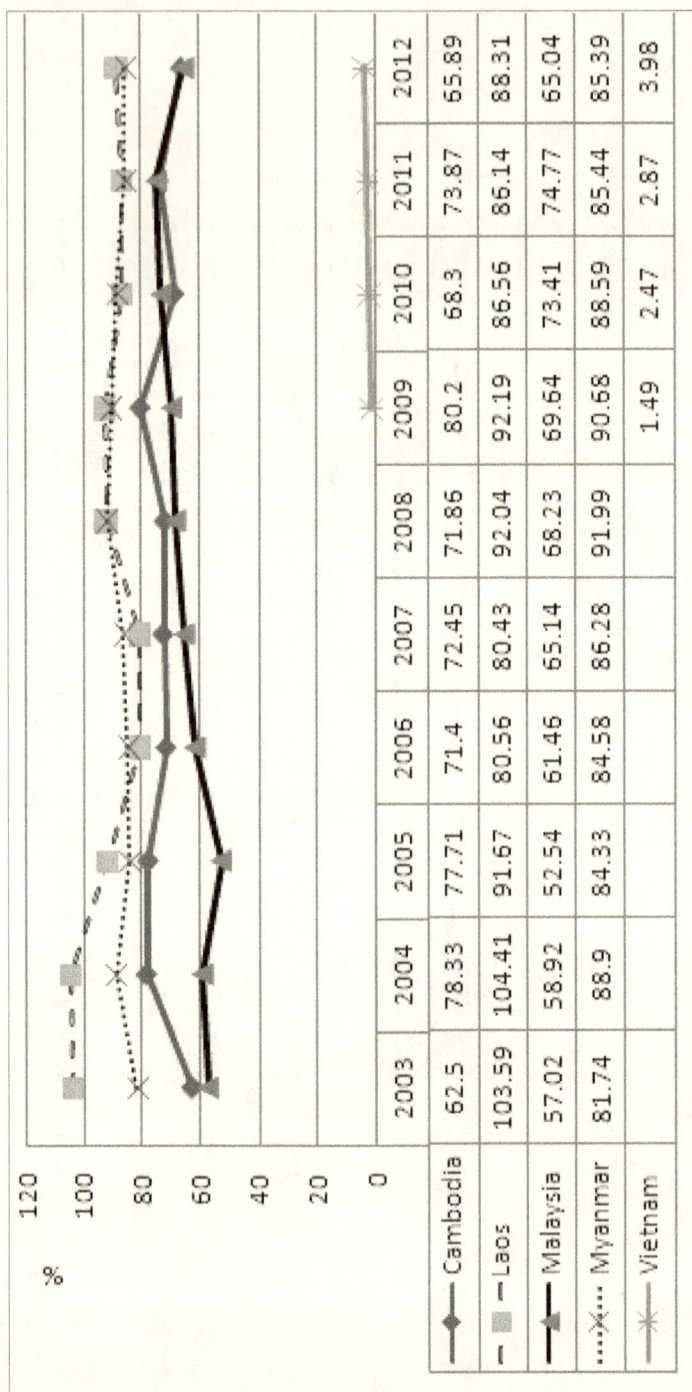

	2003	2004	2005	2006	2007	2008	2009	2010	2011	2012
Cambodia	62.5	78.33	77.71	71.4	72.45	71.86	80.2	68.3	73.87	65.89
Laos	103.59	104.41	91.67	80.56	80.43	92.04	92.19	86.56	86.14	88.31
Malaysia	57.02	58.92	52.54	61.46	65.14	68.23	69.64	73.41	74.77	65.04
Myanmar	81.74	88.9	84.33	84.58	86.28	91.99	90.68	88.59	85.44	85.39
Vietnam							1.49	2.47	2.87	3.98

FIG. 7.3: Share of Border Trade to Total Trade

Source: 'Cross-border and Trans-border Trade Statistics', Division of Information Technology, Department of Foreign Trade with the Cooperation of the Department of Customs.

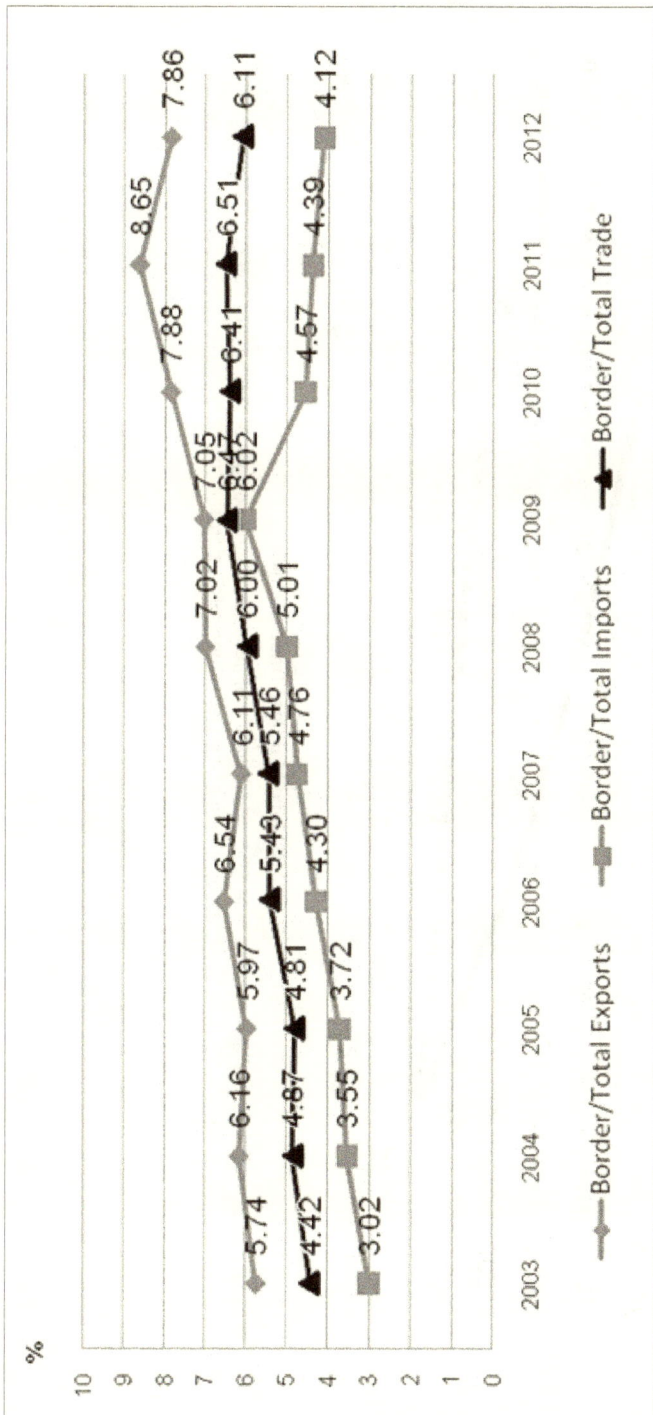

FIG. 7.4: Share of Border Trade to Total Trade, Exports and Imports

Source: 'Cross-border and Trans-border Trade Statistics', Division of Information Technology, Department of Foreign Trade with the Cooperation of the Department of Customs.

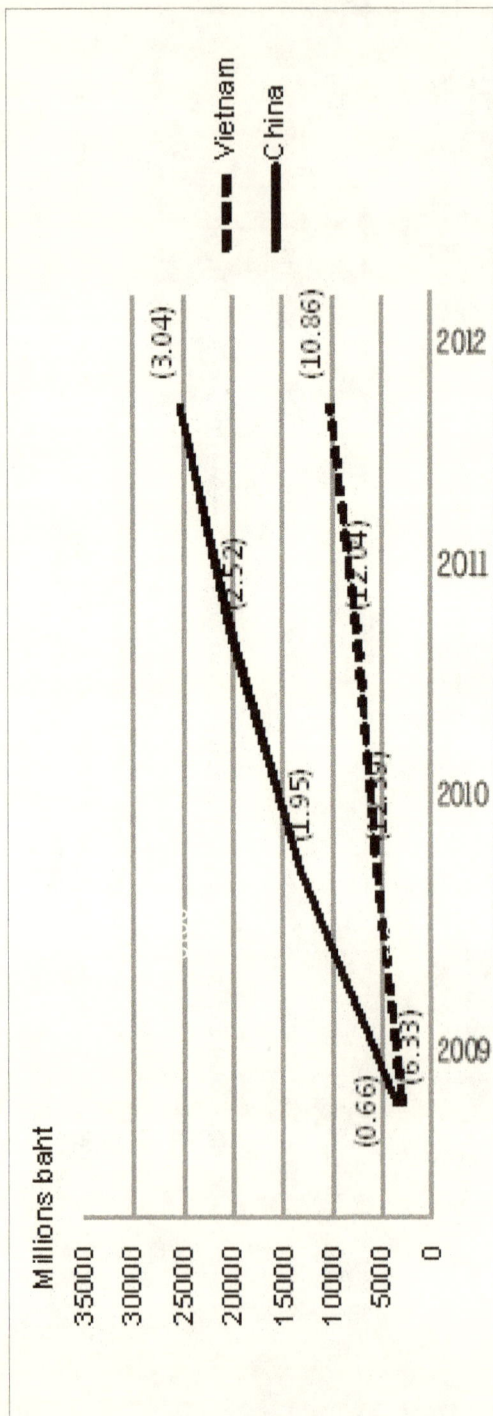

FIG. 7.5: Export Value of Border Trade to China and Vietnam

Source: 'Cross-border and Trans-border Trade Statistics', Division of Information Technology, Department of Foreign Trade with the Cooperation of the Department of Customs.

border imports from China and Vietnam to Thailand are still small (0.70 and 1.60 per cent of total trade, respectively) despite a recent increase (Fig. 7.6). This suggests a possible improvement of economic corridors, trade facilitation, and logistic arrangements, in particular to those sections linking Thailand–Lao PDR–China and Thailand–Lao PDR–Vietnam.

As noted earlier, Thailand's border trade with neighbouring countries keeps expanding quite interestingly. Particularly in the case of border imports from Myanmar, it is seen that beyond natural gas, aquatic animals come second but have a much lower value of around 1.1 billion ฿ in 2012, or less than 1 per cent of Thailand's border imports from Myanmar (Table 7.3). This is followed by other items like timber products (507 million ฿); cattle, pigs, goats, sheep (428 million ฿); other metal ores, metal waste scrap and products (355 million ฿); oil plants and products (251 million ฿); and fresh and frozen squid (118 million ฿). For Thailand's border trade with Myanmar, there is quite a variety of goods destined for both Myanmar's needs of consumption and production, starting with diesel fuel (7.2 billion ฿), gasoline (5.1 billion ฿), alcoholic beverages (4.9 billion ฿), non-alcoholic beverages (4.0 billion ฿), fabric yarn (3.1 billion ฿), palm oil (2.1 billion ฿), instant noodles and instant foods (1.9 billion ฿), iron and steel (1.8 billion ฿), cosmetics, perfumes and soaps (1.8 billion ฿), and vehicle tyres (1.7 billion ฿) (Table 7.4).

It is noted that Thailand also has a similar trade pattern with Myanmar, although not quite exactly the same as its border trade, both exports and imports, with Lao PDR and Cambodia. These countries, considered as part of CMLV countries (Cambodia, Myanmar, Laos, Vietnam) joined the rest of ASEAN, have come out from their economic isolation, and are looking for a more developed market economy in order to steer their future economic development.[6] Thus, Thailand possesses an immediate advantage as a more advanced economy and could serve as a bridge for further development and integration of these economies in the regional and global context. Malaysia is the only exception, as trade patterns look more like an exchange among these emerging economies while continuing to deepen their trading relationships with Thailand.

Moving away from Thailand's Mainland South East Asian neighbours and looking at a broader perspective in relation to South Asia and other major trading partners, it can be said that Thailand's trade with Mainland South East Asia since 2008 has always had a

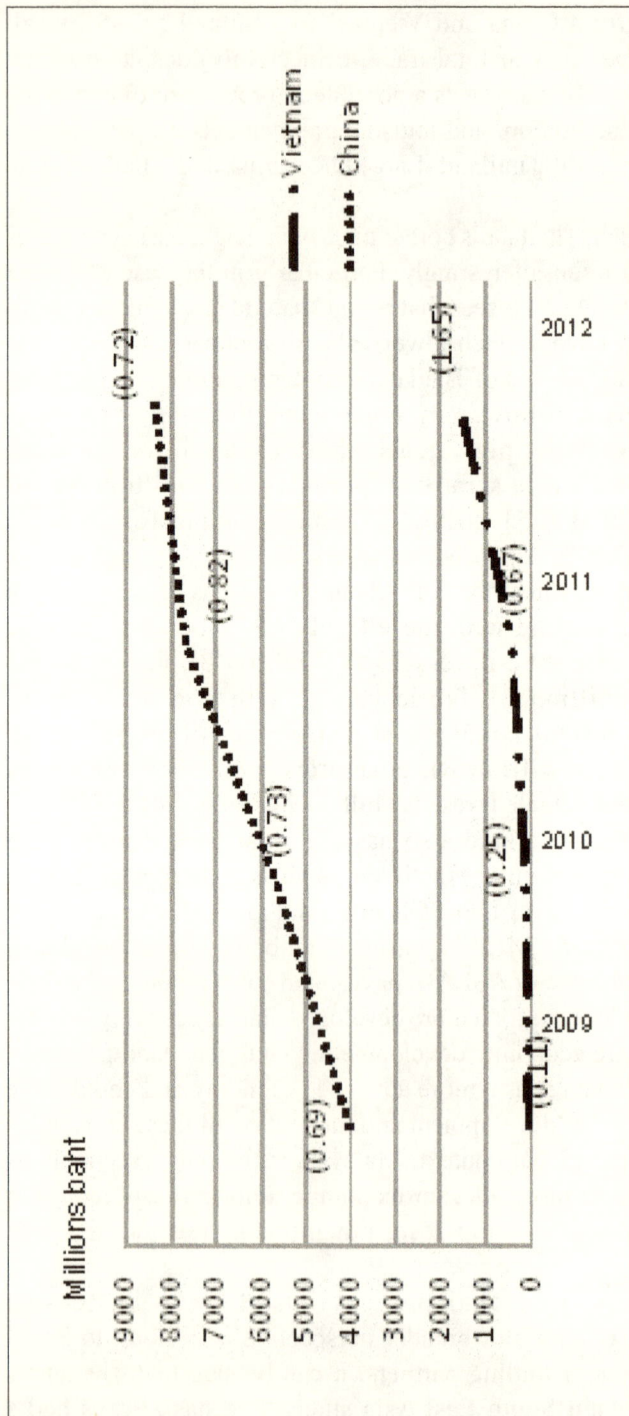

FIG. 7.6: Import Value of Border Trade from China and Vietnam

Source: 'Cross-border and Trans-border Trade Statistics', Division of Information Technology, Department of Foreign Trade with the Cooperation of the Department of Customs.

TABLE 7.3: Thailand's Top Ten Products Imported from
Myanmar (Border Trade) in 2012

(in million ฿)

Rank	Import Product	2012	12/11
1	Natural gas	106,970.14	6.33
2	Aquatic animals	1,137.22	−29.49
3	Timber products	507.07	23.90
4	Cattle, pigs, goats, sheep	428.07	43.34
5	Other metal ores, metal waste scrap and products	354.83	69.86
6	Oil Plants and products	250.64	3470.37
7	Fresh and frozen squid	118.15	−12.95
8	Fruit and fruit flavored	89.93	115.25
9	Plywood and veneer	69.33	−29.80
10	Plants and other plant products	68.47	238.29
	Total 10 products	109,993.85	6.34
	Total all products	110,495.87	6.48

Source: 'Cross-border and Trans-border Trade Statistics', Division of Information Technology, Department of Foreign Trade with the Cooperation of the Department of Customs.

TABLE 7.4: Thailand's Top Ten Products Exported to
Myanmar (Border Trade) in 2012

(in million ฿)

Rank	Export Product	2012	12/11 *(in percentage)*
1	Diesel fuel	7,191.90	−2.28
2	Gasoline	5,074.85	53.20
3	Alcoholic beverages	4,877.81	50.89
4	Non- alcoholic beverages	3,993.44	9.97
5	Fabric and yarn	3,122.91	15.80
6	Palm oil	2,057.65	24.95
7	Instant noodles and instant food	1,899.06	26.26
8	Iron and steel	1,817.18	−1.05
9	Cosmetics, perfumes and soaps	1,801.22	18.40
10	Vehicle tyre	1,700.38	25.89
	Total 10 products	33,536.40	19.38
	Total all products	69,975.66	15.47

Source: 'Cross-border and Trans-border Trade Statistics', Division of Information Technology, Department of Foreign Trade with the Cooperation of the Department of Customs.

larger share when compared to the rest of ASEAN, which takes around 10.60 per cent. This might reflect the appetite of Thai traders, particularly the small and medium enterprises (SMEs) with regard to new markets opening closer to the home country, as a result of the ASEAN Free Trade Area (AFTA), and new borders giving access to all kinds of goods and services trading. The same cannot be said, for instance for South Asia, which has seen a smaller increase of its share to Thailand's total trade, at around 2.40 per cent in 2012. Similarly, China accounts for 13.40 per cent trade volume in 2012, but is still considered smaller than the volume of ASEAN at 20.20 per cent in the same year (Fig. 7.7).

Despite the small share of South Asia as compared to the Mainland South East Asian neighbours, the region is increasingly linked to Thailand's trade, with a particular role of India. Indeed, most of Thailand's trade with South Asia is with India, as the rest of the countries are still trading very little, whether it is Bangladesh, Nepal, Pakistan, or Sri Lanka. Therefore, Thailand has ample room to trade with India, since the countries have enjoyed a free trade agreement since 2004, which has also helped Thailand to increase its trade volume and become trade surplus with India. In fact, Thailand's overall imports' share from South Asia stands at only 1.50 per cent in 2012, as compared to the exports' share at 3.30 per cent in the same year (Figs. 7.8 and 7.9). Thus, Thailand has gained quite substantially ever since these countries, and particularly India, have opened their door to the outside world.

Recent Trends of Inward and Outward Foreign Direct Investment

While examining the increasing globalization of the Thai economy, international investment is seen as a powerful force to explain its links to Thailand's international trade. For instance, the recent trend of Thailand's Foreign Direct Investment (FDI) is similar to its exports. Due to the global financial crisis, FDI has gone up and down in recent years, declining by 15 per cent in 2011 before a recovery of 10.60 per cent in 2012, or around US$8.6 billion (Fig. 7.10). This may suggest that Thailand has become more difficult as far as relying on external funding and investment is concerned, as there are more and more emerging countries looking to attract FDI, given the limits of funding available worldwide.

This issue is likely linked to how FDI is adjusting to the new reality, given Thailand's recent changes and development, and how Thailand takes the whole process of production transformation through technology

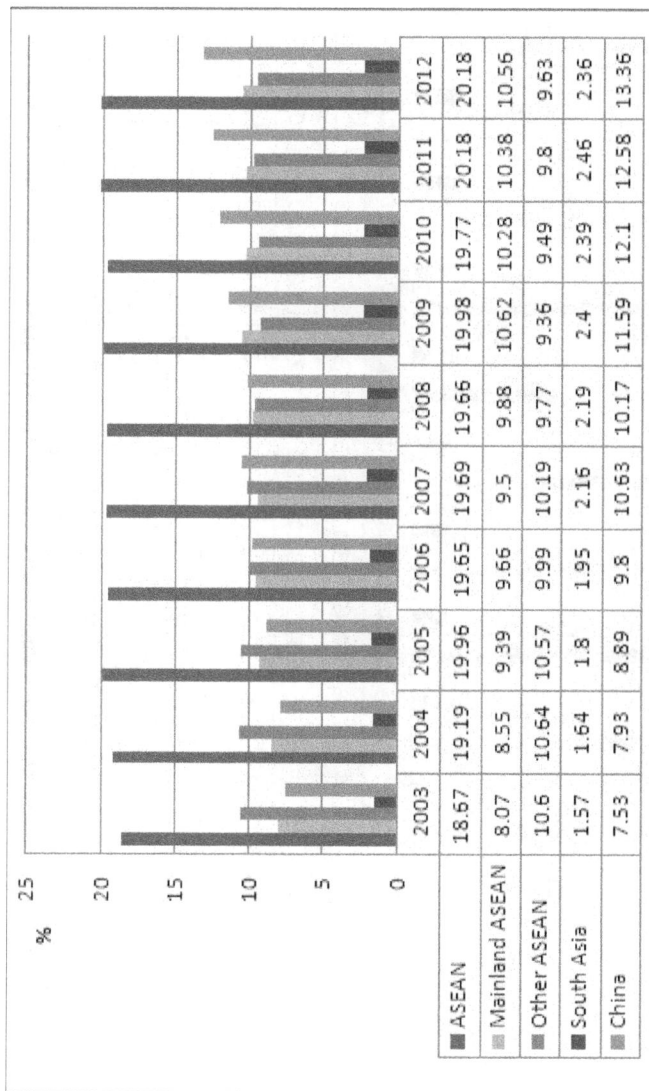

	2003	2004	2005	2006	2007	2008	2009	2010	2011	2012
ASEAN	18.67	19.19	19.96	19.65	19.69	19.66	19.98	19.77	20.18	20.18
Mainland ASEAN	8.07	8.55	9.39	9.66	9.5	9.88	10.62	10.28	10.38	10.56
Other ASEAN	10.6	10.64	10.57	9.99	10.19	9.77	9.36	9.49	9.8	9.63
South Asia	1.57	1.64	1.8	1.95	2.16	2.19	2.4	2.39	2.46	2.36
China	7.53	7.93	8.89	9.8	10.63	10.17	11.59	12.1	12.58	13.36

FIG. 7.7: Percentage Share of Total Trade

Source: Author's calculation from 'Export, Import and Trade Statistics', Global Trade Information Services, Department of International Trade Promotion, Ministry of Commerce, Thailand, see https://www.gtis.com/gta/, accessed 5 October 2014.

	2003	2004	2005	2006	2007	2008	2009	2010	2011	2012
■ ASEAN	19.44	20.25	20.42	19.17	19.58	20.54	19.15	20.46	22.04	23.13
▨ Mainland ASEAN	7.2	7.85	8.13	8.12	8.24	9.27	9.07	9.5	10.23	11.31
▤ Other ASEAN	12.23	12.4	12.28	11.06	11.34	11.27	10.08	10.96	11.8	11.82
■ South Asia	1.79	1.99	2.47	2.5	2.71	2.83	3.24	3.38	3.53	3.33
▨ China	7.09	7.29	8.3	9.02	9.74	9.09	10.56	10.99	11.8	11.72

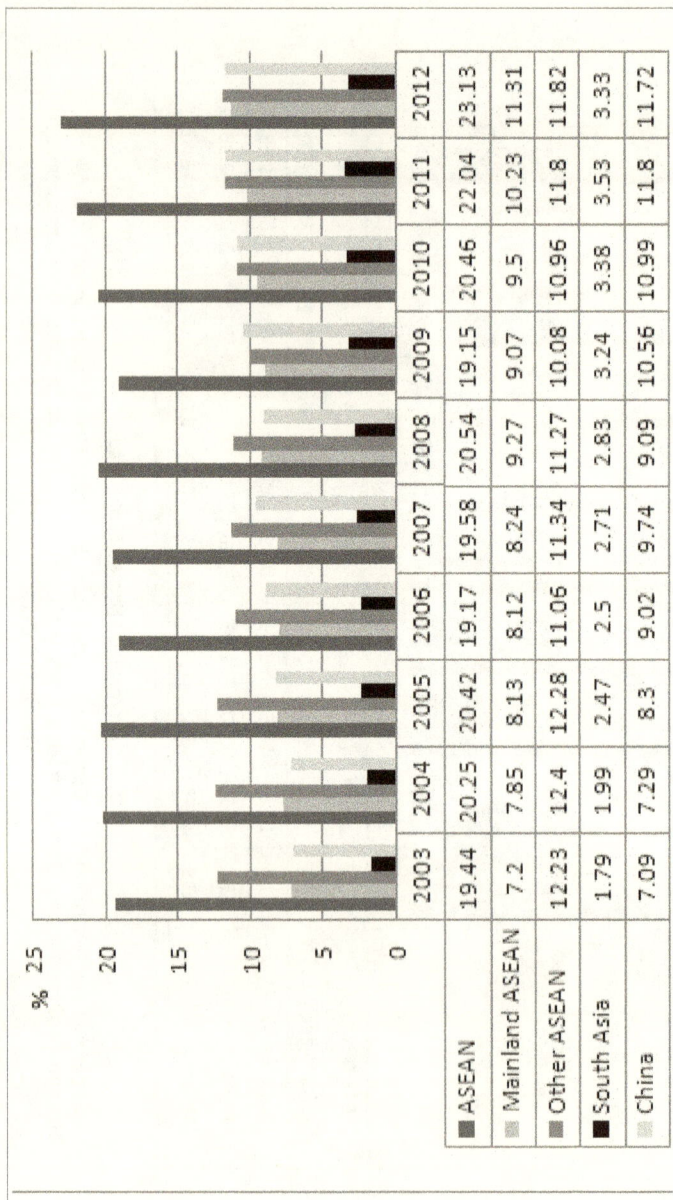

FIG. 7.8: Percentage Share of Total Exports

Source: Author's calculation from 'Export, Import and Trade Statistics', Global Trade Information Services, Department of International Trade Promotion, Ministry of Commerce, Thailand, see https://www.gtis.com/gta/, accessed 5 October 2014.

	2003	2004	2005	2006	2007	2008	2009	2010	2011	2012
ASEAN	16.64	16.52	18.3	18.43	17.91	16.81	18.5	16.63	16.24	16.14
Mainland ASEAN	7.77	7.77	9.33	9.52	8.96	8.51	9.95	8.71	8.37	8.5
Other ASEAN	8.87	8.85	8.97	8.91	8.95	8.3	8.55	7.92	7.87	7.64
South Asia	1.34	1.28	1.18	1.39	1.56	1.56	1.45	1.34	1.43	1.48
China	8	8.59	9.44	10.59	11.59	11.22	12.74	13.28	13.33	14.85

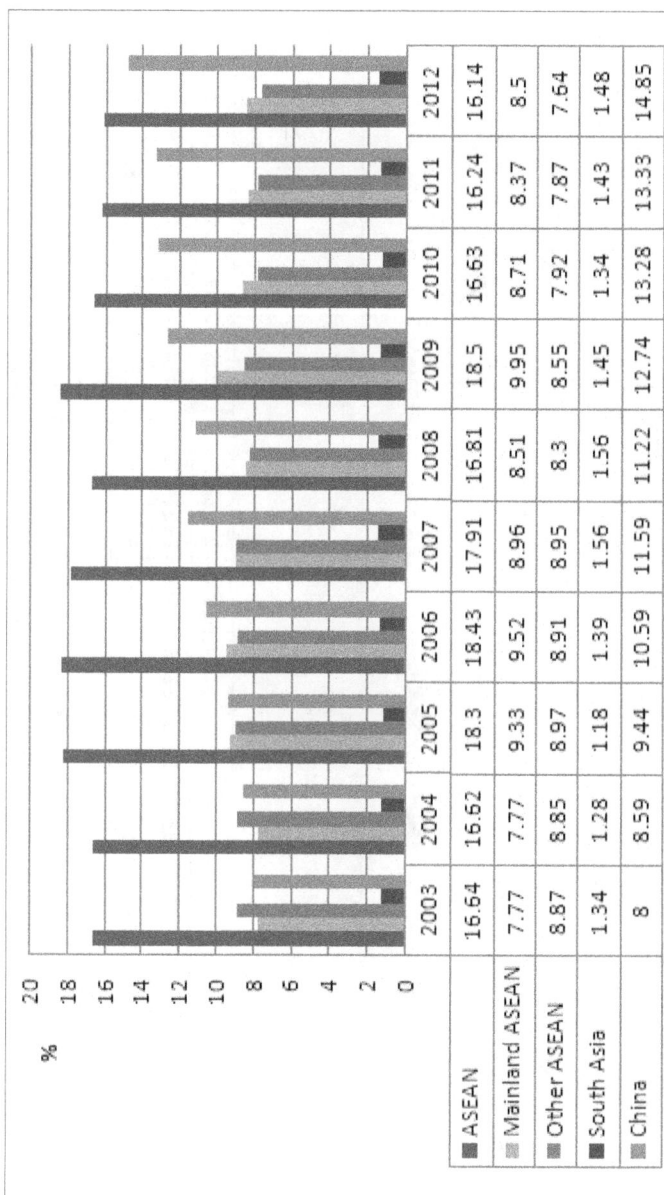

FIG. 7.9: Percentage Share of Total Imports

Source: Author's calculation from 'Export, Import and Trade Statistics', Global Trade Information Services, Department of International Trade Promotion, Ministry of Commerce, Thailand, see https://www.gtis.com/gta/, accessed 5 October 2014.

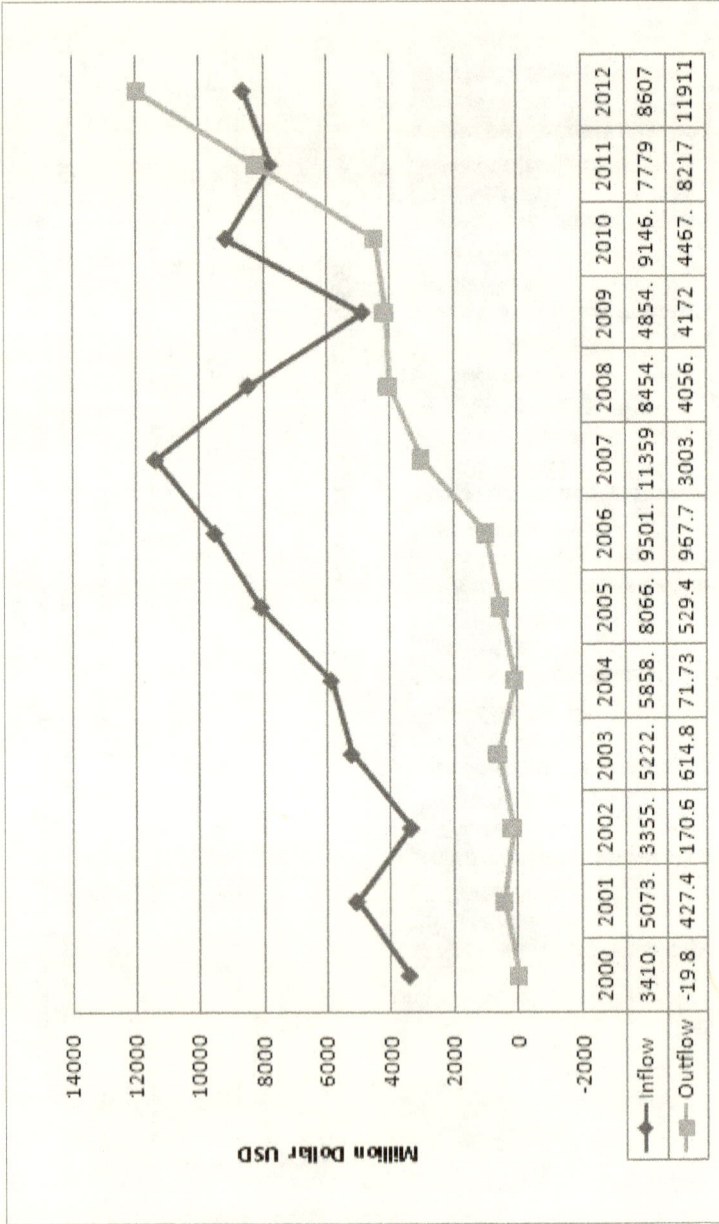

	2000	2001	2002	2003	2004	2005	2006	2007	2008	2009	2010	2011	2012
Inflow	3410.	5073.	3355.	5222.	5858.	8066.	9501.	11359	8454.	4854.	9146.	7779	8607
Outflow	-19.8	427.4	170.6	614.8	71.73	529.4	967.7	3003.	4056.	4172	4467.	8217	11911

FIG. 7.10: Thailand's FDI Inflows and Outflows

Source: UNCTAD World Investment Report, 2013.

of transfer, knowledge, and management; and more capital-intensive way of doing things, more seriously, unlike in the past. Compared to some rising ASEAN members like Indonesia, Myanmar, and Vietnam, one wonders how Thailand continues to be attractive and relies on traditional investors like Japan, the EU, and the US. In addition, an important issue is how the country can attract new investors like China, India, Malaysia, Singapore, etc.

Given such a rising trend, Thailand definitely needs to continue to improve global supply chainlinks, enhance technology, improve trade liberalization, and reduce communication and transport costs. Thailand had earlier made its links to trade in global and regional production networks, which also helped the country to expose a multitude of foreign production chains in connection with the domestic firms producing parts and components or being major suppliers for these industries, thus widening and deepening Thailand's role in the regional and global economies.

More recently, Thai firms are pursuing their business abroad, thus leading to a surge in the country's outward FDI, in addition to the inward one. This trend—emerging outward FDI—started to emerge in 2003 and rose from around US$500 million in 2005 to almost US$12 billion in 2012, making Thailand, for the first time since 2011, a net exporter of capital, meaning its outward FDI outpaced its inward FDI.[7] The appreciated baht and the extension of production facilities, in addition to more attractive low-cost and resource-rich availabilities in neighbouring countries help Thailand to allow local firms to get open access to neighbouring markets and low-cost production bases to reduce operating costs, as well as to working and sourcing for better integration within the regional and global production networks.

Policies and Initiatives in Linking with South East Asia and India

As shown earlier, because of Thailand's position with regard to its trade and FDI, the country has no option but to pursue consistent outward-oriented policies and initiatives in response to regional, dynamic changes and the global economic environment. Since the last Asian financial crisis of 1997–8, trade, and FDI have been given an even higher priority for Thai policymakers to enhance the country's foreign reserves,[18] but more importantly, productivity and competitiveness with regard to its exports in various goods, while balancing its imports in tandem with the needs of its multitude of industries, in particular foreign and multinational firms with a strong presence of its supply chains linking regionally and globally. Despite the slowdown of trade and investment as a result of the global financial crisis of 2007–8, Thai policymakers seem to weather the storms by adjusting trade orientation according to emerging economies and capital exports' reshaping in the form of outward FDI, supported by government policies both for trade and investment.

Thailand is currently involved in several regional, subregional, and bilateral trade agreements as well as a wide range of economic and technical cooperation. With increasing uncertainty in the global trading environment, it is in the interest of the country to find a way to contribute positively to its external sector. This is why a country closest to home would be the ASEAN arena, where it has finally become a central piece for a deeper and wider regional integration. Indeed, years before the end of the Cold War, Thailand was a founding member of the ASEAN. The country has remained a prominent player all along in the regional economic affairs, whether in the launching of the AFTA since 1993 or the recent start of the AEC by the beginning of 2016.

Indeed, the country had rightly foreseen the end of the Cold War, when the former Thai Premier Chatchai Choonhawan proposed to its neighbours in the late 1980s, 'turning the battlefield to the marketplace', with the conclusion to build the first Mekong Bridge linking Thailand and Lao PDR, in the early 1990s. Later, Thailand also joined the ASEAN efforts for its Hanoi Action Plan to assist the development of CMLV countries right after the crisis, until the end of 1990s. Then, by the turn of the century, Thailand proposed to its Mainland South East Asian neighbouring countries the Ayeyawady-Chao Phraya-Mekong Economic Cooperation Strategy (ACMECS), another scope of its cooperation with the CMLV countries, without the involvement of any countries or organizations outside the grouping. Another major subregional economic cooperation is the GMS, where the country plays a very active role with the help of the Asian Development Bank (ADB), for its links to the six countries involved.

At a certain level, domestic and regional changes have also shaped Thailand to become closer to South Asia, particularly India—the core country of the region. Thailand has gradually built with India a new path towards a strong economic partnership. India's Look East Policy and Thailand's Look West Policy have been instrumental right from the beginning to bridge mutual understanding and further contact. Thailand's support of India to be an ASEAN dialogue partner has led to India fostering its linkages with the region, with a recently concluded ASEAN-India Free Trade Agreement (ASEAN-India FTA), in addition to an earlier Thailand-India Free Trade Agreement in 2004. Indeed, with such a Thailand-India agreement, Thailand has been able to reverse its trade deficit with India to a position of a trade surplus since 2005, with a view to link India through Thailand to South East Asian production networks, and work with multinational firms from Japan, Korea, etc. Although recent studies have shown India's slow adjustment to ASEAN production chains,[9] Indian firms have slowly been awakening to the new business opportunities, with leading firms of India taking a sizeable business start-up in South East Asia, which could overturn the trend of the past in the near future.

Beyond the scope of Thai-India and ASEAN-India agreements, Thailand has also contributed to India fostering its linkages with the region through the ASEAN-India cooperation, and the newly set-up Regional Comprehensive Economic Partnership (RCEP) which also extends to other cooperative efforts at the subregional level, like the Bay of Bengal Initiative for Multi-Sectoral and Technical Cooperation (BIMSTEC) and the Mekong-Ganga Cooperation (MGC). Linking all these newly useful frameworks to India's Look East Policy, a new landscape of connectivity within India linking it to its neighbours in South Asia is evident, with the ambition of further linkages to South East Asia. It is worth mentioning the two major initiatives, one by India and another by Thailand, that have led to a new emerging landscape of cooperation and integration, not just for these two countries but with Myanmar figuring as a bridge connecting South Asia and South East Asia.

Myanmar's recent political changes since 2011 and in particular the new elections since November 2016, had impacted upon the new dynamics of partnerships with neighbouring countries, e.g. India and Thailand. The government of India has pursued a new 'Act East Policy' with regard to the latest development of Myanmar, and seeing it connected by land connectivity to Mainland South East Asia is an important strategy. Thailand also saw the recent changes that were sought by both Myanmar and India to work on a possible connectivity by renewing a trilateral highway project to unlock the potentials of north-east India, Myanmar, Thailand, and the rest of South East Asia. Thailand is actively pursuing its strategic border crossings with Myanmar, from Mae Sai in Chiangrai to Mae Sot in Tak, Phu Nam Ron in Kanchanaburi, Sing Khorn in Prachuap Kiri Khan, and Koh Song next to Ranong.

The second is Thailand's own initiative, the seaport and industrial development of Dawei. It was started first by the private sector and then the government was convinced to join in. The proposal had been accepted to a certain extent by the Myanmar Government, pending due to its long-term viability. Meanwhile, a joint investment was also sought out from the Thai side so the Myanmar Government could become a strong and important partner. The rationale of the whole project is to open Thailand, for its maritime connectivity to South Asia, and India, in particular, as well as a way to dislocate its heavy industrial facilities from its own East Seaboard, now quite congested, to this part of Myanmar. While Myanmar's participation will allow the country to develop and possess premier heavy industrial development as well as an alternative for deep seaport beyond the Thiwala Seaport near Rangoon. However, the impending development of Dawei has some concerns related to important issues like environmental degradation, heavy investment involvement, and requirement of more partners beyond Myanmar and Thailand, in particular the Japanese for its funding and the Indians for its linkages to South Asia.

Connectivity with North-East India

It is important for Thailand to have its own 'Look West' strategy that is adaptable to changes that are taking place in India and Myanmar. As mentioned earlier, economic relations between Thailand and both India and Myanmar have been undergoing major expansion. In case of India, Thailand's trade has expanded beyond trade in goods to cover services and investment as well, looking from both Thailand-India and ASEAN-India agreements in current operations. For Myanmar, Thailand has become even more active with the political and economic changes inside the country. Given the current trend of change in Myanmar, Thailand-Myanmar economic relations will surely be transformed.

Looking at this perspective and given the increase in connectivity between India-Thailand and the neighbouring countries, it is natural to see improvement of trade and investment and logistical arrangements becoming detrimental to future economic relationships. Thus, it is perhaps realistic to revive the concept of bringing Mainland South East Asia closer to north-east India. The trilateral highway, once completed, will help linking north-east India to Myanmar and then Thailand, resulting in closer ties for the people and business community.[10]

Thailand's trade with north-east India has been difficult to assess, but is believed to have a small value. Relatively few contacts in the recent past blocked by the infrastructural bottlenecks and discouraged by both traders and investors, prohibited any further economic improvements, with no option but to wait for policy changes. Indeed the shortest distance from north-east India to reach the Thai borders is around 1,400 km., shorter than to reach New Delhi. After both Indian and Thai Governments expressed their intention in various fora to address the increasing needs to develop a 'rapprochement' in economic linkages, it is a good time to reap benefits of these changes as both could use the scope of trilateral relationships, involving Myanmar more actively in the change process.

As for north-east India including West Bengal, Thailand also has a good chance in the long run to further develop an economic relationship. At the moment, China has a strong presence in this region of India with both trade and people contact, and India has a policy to develop an economic corridor through Nagaland, linking India and China through Myanmar.[11] Also, India expresses clear strategies to link India and Mainland South East Asia through economic corridors that are already functioning in the GMS, starting from the Indian border town of Moreh, Manipur and Myanmar's border town of Tamu. For sea transport development, Thailand expects the future development of Dawei, Myanmar's port town on the Andaman Sea, and linking directly to Bangkok by land transport development.

In practice, trade and investment obstacles between the two countries remain high at the regional level. There is a need for coordination between the central and local administrations which often causes confusion for the business sector. The list includes among others, transport and logistical arrangements, customs procedures and facilities to meet the changes, information and knowledge about both sides' business practices and laws, and for north-east India in particular, insufficient infrastructure.

Conclusion

Due to internal and external factors contributing to uncertainties for the Thai economy, the country is looking forward to moving ahead with a strong middle class demand, a large industrial base and strong supply chains, and a new path of greater connectivity to the regional economies. While examining changes in economic structure, the extension of manufacturing activities and the emergence of regional economies beyond Bangkok is evident, whether it is north-eastern, southern, northern, or eastern, which serve Thailand's new foundation for growth as well. Thus, improving connectivity, both soft and hard infrastructures, inside Thailand, within ASEAN, and between South Asia and Mainland South East Asia, could become the key for Thailand's future development.

Recent trade trends with its Mainland South East Asian neighbours support a trend of new connectivity, particularly for import and export border trade with its four main neighbouring countries of Cambodia, the Lao PDR, Malaysia, and Myanmar. Border trade with these four countries expanded more than the average of other ASEAN countries and Thailand's total trade. Private sector communities along the border areas have taken advantage of trade facilitation improvement and the relaxation of border controls. It is also evident that countries like China and Vietnam, although not having an immediate border with Thailand, have still been able to substantially increase their border trade with Thailand, particularly in terms of Thai exports to these two countries.

Therefore, it is important to observe the trends of Thailand's trade with Myanmar that could have strong implications for connecting trade with South Asia through land connectivity with this country. At present, Thailand's border trade with Myanmar in various kinds of goods and services has helped Myanmar integrate its own economy with the rest of ASEAN. It remains to be seen how improving connectivity inside Myanmar could serve for Thailand's future trade and development with Myanmar and possibly serve as land connectivity to South Asia, through north-east India.

Thailand has several physical transport infrastructure projects linking it to Myanmar and India. The most notable one is the Dawei Special Economic Zone, which is delayed due to financing issues. The Thai Government also provides low-interest loans and development assistance from Neighbouring Countries Economic Development Cooperation Agency (NEDA) for road construction projects in Myanmar and bridge constructions linking Thailand and Myanmar. The India–Myanmar–Thailand Highway has been initiated to improve connectivity among three countries.

Notes

1. Asian Development Bank, October 2012, see http://www.adb.org/sites/default/files/myanmar-energy-sector-assessment.pdf., accessed 11 October 2013. Also see Asian Development Bank, Asian Development Bank Institute, 31 August 2013, see http://www.adbi.org/files/2009.08.31.book.infrastructure.seamless.asia.pdf., accessed 13 October 2013.

2. B.N. Bhattacharyay et al., *Infrastructure for Asian Connectivity*, Cheltenham: Edward Elgar, 2012.
3. S. Chirathivat, 'China's Rise and Its Effects on ASEAN-China Trade Relations', in *China, the United States and Southeast Asia: Contending Perspectives on Policies, Security, and Economics*, eds. E. Goh and S. Simon, New York: Routledge, 2008, pp. 38–55.
4. S. Chirathivat and C. Sabhasri, 'Thailand', in *National Strategies for Regional Integration: South and East Asian Case Studies*, eds. J. Francois et al., London: Anthem Press and Asian Development Bank, 2009, pp. 383–481.
5. S. Chirathivat, 'Prospering Thailand-India Economic Partnership', Mekong-Ganga Policy Brief, Research and Information System for Developing Countries, New Delhi, 2009, pp. 1–2.
6. Neighbouring Countries Economic Development Cooperation Agency, 31 October 2009, see http://www.neda.or.th/eng/contentviewfullpage.aspx?folder=88&subfolder=&contents=1167, accessed 14 October 2013. See also Neighbouring Countries Economic Development Cooperation Agency, 2013, see http://www.neda.or.th/eng/contentviewfullpage.aspx?folder=87&subfolder=&contents=1037, accessed 14 October 2013.
7. Y. Tanaka, 'Asian Development Bank', 26 September 2013, see http://www.adb.org/projects/41682-013/details, accessed 14 October 2013.
8. C. Sussangkarn, 'United Nations Economic and Social Commission for Asia and the Pacific', 4 October 2007, see http://www.unescap.org/ttdw/ppp/PPP2007/bf_thailand.pdf, accessed 14 October 2013.
9. M. Kawai and G. Wignaraya, 'Policy Challenges Posed by Asian Free Trade Agreement: A Review of the Evidence', in *A World Trade Organization for the 21st Century: The Asian Perspective*, Glos: Edward Elgar, 2014, pp. 182–238.
10. P. De, *ASEAN-India Connectivity Report*, India Country Study, Research and Information System for Developing Countries, Bookwell, 2012.
11. S. Chirathivat, 'Thailand's Greater Mekong Sub Region: Role and Potential Linkages to South-West China and Northeast India', *Millennial Asia*, vol. 1, no. 2, 2010, pp. 171–95, see also M. Epao, 'Ministry of Development of the North Eastern Region', June 2012, see http://www.mdoner.gov.in/content/myanmar, accessed 26 October 2013.

8

Connectivity and Subregional Cooperation in the East of South Asia

Importance of India's North-East Revisited

Anasua Basu Ray Chaudhury

THE SOUTH ASIAN ASSOCIATION for Regional Cooperation (SAARC) completed thirty years of existence in December 2015. Born out of a fractured South Asian psyche, SAARC has yet to become an active regional organization in this part of the world. Economic integration and mutual understanding among its members always suffer because of nagging bilateral disputes, political tension between India and Pakistan, and India's 'big brotherly' attitude towards its neighbours. Though a majority of the disputes of this region are in most cases 'India-centred', the disputes between India and Pakistan dominate the South Asian scenario.

Since 1990, there has been a major attempt in the eastern part of South Asia to promote subregional cooperation for the mutual benefit of the people. It was expected that Pakistan's tactical elimination would lead to better cooperation among the remaining states of South Asia. The supporters argued that subregional cooperation would facilitate the smaller states to have more access to world trade, and would help them to speed up the transformation of the South Asian Preferential Trading Arrangement (SAPTA) into South Asian Free Trade Area (SAFTA). However, initially Pakistan, Sri Lanka, and Maldives vehemently opposed the idea of such a subregional grouping within the SAARC as they were left out of such an initiative.

The World Bank and Asian Development Bank (ADB), being impressed with the Association of South East Asian Nations' (ASEAN's) experience of the Indonesia–Malaysia–Thailand Growth Triangle, intended to support a similar cooperative venture in the eastern part of South Asia in the 1990s. Under the banner of this growth triangle, three major initiatives were taken—the Southern Growth Triangle (SGT), the Northern Growth Triangle (NGT), and the East ASEAN Growth Area (EAGA). Perhaps, the success story of the Greater Mekong Subregion (GMS), named after the Mekong River, comprising Cambodia, Laos, Myanmar, Thailand, Vietnam, and the Yunnan province of the People's Republic of China in South East Asia since 1992, influenced the ADB mostly to promote the idea of a similar type of multilateral subregional cooperation in South Asia. It was decided that under the guidance of the foreign officers of the member states, the establishment of the proposed South Asian Growth Quadrangle (SAGQ) comprising Bangladesh, Bhutan, Nepal, and India's north-eastern region would take place within a stipulated time frame and it would not only strengthen political and cultural ties, but would also foster economic benefits. Indeed, such an initiative increased the importance of India's north-east while creating a subregion in the east of South Asia. However, the initiative could not take off due to not having a congenial political situation in India's neighbourhood.

As India has been looking eastward in its foreign policy since the 1990s, India's north-east has become a key strategic point through which India can really look farther east towards South East Asia. In this context, the Bay of Bengal Initiative for Multi-Sectoral Economic Cooperation (BIMSTEC) comprising Bangladesh, India, Myanmar, Sri Lanka, and Thailand along with the two Himalayan states of Nepal and Bhutan, has become a perfect synergy between India's Look East Policy, and Thailand and Myanmar's Look West Policy. Here also, India's north-east plays a role of a bridge-builder between these two regions. Similarly, initiatives in the recent past have been taken to form cross-border multilateral forums like the Bangladesh, China, India, and Myanmar Economic Corridor (BCIM-EC) since 1999, supporting the overland connectivity between India's north-east and the countries of East and South East Asia. To improve infrastructure, building and establishing an appropriate legal and regulatory framework for development of multimodal transports (road, rail, waterways, and airways) by developing and accelerating transportation interconnectivity is one of the aims of the BCIM-EC forum. It has been expected that once these roads and railway lines become operational and interlinkages are established with this corridor, it will be a game changer for landlocked regions like Barak Valley, of

Assam, Tripura, and Mizoram, of India's north-east. Currently, most of the landlocked states of the region are paying higher transportation price for not having easy access to sea ports. Lack of proper infrastructural facilities has led to economic isolation of the region.

Against this backdrop, this essay intends to evaluate the initiatives for cross-border subregional cooperation in eastern South Asia and the scope of exploring India's north-east, keeping three dimensions in consideration—connectivity within the north-east of India, connectivity between the north-east and the rest of India, and connectivity with immediate neighbours and beyond for promotion of trade and commerce. This essay is confined to the hard infrastructural connectivity comprising rail, road, air, and water, which passes through India's north-east.

Initiatives to Improve Connectivity within the North-Eastern Region of India

The Ministry of Road Transport and Highways has initiated a mega road development programme in the north-eastern region under the programme 'Special Accelerated Road Development Programme in North East' (SARDP-NE) (Map 8.1). The scope of the programme has been enlarged from time to time since September 2005. SARDP-NE Phase 'A' covering 4.099 km. and Arunachal Pradesh Package of Roads and Highways covering 2,319 km., is presently under implementation (Map 8.2). In addition, improvement of roads in the states of Assam and Meghalaya has been taken up.[1] The government has also approved road projects worth ₹64,413,40 million for construction of 12 road stretches in the north-eastern state of Nagaland. The land for these projects is said to be provided by the state government.[2] Apart from the above, the government has also given approval to the preparation of a detailed project report for 3,723 km. of roads under Phase 'B' so as to enable the government to plan the expenditure on these roads during the next five-year plan.[3]

In parallel projects, the ADB-funded South Asia Subregional Economic Cooperation (SASEC) is also providing support to an Indian government initiative to upgrade old roads and build new ones in the north-east. These projects are being designed to improve connectivity in this part of India where movement is often hindered by hilly terrain and climatic elements, such as heavy rains. Under the programme, the ADB is set to lend US$300 million to India for improving regional road

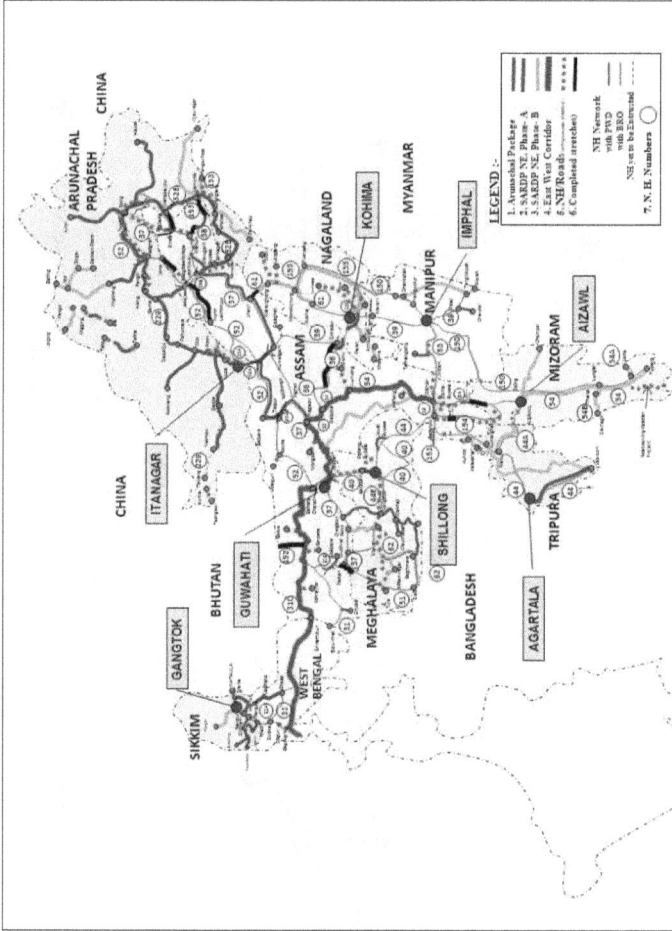

MAP 8.1: Major Road Development Programmes in the North-east Region

Source: See http://mdoner.gov.in/sites/default/files/silo3_content/roads/mrdp.jpg, accessed 14 September 2015.

Note: Map not to scale. The international boundaries of India as shown in this map are neither correct nor authentic.

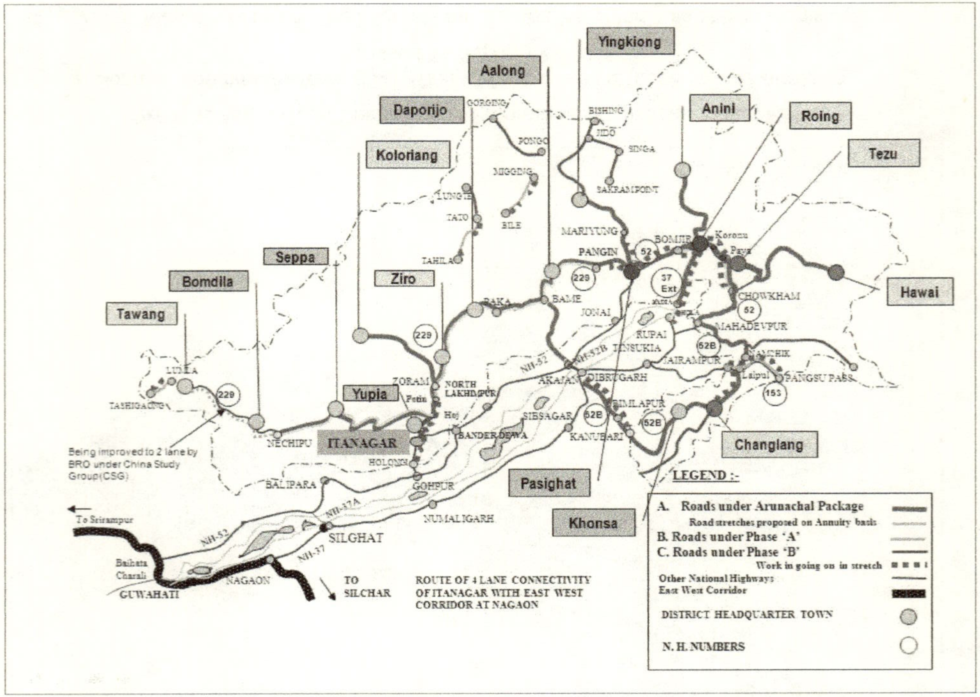

MAP 8.2: Arunachal Pradesh under the SARDP-NE Programme

Source: See http://mdoner.gov.in/sites/default/files/silo3_content/roads/rcfi.jpg, accessed 12 August 2015.

Note: Map not to scale. The international boundaries of India as shown in this map are neither correct nor authentic.

connectivity in the north-east. The country signed an agreement with the ADB on 26 March 2015 for developing 500 km. of roads in the north-eastern region along north Bengal. The ADB is funding road projects in India's north-east to establish transport linkages with neighbouring countries.[4]

Connectivity, Subregionalism and the Asian Highway

Subregional cooperation across the international borders has been used as a strategy to promote growth and development of the peripheral areas in different parts of the globe. At the same time, in an age of economic interdependence and cooperative security, connectivity has become a buzzword. This is primarily because, while reflecting globalization's second wave, the importance of giving a fillip to regional and/or subregional cooperation is being appreciated and acknowledged at political, economical, and social levels. Physical connectivity comprising land, water, and air components has been envisaged to further bilateral and multilateral ties among the nations in a region or subregion, in order to better understand each other and also to complement each other's strengths and weaknesses. With these facts in mind, we shall discuss the Asian highway and importance of India's north-east.

The proposed Asian Highway (AH) is a network of 141,000 km. of standardized roadways, criss-crossing thirty-two Asian countries (Map 8.3). Although the Asian highway project was conceived in the 1960s, the Intergovernmental Agreement on the Asian Highway Network was adopted only in 2003 and signed in 2004 among thirty-two countries. India became the twenty-fourth country to sign the agreement in April 2004. Two of the principal routes, viz., AH 1 and AH 2 pass through India. AH 1 enters India from Pakistan at Atari and terminates at Bangladesh's border at Petropol (Benapol in Bangladesh). After traversing through Bangladesh, it again enters India at Dawki, Meghalaya; and Myanmar at Moreh, Manipur; passing through Shillong, Nagaon, Dimapur, Kohima, and Imphal and further connecting the network in South East Asia. The other route, i.e. AH 2 originates from Delhi and enters Nepal after passing through Ghaziabad, Moradabad, Ramnagar, and Banbasa. It re-emerges in India in West Bengal, enters Bangladesh, and further connects Myanmar, Thailand, Malaysia, and Singapore. Thus, it is AH 1 that connects India through her north-eastern region with South East Asia.

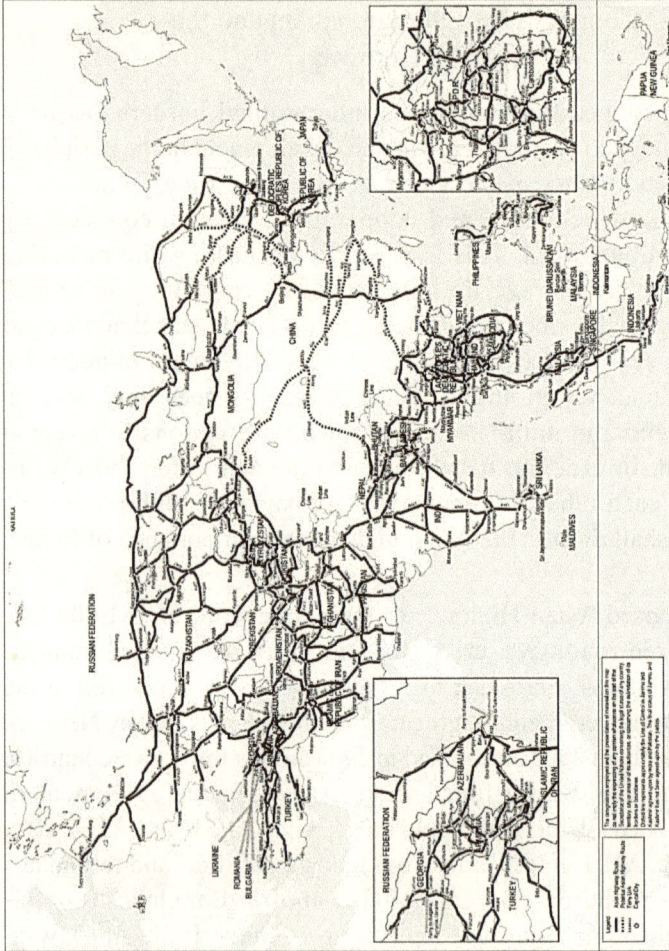

MAP 8.3: Asian Highway Network

Source: https://sites.google.com/site/indianoceancommunity1/trans-asian-highway, accessed 15 March 2018.

Note: Map not to scale. The international boundaries of India as shown in this map are neither correct nor authentic.

AH 1 runs from west to east through four states of India's north-east, viz., Meghalaya, Assam, Nagaland, and Manipur; before entering Myanmar. Thus, AH 1 enters India from Bangladesh at Dawki, Meghalaya and follows National Highway (NH) 40 up to Jorabat and then enters Assam and follows NH 37 up to Nagaon, Assam. It then follows NH 36 (some parts of Karbi Anglong) and enters Nagaland (Dimapur-Kohima). From Nagaland, it follows NH 39 via Imphal-Moreh, Manipur and then enters Myanmar and further connects the AH network in South East Asia.

There has also been a strong demand in India's north-east to repair and restore the 'Stillwell Road' to connect India with Myanmar and China. However, the Government of India has not considered the matter seriously, despite certain reports that the central and the state governments are keen on reopening it for improving trade relations with ASEAN countries.[5] It is worth mentioning here that the East–West Corridor road network, which runs from Silchar in Assam to Porbandar in Gujarat under National Highways Development Project (NHDP), covers some stretches of AH 1 in the north-east. The overlapping sections are Doboka-Nagaon (NH 36) and Nagaon-Dharamatul-Sonapur (NH 37) (Map 8.2).

It may be noted here that the widening/improving work of the existing national highways in India's north-east that fall under AH 1 are not likely to cause any major displacement of people, as there is no need to acquire additional land for this purpose—there exists enough space for widening the roads. The Government of India had already acquired enough land for building highways during the 1960s, keeping future widening in view. Those that are likely to be displaced are the people who are illegally occupying the land alongside the highways. Wherever, there is defacto ownership of land adjacent to the proposed AH, there might be some political problem. The question of community ownership of tribal land might cause problem in Karbi-Anglong, Nagaland and some districts of Manipur.

India's north-east region, with an area of a little over 255,000 sq. km. (excluding Sikkim) is considered as a landlocked region of the country and is still underdeveloped in terms of almost all socio-economic indicators even after 68 years of India's Independence. All the symptoms of underdevelopment and syndromes of civil unrest are evident in the region. The proposed AH in conjunction with the Look East Policy, now refurbished as the Act East Policy, is an attempt to develop the region by opening it up to the global order. However, in the backdrop of the prevailing scenario of underdevelopment, opening up of the region and connecting it with the world through a transnational highway like the AH, is likely to have both a positive as well as negative socio-economic impact on the region. It is expected that this transborder road connectivity will play an important role in the economic development of the region through cheaper transportation of goods and people, increased exports, industrial development, development of tourism sector, employment generation, etc.

However, there is a growing suspicion that the absence of industrial infrastructure and any significant large-scale industries in the region may reduce India's north-east to a mere transit point for human and commercial traffics. Moreover, unless the insurgency problem in the region is managed and peace transformation is activated, mere construction of a transnational highway will not facilitate the flow of expected benefits. Drug and small arms trafficking may increase due to quick and easy movement of people because of the AH.

It is also alleged that in absence of local entrepreneurs, people from other parts of the country will capture the benefits that would emerge from the AH. The project may also lead to haphazard urbanization in the region, which may be problematic.

Till now, no serious problem of displacement has been voiced in the areas where widening works have already been started (see Table 8.1 for information on population and ethnic affiliation of the inhabitants of the districts through which AH 1 passes). However, there are reports of inadequate compensation for ravaging paddy fields and felling valuable trees along the East–West Corridor in Bongaigaon District (Map 8.4). Certain public committees have been formed to get adequate compensation not only for the present loss but also for realization of compensation for acquisition of land in 1967. Such reports do not talk of displacement of people.[6]

Pros and Cons of the Proposed Transport Corridor in the BCIM-EC through the North-East

Physical connectivity is the bedrock of all of other forms of connectivity such as economic links, social links, and people-to-people interactions. Given the geographical proximity of the Bangladesh-China-India-Myanmar or BCIM countries, the establishment of road, rail, inland waterway, and maritime links is vital for integrating the subregion as well

TABLE 8.1: Some Basic Information on Population and
Ethnic Affiliation of the Inhabitants of the Districts
through which AH 1 Passes

State	District	Ethnic Community
Meghalaya	East Khasi Hills/Ri-Bhoi	War Khasi/Bhoi Khasi, Nepali
Assam	Kamrup/Morigaon/Nagaon/ Karbi Anglong	Nepali/Karbi/ Tiwa/Non-Tribal
Nagaland	Dimapur/Kohima	Sema, Angami
Manipur	Senapati/Imphal/Thoubal/Chandel	Kuki, Maram, Mao, Nepali, Meitei, Pangal, Naga, Kuki, Anal Naga, Meitei, Nepali, Tamil, Pangal, Kuki, Bengali Hindus (Moreh)

Source: Cited in a report entitled *Socio-economic Impacts of the Proposed Asian Highway on India's Northeast with Special Reference to Assam: A Preliminary Study*, coordinated by Annada Charan Bhagabati and Abu Nasar Saied Ahmed under the auspices of OKD Institute of Social Change and Development, Guwahati, July 2006, p. 11.

as to encourage and develop economic interactions that would contribute to the socio-economic improvement of the contiguous zone. Beyond this, it implies 'linear connectivity' along a physical-transportation artery within a defined space or location, linking various modes of production, distribution, and consumption; and supported by programmes, policies, institutions, and agreements that facilitate cooperation among the economic clusters along the corridor route.[7]

The focus on linking provinces in the BCIM—in this case, Yunnan and West Bengal—seems to have given a new impulse to galvanizing the plan. It has been reported that the member states have taken serious steps to build the 2,800 km. long main artery, K-2-K transport corridor. The corridor will pass through the nodes of Kolkata-Petrapole/Benapole-Jessore-Dhaka-Sylhet-Deola/Sutarkandi-Silchar-Imphal-Moreh/Tamu-Kalay-Mandalay-Muse/Ruili-Tengchong-Dali-Kunming. The point to be noted is that not all of the roads connecting the nodes are in good condition. Therefore, one of the primary tasks is to upgrade the existing network and improve them, they are able to withstand traffic. Existing roads which connect international highways should also be improved and made durable enough to bear the load of cross-country trade and traffic. According to a news report, a stretch of about 200 km., from Kalewa to Monywa in Myanmar, needs to be upgraded as an all-weather road. More so, the segment between Silchar in Assam and Imphal in Manipur needs immediate upgradation (which India is upgrading presently). From

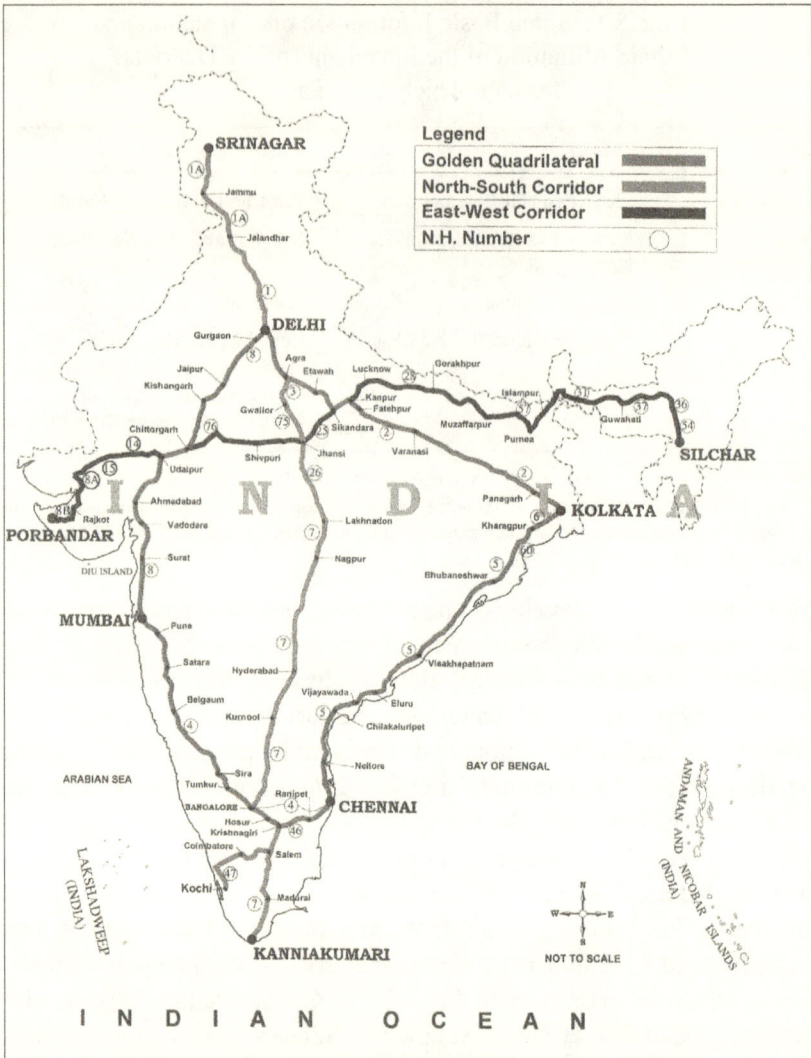

MAP 8.4: East–West Corridor (National Highways Development Project)
Source: http://senthil-studynotes.blogspot.in/2015/09/indian-geography-north-south-east-west.html, accessed 15 March 2018.

Note: Map not to scale. The international boundaries of India as shown in this map are neither correct nor authentic.

Adviser Mashiur Rahman. The goods were unloaded at Ashuganj Port and then reloaded onto Bangladeshi trucks before travelling Akhaura in Tripura. The entire duration of the trans-shipment was ten days.

The trans-shipment fee has been fixed at ৳192.25/ton and India has to pay an additional ৳50 ton for transporting goods from the Ashuganj

Kolkata, the capital of West Bengal, the corridor will head towards Benapole, a border-crossing town in Bangladesh. As far as the corridor route is concerned, after passing through Dhaka and Sylhet, it will re-enter the Indian territory near Silchar in Assam.

The rest of the passage will be connected to Imphal and then pass through the India-built 160 km. long Tamu-Kalewa Friendship Road in Myanmar (Map 8.5). However, there are seventy weak bridges, of which only one has been repaired by Myanmar till date. The remaining need upgradation and repair. These will not be repaired by the Government of India through Border Roads Organisation (BRO), but by the Myanmar government instead.[8] It is part of the 1,360 km. long cross-border trilateral highway.[9]

Mandalay will be the next focal point of the corridor before the road enters Yunnan, after crossing Lashio and Muse in Myanmar. The Chinese stretch of this arterial road extends from Ruili to Kunming through Longling and Dali. The central corridor can be connected with two supplementary passages to the north and south. Starting from Kunming, the northern passage heads towards Myitkyina, the capital of Kachin state in Myanmar before extending to Ledo in Assam. After crossing Dibrugarh and Guwahati, this road enters northern Bangladesh and joins the central corridor inside the country before reaching Kolkata. At present, this route is problematic because it enters a small portion of Arunachal Pradesh over which India and China are in a territorial dispute. Besides, a part of this stretch is insurgency prone, and therefore, unsafe.[10]

The BCIM corridor would be incomplete without drawing Mizoram into the framework through the Kaladan Multimodal Transit Transport Project (KMTTP) (Map 8.6). Under this plan, Mizoram would be connected with Myanmar's port of Sittwe through the Kaladan River, and the passage will provide all the landlocked north-eastern states access to the sea. Compared to the land route, Sittwe provides these states direct access to Kolkata, just 539 km. away. The goods destined for the north-east will be unloaded at the Sittwe Port and then travel 160 km. along the Kaladan River to Paletwa and then along a 210 km. highway connecting to the Indian border at Lawngtlai, Mizoram. A Land Customs Station (LCS) at Zorinpui in the Lawngtlai District of Mizoram would be established.[11] The KMTTP, currently under construction under the auspices of India's Ministry of External Affairs, is combining overland (road/rail), inland waterway or maritime passageways together, as proposed in the Mekong-India Economic Corridor (MIEC) linking southern India with the GMS countries via Dawei Port in southern Myanmar.[12] Though in terms of cost-benefit analysis the maritime

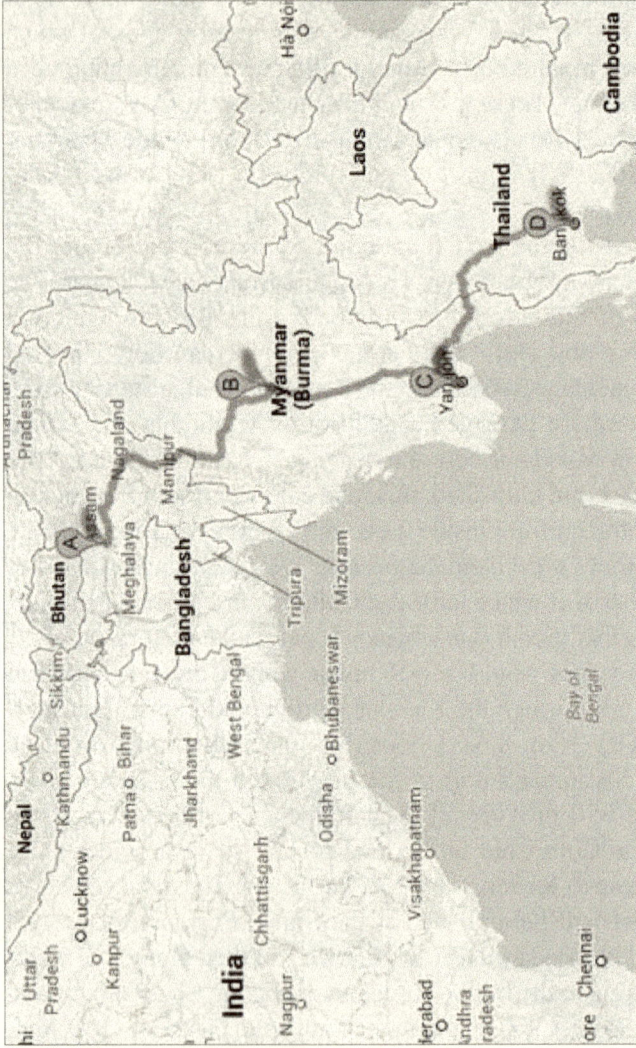

MAP 8.5: India-Myanmar-Thailand Trilateral Highway

Source: Cited in https://www.newsgram.com/india-myanmar-thailand-highway-starts-operation, accessed 24 August 2018.

Note: From India's Moreh to Thailand's Maesot via Myanmar's Tamu, Mandalay, and Myawaddy. The stretch along Tamu–Kalewa–Kalemyo is a part of the Trilateral Highway.

Map not to scale. The international boundaries of India as shown in this map are neither correct nor authentic.

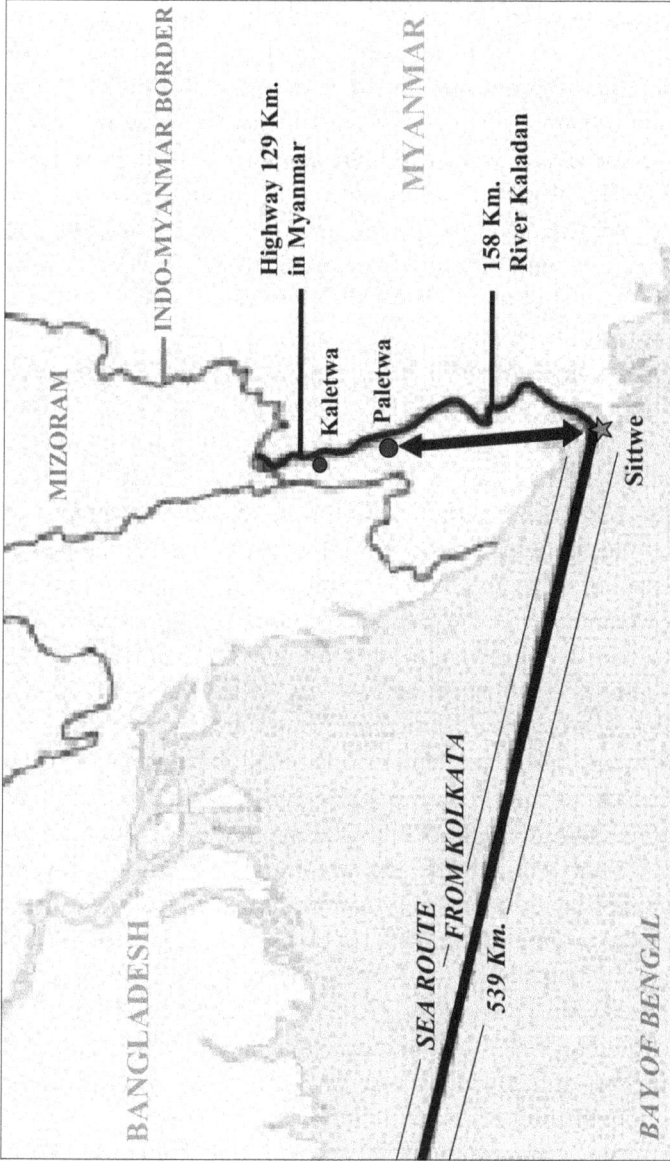

MAP 8.6: The Route of the KMTTP

Source: http://coastalnewstoday.com/myanmar-kaladan-waterway- phase-to-be-completed-by-next-march, accessed 15 March 2018.

Note: Map not to scale. The international boundaries of India as shown in this map are neither correct nor authentic.

route appears to be favourable over the land-based routes, it is always advisable to see these two modalities as complementary rather than oppositional.[13]

A crucial logistical issue has been identified in the KMTTP that needs to be addressed for the project to realize its objectives. The KMTTP comprises a complex process of disembarkation and re-embarkation at Setpyitwin in Myanmar.[14]According to the rules at present, goods travelling to Mizoram and further into the north-eastern states in India need to be transferred into land-vehicles from waterway containers. This is because the Kaladan River is navigable only up to Paletwa and the route towards Mizoram is a surface-transport route. Hence, to make the muiltimodal aspect of the project fruitful, there needs to be smooth operations and facilities in place.[15]

According to a news report, China proposes to build a high-speed railway line between Kunming in the southwest of the country and Kolkata. The link would be part of the BCIM-EC aimed at boosting the trade and relations. The proposed 3,000 km. rail corridor, starting from the capital city of Yunnan Province and passing through Myanmar and Bangladesh, could be funded through China's Silk Road development fund or the Asian infrastructure fund. The rail corridor will pass through Mandalay in Myanmar and the Bangladeshi cities of Chittagong and Dhaka before entering West Bengal and ending in Kolkata (Map 8.7).[16]

India has already established connectivity with Myanmar (Moreh–Tamu–Kalewa Road, as well as trade points at Moreh-Tamu and Zowkhathar-Rhi besides the implementation of the Kaladan project), but the same is yet to be arrived at with Bangladesh. The landlocked India's north-east forms the hinterland of the Chittagong Port in Bangladesh and access to this port would be beneficial for trade from the north-east. The importance of land connectivity can be best realized when these links are extended to the nearest ports. In this sense, another important port is Ashuganj which sits on the Meghna River in the Brahmanbaria District of Bangladesh. The port is 37 km. from Agartala, the capital of Tripura, and would be a vital link among India's north-eastern states. It is still in the process of being modernized and there is an imperativeness for the institutionalization of infrastructural support.

It is noteworthy that a Bangladeshi ship arriving from the Kolkata port and carrying 1,000 tons of corrugated-iron sheets was scheduled to leave Ashuganj Port in Bangladesh for Tripura on 22 June 2016, as transit between India and Bangladesh became operational.[17] The consignment was inaugurated for trans-shipment by the then Shipping Minister Shajahan Khan and Prime Minister Sheikh Hasina's Economic Affairs

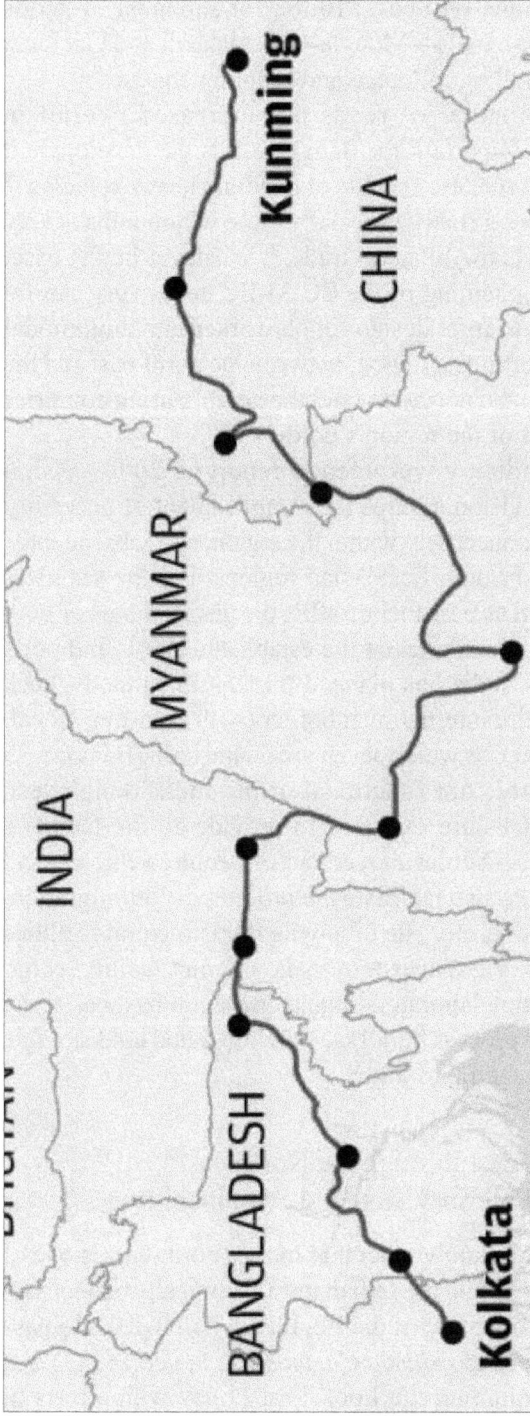

MAP 8.7: The Route of BCIM Transport Corridor

Source: Deccan Chronicle, 'BCIM Economic Corridor Beneficial for North-East Economy', 25 November 2014, see http://www.deccanchronicle.com/141125/nation-current-affairs/article/%E2%80%98bcim-economic-corridor-beneficial-north-eastern-regions, accessed 12 September 2015.

Note: Map not to scale. The international boundaries of India as shown in this map are neither correct nor authentic.

port to Akhaura. Also, India will pay ৳10 ton for shipment of goods through Bangladesh's two canals—Mongla-Ghashiakhali and Gabkhan Canal, besides labour handling, pilotage and berthing charges.[18]

It is true that the number of roads has increased overall in Bangladesh. Yet, what is important for Bangladesh is the development of more durable roadways that are capable of handling heavy vehicles.[19] The condition of cross-border roads, especially those within India is very poor, and therefore, affects the bilateral trade.[20] Whatever be the case, it is clear that the spatial planning of the BCIM-EC needs very careful thought with respect to the larger design for networked and multimodal connectivity within the north-east region; between the north-east and the rest of India; and between the north-east and the neighbouring countries that comprise 98 per cent of the region's borders.[21]

According to the Indian government's report of 2008 'Vision 2020', the government's vision assures the establishment of necessary infrastructure and better connectivity within the region, and subsequently, with the larger South and South East Asian regions. For the seamless movement of trade as well as passenger traffic, the governments of both India and Bangladesh have undertaken the establishment of land ports and land custom stations. India has planned thirteen Integrated Check Posts (ICPs) along its entire international border (with Pakistan, Nepal, Bangladesh, and Myanmar), of which seven are on the India-Bangladesh border. About two or three are functional at the India-Bangladesh border at the moment. ICPs are expected to provide all the facilities necessary for smooth cross-border movement of people, vehicles, and goods under one roof. ICPs also facilitate the processes of immigration, customs, security, quarantine, etc. The following infrastructural facilities are provided at the ICPs: Passenger terminals, internet facility, cargo inspection sheds, quarantine laboratory, banks, isolation bay, cafeteria, currency exchange, cargo process building, warehouse and cold storage, clearing agents, scanners, and parking.[22]

Looking East through the North-east
Need for Long-term Vision and Sustainability

It has become almost a well-known fact that India's north-east is one of the most complex regions within the Indian territory and all connectivity projects under the larger initiative of the Look East Policy have to pass through this region.[23] It was the *Shukla Commission Report* (1997) that became instrumental in aligning the Look East Policy with efforts of developing the north-east, after a study group headed by S.P. Shukla and comprising B.G. Verghese and Jayanta Madhab among others, toured the states of the north-east to appraise the gaps in infrastructure and development in the states and offered recommendations for improving the same. The fundamental realization being that a policy of 'Looking East' will be incomplete without bringing the country's north-eastern region within the purview of the policy framework. It is this realization that has made the way for various connectivity projects through north-east India and also of subregional organizations such as the BIMSTEC and BCIM forum.[24]

According to the 'Vision 2020' document, the development of India's north-east is visualized 'in terms of its ability to cater to'[25] the markets in the countries of South and South East Asia, and the ethnic or cultural similarities between the people of the north-east and those across the border often become a means to an end to the 'acceptability and salability'[26] of emphasizing the importance of the north-east to establishing connectivity with India's east. India's north-east, therefore, becomes not more than a conduit of potential economic benefits.[27]

It is thus vital to engage the people of the states sharing their borders within the BCIM framework to understand their gains out of the road and communication networks being envisioned. Therefore, there is an urgent need to set up a consultative mechanism to integrate India's Look East Policy with the requirements of the north-east. There is a need to study the export potential of the north-east and to match that with the demand conditions in markets, such as Bangladesh, China, and Myanmar. While highlighting the significance of congenial circumstances in the north-east for such exports to take place, it is also important to create sustainable projects in the region in collaboration with the other countries in the BIMSTEC, as well as BCIM groupings. It is true that some steps have already been taken in terms of road connectivity but much more must be done to take full advantage of trans-national connectivity. Local capacities needed to be built up according to the priority of the projects.

The BCIM-EC would link two least developed countries (Bangladesh and Myanmar) with two of the world's largest and fastest growing economies like India and China. The transport corridor traverses areas which are relatively underdeveloped, particularly the landlocked south-western part of China and north-eastern states of India, a distinct subregion whose backwardness can be addressed not merely through national developmental programmes, but also through trans-national connectivity, economic integration, and cross-border cooperation.

Therefore, planning for the BCIM-EC, and particularly for the routing of the backbone of transport corridor, must be simultaneously grounded in a national and a regional perspective.[28]

The issues like non-tariff barriers, the harmonization of standards, and the whole range of trade-facilitation measures are to be dealt with high priority not only for the BCIM corridor, but also for other cross-border connectivity projects; and these would need to be further buttressed with trans-national arrangements for transit and movement of cargo and passenger vehicles and other forms of transportations across the national borders. After all, good infrastructure is crucial for people-to-people contacts in fostering greater understanding, cooperation, and goodwill. For the BCIM project; the key nodes in the development of 'mini-corridors' are the border-crossing points, gateway nodes (very often sea-ports) and interchange nodes, along with commercial nodes, both industrial and agricultural. In this, and in the development of value chains along the corridor, small and medium enterprises (SMEs) will have a special role to play as the fulcrum of local enterprise and entrepreneurship.[29]

It is indeed true that since its inception in 1999 with the primary aim to boost the economic prowess of the region and increase connectivity, the BCIM has not been productive in any substantial manner. Despite the apparent willingness of the four countries, they have been limited by several factors in their endeavour to make the initiative prosperous. One of the prime reasons for this is the considerable political reluctance that hinders its success. The border regions of the BCIM countries have a complex development-security conundrum. The protracted ethnic conflicts in India's north-east and northern Myanmar have had serious security concerns, which have impacted the border areas of the BCIM region.[30]

The state of affairs between India and China is the most vital aspect, influencing the proper functioning of the BCIM. From India's perspective, a couple of causes are pointed out with respect to the 'Sino-phobia'. First, the concerns that opening up of the north-east would flood the Indian markets with Chinese goods and second, it would make the north-eastern border security vulnerable. Many believe that it is part of Chinese policy to keep the border issues unresolved, wean off Nepal, Bangladesh, and Myanmar; and arm Pakistan, thereby limiting India's influence in the subcontinent. On the other hand, there is the much talked about the 'Asian Century' and the view that 'India and China need not fear each other, as it is not "India or China" but "India and China" which would redefine the global economy'.[31]

With the political and constitutional changes that have taken place, Myanmar is keen to balance its position with other countries and reduce its reliance on Beijing. There are in fact several areas of convergence between India and Myanmar with regard to energy investments, geo-strategic and maritime security. Indian policy with respect to Bangladesh is vital, as India shares the longest border with the latter and also because it is often acknowledged that 'India's north-east is Bangladesh-locked'. Against this backdrop, utilization of Chittagong, Kolkata, Haldia, and Kulpi Ports for enabling the exchange of both trade and passenger movements is to be considered. It is also important to encourage large-scale transportation of goods through Bangladesh to the north-eastern region.

While concluding, one can say that any cross-border connectivity project—be it under the banner of BIMSTEC or the BCIM Economic Corridor—has the potential of transforming a conflict zone into a cooperation zone. This can happen only if adequate regulatory measures are taken to check any possible negative impact by emphasizing the importance of dialogue with all the stakeholders at different levels to engage them in the process of policymaking, importance of understanding the role of perception of the neighbouring countries across the border, and importance of functional synergy between planning and execution of the projects on sectoral basis.

Notes

1. 'Transportation Infrastructure for North Eastern States', Press Information Bureau, Ministry for Development in the North Eastern Region, Government of India, New Delhi, 30 March 2017.
2. 'Govt approves Rs 6,441 crore road projects for Nagaland', *livemint*, 14 March 2018, see http://www.livemint.com/Politics/4gIGAZC95pbGhOxxiKFTDO/Govt-approves-Rs6441-crore-road-projects-for-Nagaland.html, accessed 19 March 2018.
3. See http://www.mdoner.gov.in/content/sardp-ne, accessed 20 September 2015.
4. Anasua Basu Ray Chaudhury, Pratnashree Basu and Mihir Bhonsale, *Driving Across the South Asian Borders: The Motor Vehicle Agreement Between Bhutan, Bangladesh, India and Nepal*, Occasional Paper 59, New Delhi: Observer Research Foundation, September 2015, pp. 11–12
5. In this context, see also Jaipati K. Pattanaik, 'Should the Stilwell Road be Reopened?', *Economic and Political Weekly*, vol. 51, no. 15, 9 April 2016, https://www,epw.in/journal/2016/15/reports-states/should-stilwell-road-be-reopened.html, accessed 12 August 2017.

178   *Anasua Basu Ray Chaudhury*

6. Cited in a report entitled S*ocio-economic Impacts of the Proposed Asian Highway on India's Northeast with Special Reference to Assam: A Preliminary Study*, coordinated by Annanda Charan Bhagabati and Abu Nasar Saied Ahmed, OKD.

7. Patricia Uberoi, *The BCIM Economic Corridor: A Leap into the Unknown?*, Working paper, New Delhi: Institute of Chinese Studies, November 2014, p. 7; see also Kishan S. Rana and Patricia Uberoi, *India's Northeast States, The BCIM Forum and Regional Integration*, New Delhi: Institute of Chinese Studies, 2012.

8. Ministry for the Development of the Northeast, see http://www.mdoner.gov.in/node/1505, accessed 20 February 2015.

9. The 1,360 km. cross-border transportation network would link Moreh, India to Mae Sot, Thailand through Bagan, Myanmar. It is expected that the project will be completed by December 2019.

10. 'China, India Fast-track BCIM Economic Corridor Project', *The Hindu*, 26 June 2015, see http://www.thehindu.com/news/national/china-india-fasttrack-bcim-economic-corridor-project/article7355496.ece, accessed 11 September 2015.

11. Interview with Anil Viswakarma, Project Incharge, Essar, Sittwe, Myanmar, 27 March 2015.

12. The corridor proposes to connect Ho Chi Minh, Vietnam with Dawei, Myanmar via Bangkok, Thailand and Phnom Penh, Cambodia, and further linking it to Chennai, India.

13. Uberoi, *The BCIM Economic Corridor*.

14. 'Kaladan Multi-modal Project in Myanmar', *Manipur Online*, December 2010; see http://manipuronline.com/look-east-policy/kaladan-multi-modal-project-in-myanmar/2010/12/19, accessed 10 June 2015.

15. Interview with U Tun Htay, Port Officer, Senior Pilot, Myanmar Port Authority, Rakhine State, Sittwe Port, 25 March 2015.

16. 'New Silk Route? China Plans Kunming-Kolkata Railway Link', *The Economic Times*, 18 June 2015, see http://articles.economictimes.indiatimes.com/2015-06-18/news/63567726 1 rail -corridor-new-silk-route-bangladesh-china-india-myanmar, accessed 15 September 2015.

17. Rejaul Karim Byron and Md Fazlur Rahman, 'Transit gets Operational', *The Daily Star*, 14 June 2016, see http://www.thedailystar.net/backpage/transit-gets-operational-1239373, accessed 17 June 2016.

18. Sahidul Hasan Khokon, 'Indo-Bangladesh Transshipment Formally begins Today', *India Today*, 17 June 2016, see http://indiatoday.intoday.in/story/indo-bangladesh-transshipment-formally-begins-today/1/694040.html, accessed 17 June 2016.

19. Mustafizur Rahman, Khondaker Golam Moazzem, Mehruna Islam Chowdhury, and Farzana Sehrin, 'Connecting South Asia and Southeast Asia: A Bangladesh Country Study', Asian Development Bank Institute (ADBI) Working Paper Series, September 2014, p. 16.

20. Anasua Basu Ray Chaudhury and Pratnashree Basu, *India-Bangladesh Connectivity: Possibilities and Challenges*, New Delhi: Observer Research Foundation, 2015, p. 28.
21. Uberoi, *The BCIM Economic Corridor*, p. 15.
22. Ibid., p. 67.
23. Subir Bhoumik, *Look East through Northeast: Challenges and Prospects for India,* New Delhi: Observer Research Foundation, 2014, pp. 1–3.
24. Pratnashree Basu, 'Looking East through the Northeast: Challenges and Viabilities', in *North East in India's Look East: Issues and Opportunities*, ed. Imankalyan Lahiri and Pahi Saikia, Indian Council for World Affairs (ICWA) and Jadavpur Association of International Relations (JAIR), New Delhi: Varti Publications, 2015, pp. 250–60.
25. Samir Kumar Das, 'Between South and Southeast Asia: Recasting India's Northeast in the Age of Globalization', in *Society, Politics and Development in Northeast India*, ed. Ashok Kumar Ray and Satyabrata Chakraborty, New Delhi: Concept, 2008, pp.149–65.
26. Ibid., p. 152.
27. Basu, 'Looking East through the Northeast', p. 255.
28. Uberoi, *The BCIM Economic Corridor*, p. 11.
29. Hans-Peter Brunner, *North East India: Local Economic Development and Global Markets,* New Delhi: Sage Publications, 2010, pp. 24–8; see also 'What is Economic Corridor Development and What can it Achieve in Asia's Sub-regions?', Asian Development Bank (ADB) Paper Series on Regional Economic Integration, no. 117, Manila: Asian Development Bank, 2013.
30. K. Yhome, 'The BCIM Economic Corridor: Prospects and Challenges', see http://www.orfonline.org/research/the-bcim-economic-corridor-prospects-and-challenges/, accessed 9 September 2015.
31. Pratnashree Basu, 'From Kunming Initiative to BCIM Corridor', see http://www.orfonline.org/research/from-kunming-initiative-to-bcim-corridor/, accessed 10 September 2015.

9

India's 'Look East' Policy

The Imperatives of Overland Connectivity

Rajen Singh Laishram

T HE IMPERATIVE of north-east India as a component in India's
Look East Policy was envisaged by the former External Affairs
Minister Pranab Mukherjee.[1] Following the Act East Policy,
a new avatar of the 'Look East' one with an enhanced ambit,
Prime Minister pronounced that 'India's Eastern journey begins
on the Western boundary of Myanmar',[2] attention is on India's
north-eastern provinces that share their border with Myanmar. As the
projected gateway to the East and South East Asia, Manipur continuously
hosts policymakers, corporate honchos, and members of the academia
from across the globe. Representatives from the Association of South
East Asian Nations (ASEAN), Cambodia, the EU, Germany, Japan,
Myanmar, Sweden, Thailand, the UK, the US, and Vietnam assess
preparedness of north-east Indian provinces for the impending Act East
Policy. Many of the visitors question, in private, the persisting pathetic
overland connectivity within India's north-eastern provinces and with
Myanmar, the apparent lack of commitment and political will on the
part of the Government of India, and inquire how and in what way the
provincial authorities and intelligentsia partake in development and
foreign policy process.

This essay presents a ringside view from the periphery that for
pushing the agenda of development in the frontier provinces, connectivity
is a must; and contends how overland connectivity through north-eastern
India can be an intrinsic component of India's engagement with the
East Asian and ASEAN countries. Substantiating the argument for
connectivity is informed by periodic academic sojourn to some of the

East Asian and South East Asian borders, and the fact that north-east India's linkages to East and South East Asia does not entail only fresh connectivity but also reviving the old routes anew. In addition, proper overland connectivity has the potential that can erase the prevailing perception of participation denial—real or imagined—of India's north-east region, open vista as active participants, and stakeholders in India's increasingly 'proactive' foreign policy.

The visible lack of development in these frontier provinces is perceived as part of a grand strategy by successive regimes at the centre for systematic domination and denial of rights of the communities in north-east India on cultural and racial differences. We also find that in those frontier provinces that have the same ethnic, linguistic, or cultural stocks as that of the ruling elites, there are less problems of legitimacy and even if there are some issues, the nature of the legitimacy does not pose as serious a challenge as in ethnically, racially, or culturally different provinces.[3] Hence, while combating participation denial or deficit, the potential gains from connectivity includes contributing to processes of political reconciliation of the north-east region of India.[4]

India's North-East as Pivot

India's north-east provinces are straddled—96 per cent of its border—by South Asia, South East Asia, and East Asia. At this strategic tri-junction, interspersed communities sustain traditional sociocultural, politico-economic activities, and normal patterns of relationships alongside memories of bloody wars and incursions. Four provinces in India's north-east—Arunachal Pradesh, Nagaland, Manipur, and Mizoram—share a border, 1,648 km. long, with Myanmar. At the height of the colonial contest for domination of Asia, north-east India was the route taken by the Imperial Japanese and the Indian National Army, connected to China through the Stillwell (Ledo) Road and Old Burma Road, and used to be an important supply route during the Second World War.

The post-Second World War political alignments continue to curtail the 'normal pattern of relationships', natural growth, and intensification of exchanges. And the political tradition of minimal provincial participation in foreign policy formulation hinders the cultivation of ties with India's East and South East Asian neighbours. Nonetheless, in India's National Transport Policy, for the first time attention has been paid to intra-regional, as well as interregional needs along with transborder movement in India's north-east as a response to the Look East Policy,[5] and possibly finding merit in the inchoate, provincial demands to revive the old links.

It would be economically and strategically viable to revive the Stillwell Road and Old Burma Road, the South Silk Road, and the Tea and Horse Trade Routes that can potentially link India to the vibrant markets and technology hubs of East and South East Asia. India is also involved in the Trans-Asian Highway, Trans-Asian Railway, the India-Myanmar-Thailand Trilateral Highway projects, as well as the Kaladan Multimodal Transport Project designed to provide north-east Indian provinces maritime access through Mizoram.

Overland connectivity, besides augmenting trade and economic activities, can provide access to a large population to tourism, and enhance people-to-people interactions through sports, culture, and academic and medical researches.[6] The existing trading posts along Indian and Myanmar borders at Moreh in Manipur, Champhai in Mizoram, Nampong in Arunachal Pradesh, and Awangkhu and Lungwa in Nagaland can augment the supply of basic needs for both sides of the border. To make these posts operational, connectivity is required as 'a place needs to have well-functioning roads before it can get rich'.[7]

The Indian Institute of Foreign Trade estimated the informal trade through these border points to the tune of ₹20 billion annually. As of today, Moreh in Manipur handles a major bulk of the formal overland trade between India and Myanmar, and also the informal and/or illegal trade somewhere in billions of rupees, far above the hundreds of millions of rupees in annual formal trade.[8] Why cannot we legalize these economic exchanges? Besides, in north-east India there are 42 Land Customs Stations (LCSs) bordering with Bangladesh, Bhutan, China, and Myanmar, out of which 26 are functional.[9] Yet, all these LCSs lack essential infrastructure necessary to promote border trade.[10]

Overland Connectivity and Transport

The Bangladesh, China, India and Myanmar Economic Corridor (BCIM-EC) has US$1,025 billion trade capacity and the ASEAN economic vitality is US$1,710 billion. If a small percentage of these trade activities are conducted through the provinces of north-east India, it will help the region to avoid paying more due to transport and damage costs. For instance, the distance of many north-east Indian provinces to India's trade centres like Mumbai is more than 3,000 km., Delhi is

2,000 km., and Kolkata is 1,700 km., measured from places like Imphal and Ledo. Kolkata is more than 1,800 km. from Agartala, the capital city of Tripura. Surface travel from Aizawl to Kolkata is a 1,547 km. long journey. This physical distance of the north-east provinces, 'even if tariff and institutional obstacles are removed,' and being landlocked, means they pay about 5.60 per cent more for shipping than a coastal economy, representing as much as 63 per cent in freight and insurance.[11] Besides, costs of logistics and damages add 60 per cent to the cost of a bag of cement and 14 per cent to general cargo moved from Kolkata to north-east India.[12]

Road transport or overland connectivity is a fast and relatively reliable mode that provides door-to-door services, as well as offsets higher costs vis-à-vis maritime or rail modes.[13] In South Asia, road transport caters to at least 70 per cent of freight movement and is the dominant mode in the overall regional transport system.[14] Improved infrastructure can connect remote areas and landlocked countries with regional and global markets. The median landlocked country bears 55 per cent higher transport costs than the median coastal one.[15] That is the fate of India's north-eastern provinces. Since transporting goods over land is around seven times more costly than over a similar distance by sea, connectivity through the borders will make things easily available at competitive prices, and open new vistas for marketing agricultural, horticultural produces, handloom products, and crafts.

The cost factors of transportation by detour must be taken into account while framing trade policies, particularly by countries of continental size like China and India. Since the distance between Yunnan and India is only 500 km. via Trunk Road,[16] the opening up of border trade may offer many advantages for both countries. Moreover, linking with Thailand and other countries of South East Asia is a possibility; the connectivity with Thailand is already there and is being replenished through the India-Myanmar-Thailand Trilateral Highway project. It is time to experiment and see whether 'border trade could fulfill local demands at reasonable rates'.[17] Such realities make Myanmar the key to overland connectivity of north-east India to the economies of East and South East Asia.

Myanmar to Cambodia, Laos, and Vietnam

Myanmar is the second largest country in South East Asia. It shares 5,858 km. of borders with Bangladesh, the People's Republic of China,

India, the Lao PDR, and Thailand with a coastline of 2,800 km. Myanmar has a huge reserve of natural resources and is the physical link among East Asia, South Asia, and South East Asia. Its strategic location makes Myanmar indispensable to the emerging economic corridors such as the East–West Economic Corridor among Lao, Myanmar, Thailand, and Vietnam; the North–South Economic Corridor among Kunming (China), Chiang Rai (Thailand) via Lao PDR, India-Myanmar-Thailand Trilateral Highway, and Kaladan Multimodal Transport Project linking India's Mizoram to Sittwe Port of Myanmar. India needs to keep pace with the dynamic foreign policy of the new regime in Myanmar. Manipur is connected to Myanmar through the Asian Highway 1 and the Trans-Asian Railway project is expected to be complete by 2020. A trial bus service between Manipur and Mandalay was formally inaugurated on 9 December 2015. In addition, a tour operator in Manipur has been successfully operating two-way tourism between Moreh (India) and Yangon through Mandalay.

Stronger economic cooperation and coordination between the late-developing countries of the Greater Mekong Subregion (GMS) and India under the Look East Policy and South Asia Subregional Economic Cooperation (SASEC) can usher in an era of inclusive growth. Improved connectivity between Myanmar and north-east India could open new opportunities for development of the border area, which in turn would contribute to narrowing the developmental gaps.[18] Surface connectivity through Myanmar has the potential to link Cambodia, Laos, Thailand, and Vietnam in the educational sector, cultural domain, and sports; enhance people-to-people cooperation; tourism, including medical tourism; besides trade and economic exchanges. Such policy orientation is in consonant with the 'Look West' orientation of Thailand and has the potential to cater to the rising market demands of south-western provinces of China.

India's north-east has a comparable cost advantage in medical treatment of general ailments vis-à-vis of South East Asia. This is an area which requires immediate intervention, particularly keeping in perspective the interior provinces of Myanmar. Facilitation of educational, medical, and religious tourisms will open north-east India to the needs and expectations of South East Asia. Encouraging such ventures will provide ample opportunities for north-east India as a stakeholder to the booming economic and conjoined activities of South East and East Asia, besides creating an enabling environment for participation, and thereby erasing the perception of neglect of India's north-east provinces.

India appears to be not harping on its rich cultural influence over South East Asia. New Delhi has consistently overlooked the centuries of 'deep and enduring' interactions that 'for most of the past 2000 years it was India, not China that enjoyed the closest connections with South East Asia and was by far the premier source of outside cultural and religious inspiration'.[19] New Delhi's missed opportunity in South East Asian countries can be rectified by taking into account the presence of 2.5 million people of Indian origin (PIO) in Myanmar and 250,000 in Thailand.[20]

Economic Integration

Institutional studies identify a huge potential through economic integration and cooperation of the small provincial economies of Myanmar, north-east India, Bangladesh, and south-west China. Effective integration of this geographically contiguous areas with other neighbouring provinces and countries involves several countries, requires proper execution, and negotiation for vexed political disputes.[21] Major commonalities of the region are the rural background of most people in this region and heavy dependence on agriculture as a major platform for stimulating economic development and alleviating poverty. Integrating these areas will provide the economic impetus to stimulate infrastructure development.[22] In spite of the potentialities and twenty years having passed since India announced the Look East Policy, mistrust between India and its neighbours, and poor infrastructure and connectivity have hindered the development of links between South and South East Asia.[23] Yet, greater connectivity can usher in inclusive growth, reduce poverty, and close developmental gaps among the hitherto marginalized nationalities, ethnicities, tribes, or communities. Therefore, a more integrated subregion will have many benefits.[24]

The fruits of cooperation will include improvement in regional connectivity, easier movement of people and goods across borders, and enhanced competitiveness of regional production networks, besides attracting greater investment. Poverty alleviation of excluded communities can ensue through improved access to economic opportunities, lower cost of goods and services, and better access to essential infrastructure services. Regional developmental gaps within a country will narrow with better access to regional and global markets and production networks, as well as reduce regional conflict.[25]

Cooperation leads to greater integration, expanded markets for goods and services increase the scope for economies of scale and greater competition. It provides opportunities for expansion of production networks with countries with comparatively low wages but inadequate connectivity. A more integrated region could possibly attract Foreign Direct Investment (FDI) along with technology and knowledge transfer, and higher productivity. Cooperation in infrastructure and trade facilitation can potentially reduce trade costs and 'result in welfare gains well in excess of gains from tariff liberalization'. In addition, integrated subregional groupings could lead to formation of resilient economic corridors, and provide the basis for more inclusive growth with greater potential for reducing poverty and closing developmental gaps. This includes 'minority groups that have been marginalized in the past, which often led to conflict'.[26]

Provincial Initiatives

The Manipur Chief Minister Okram Ibobi Singh has been exploring possible areas of cooperation and investment with Myanmar, China, and Japan as a part of the Look East Policy. For the first time, he visited Myanmar during May 2013 and explored ways to forge links with Myanmar.[27] Ibobi Singh proposed to the Sagaing Division counterpart to supply forest products and raw precious stones and gems to the multi-special economic zone.[28] He also sought investments, both from China and Japan, for the infrastructure development of Manipur and discussed about bilateral trade and commerce, investment, tourism, and city development.[29]

On 21 November 2013, Manipur had its first international flight from Myanmar, coinciding with the annual Sangai Festival. The chartered Golden Myanmar Airlines aircraft arrived with over 100 passengers including the Chief Minister of Mandalay region U Ye Mint, Chief Minister of Sagaing region U Thar Aye, several Meetei diaspora, and media persons. As a goodwill gesture, 23 November was celebrated as Myanmar Day during the festival. The Sangai Festival is the biggest annual tourism festival of Manipur, showcasing its cultural heritage, eco-adventure activities, indigenous food, and handicraft, with participants from Bangladesh, China, Japan, Thailand, the UK, and the USA. Similarly, in the annual Hornbill Festival of Nagaland, the provincial government invites tourists and entrepreneurs from India's neighbours, the USA, and the UK. Through such ventures, people-to-people relationships are revived, and business and economic interaction follows.

Mizoram shares 510 km. and 318 km. of borders, respectively with Myanmar and Bangladesh. As a rugged mountainous area, Mizoram encounters shortage of essential items and continues to be one of the most expensive states in north-east India. Yet, Mizoram can source its basic needs from Myanmar, thereby reducing transport cost, besides catering to interior, inaccessible areas. A reassuring instance of closer cooperation at the provincial level to enhance trade and investment through augmenting connectivity and banking arrangements, was signed at the Fifth India-Myanmar Joint Trade Committee meeting in Nay Pyi Taw.[30] Moreover, the World Bank has agreed to a US$107 million credit to Mizoram to improve its transport linkages with Myanmar and Bangladesh, keeping in perspective the potential for regional trade. The initiative from the World Bank was influenced by an estimate that investments in transport infrastructure could reduce trade costs by more than 20 per cent in India and 12.50 per cent in Bangladesh.[31]

Nagaland has also inaugurated the international trade road from Myanmar, connecting Longwa under Mon District of Nagaland via Lahe in Myanmar at zero point Longwa in April 2013. For the first time, Chairman of the Naga Self-Administrative Zone of Myanmar U Ru San Kyu, whose rank is equivalent to a chief minister in any Indian states, visited Longwa from Myanmar, thus signalling the interest on the part of Myanmar.

There have been periodic mutual business summits involving north-east Indian provinces: Thailand, Myanmar, and Vietnam. The states of Assam and Arunachal Pradesh are constantly appealing for revival of the Stillwell Road. As nationalities or communities are interspersed on both sides of the border, rather embedded, they can be made to play a proportionate role in translating ethnic affinities into a lasting, effective, and substantial cooperation; transgressing the state-centric security paradigm. For instance, ethnic groups like the Naga, Chin-Kuki-Mizo, Meitei, and Tai-Ahoms can be encouraged with institutional support to play a constructive role in developing people-to-people relationships. Agricultural training and capacity building programmes can enhance productivity that can benefit the subregion.

In educational sectors, like in medical treatment, India's north-east provinces can take advantage of the educational mismatch, as presently experienced in many pockets of South East Asia. For instance, students from Myanmar and Thailand choose, rather prefer, to study in Manipur as educational standards and cost in New Delhi, Mumbai, or Kolkata are high and experience no 'cultural shock' in Manipur as they do in many other parts of India. Above all, there is need to separate inter-country agricultural, cultural, educational, and sports interactions from political, economic, and trading calculations. Though there will be competing interests, requiring multiple idioms for mediation for the sake of subregional prosperity, capitulation of national pride or national interest may set the pace in this era of globalization. Above all, nurturing relationships among involving countries is a great challenge and is like joining a broken mirror as the Chinese adage has it, '*pò jìng chóng yuán* (破镜重圆)'. But no statesman can ignore the wishes of the people and towards that end, we in the academia have intellectual social responsibilities.

Notes

1. 'October 2007 meeting of the then Foreign Minister Shri Pranab Mukherjee and the chief ministers of the north-eastern states on the initiative of the Ministry of DONER at Shillong', *Look East Policy and North Eastern States*, Government of India, MDoNER, 2011, see http://www.mdoner.gov.in/content/aspects-of-lep, accessed 9 November 2013.

2. 'Opening Statement by Prime Minister at the 12th India-ASEAN Summit, Nay Pyi Taw, Myanmar', 12 November 2014, see http://www.mea.gov.in/aseanindia/Speeches-Statements.htm?dtl/22566/Opening+Statement+by+Prime+Minister+at+the+12th+IndiaASaEAN+Summit+Nay+Pyi+Taw+Myanmar, accessed 27 March 2016.

3. Rajen Singh Laishram, 'Knowledge and Development Disparity in the Frontier Provinces of China and India', in *Perspectives: Asia-Pacific*, Kolkata: Indian Association for Asian and Pacific Studies, Proceedings of the Fifth Biennial International Conference, 2012, pp. 514–30.

4. 'Opening Remarks by Asian Development Bank Vice-President Stephen P. Groff on 5 May 2013 at the ADBI Seminar on Connecting South Asia and Southeast Asia', see http://www.adb.org/news/speeches/opening-remarks-adbi-seminar-connecting-south-asia-and-southeast-asia, accessed 24 May 2013.

5. *Report of the Working Group on Improvement and Development of Transport Infrastructure in the North East for the National Transport Development Policy Committee*, see www.mdoner.gov.in/sites/default/files/.../Final_Report_13.6.2012.pdf, accessed 20 August 2013.

6. *Look East Policy and North Eastern States*, Government of India: MDoNER, 2011, see http://www.mdoner.gov.in/content/aspects-of-lep, p. 1, accessed 21 August 2013.

7. Shannon Tiezzi, 'The New Silk Road: China's Marshall Plan?', *The Diplomat*, 6 November 2014, see http://thediplomat.com/2014/11/the-new-silk-road-chinas-marshall-plan/, accessed 27 March 2016.

8. Edmund Downie, 'Manipur and India's "Act East" Policy', *The Diplomat*, see http://thediplomat.com/2015/02/manipur-and-indias-act-east-policy/, accessed 27 March 2016.

9. *Look East Policy and North Eastern States*, Government of India: MDoNER, 2011; see http://www.mdoner.gov.in/content/aspects-of-lep, p. 23, accessed 21 August 2013.

10. 'Expansion of Northeast India's trade and investment with Bangladesh and Myanmar: An Assessment of the Opportunities and Constraints RIS, MDoNER and NEC', see http://www.ris.org.in/sites/default/files/NER_report-17-9-2012-final.pdf, accessed August 2013.

11. Manabu Fujimura, 'Cross-border Transport Infrastructure, Regional Integration and Development', ADB Institute Discussion Paper, no. 16, November 2004, p. 6, see http://www.adb.org/sites/default/files/publication/156764/adbi-dp16.pdf, accessed 28 March 2016.

12. Sushil Khanna, 'Economic Opportunities or Continuing Stagnation', see www.india-seminar.com/2005/550/550%20Sushil%20Khanna.htm, accessed 20 February 2007.

13. *Connecting South Asia and South East Asia: Interim Report*, Tokyo: Asian Development Bank Institute, 2013, p. 16.

14. 'Transport Sector Overview', see http://sasec.asia/web/index.php/en/projects/transport/transport-sector-overview, accessed 10 November 2013.

15. *Infrastructure for a Seamless Asia*, Tokyo: Asian Development Bank Institute, 2009, p. 62.

16. Hangao Chen, 'Cooperation and Prospects of Yunnan-India Trade', in *India and China in an Era of Globalisation: Essays on Economic Cooperation*, ed. Jayanta Kumar Ray and Prabir De, New Delhi: Bookwell, 2005, p. 117.

17. Prashant Jha, 'A Break in the Ridgeline', *Himal*, see www.himalmag.com/2006/august/special_report_1.htm, accessed 28 March 2016.

18. Fukunari Kimura and So Umezaki, 'ASEAN-India Connectivity: A Regional Framework and Key Infrastructure Projects', in *ASEAN-India Connectivity: The Comprehensive Asia Development Plan, Phase II, ERIA Research Project Report*, 2010, no. 7, Jakarta: ERIA, 2011, p. 4.

19. Thant Myint-U, *Where China meets India: Burma and the New crossroads of Asia*, London: Faber and Faber, 2011, p. 240.

20. 'India-Myanmar Relations', see http://www.mea.gov.in/Portal/ForeignRelation/Myanmar_May-2014.pdf, p. 1; and http://www.mea.gov.in/Portal/ForeignRelation/Thailand_11_01_2016.pdf, p. 4, accessed 27 March 2016.

21. Ponciano S. Intal, Jr Sothea Oum, and Mercy J.O. Simorangkir, 'Integrating Myanmar with its Western and Northern Neighbours: A Shared Vision

through the Promotion of Sustainable Agricultural Development', in *Agricultural Development, Trade and Regional Cooperation in Developing East Asia*, ed. P.S. Intal, Jr et al., Jakarta: ERIA, 2011, p. 627.

22. Ibid., p. 634.
23. Amb Karl F. Inderfurth and Ted Osius, 'India's "Look East" and America's "Asia Pivot": Converging Interests', *U.S.-India Insight*, vol. 3, no. 3, March 2013, p. 1.
24. *Connecting South Asia and Southeast Asia: Interim Report*, Tokyo: Asian Development Bank Institute, 2013, p. xi.
25. Ibid., p. 9.
26. Opening Remarks by ADB Vice-President Stephen P. Groff, 5 May 2013, ADBI Seminar on Connecting South Asia and Southeast Asia, see http://www.adb.org/news/speeches/opening-remarks-adbi-seminar-connecting-south-asia-and-southeast-asia_accessed 24 May 2013.
27. State CM meets Manipuri communities at Mandalay', 31 May 2013, Imphal Free Press, see http://kanglaonline.com/2013/05/state-cm-meets-manipuri-communities-at-mandalay/, accessed 28 March 2016.
28. *The Sangai Express*, 'Business Condane with Myanmar Sangai Fest Explores Free Trade Regime Idea', 23 November 2013.
29. *The Sangai Express*, 1 October 2013, see http://www.thesangaiexpress.com/tseitm-30912-trip-to-china-ibobi-opens-investment-doors/, accessed 28 March 2016.
30. 'India, Myanmar to Start Border Trade through Mizoram', 18 March 2015, see http://www.business-standard.com/article/news-ians/india-myanmar-to-start-border-trade-through-mizoram-115031800425_1.html, accessed 28 March 2016.
31. 'US$107 Million World Bank Project to Connect Mizoram with Bangladesh and Myanmar via Roads', 12 June 2014, see http://www.worldbank.org/en/news/press-release/2014/06/12/107-million-world-bank-project-to-connect-mizoram-with-bangladesh-and-myanmar-via-roads, accessed 28 March 2016.

Bibliography

Primary Sources

Annual Report: 2000–1, Policy Planning and Research Division, Ministry of External Affairs, New Delhi: Government of India, 2001.

Annual Report: 2003–4, Policy Planning and Research Division, Ministry of External Affairs, New Delhi: Government of India, 2004.

Annual Report: 2005–6, Policy Planning and Research Division, Ministry of External Affairs, New Delhi: Government of India, 2006.

Annual Report: 2007–8, Policy Planning and Research Division, Ministry of External Affairs, New Delhi: Government of India, 2008.

Annual Report: January 2003–March 2004, Policy Planning and Research Division, Ministry of External Affairs, New Delhi: Government of India, 2004.

Baxter, James, *Report on Indian Immigration*, Rangoon: Office of the Superintendent, Government Printing and Stationery, Burma, 1941.

Connecting South Asia and South East Asia: Interim Report, Tokyo: Asian Development Bank Institute, 2013.

High Level Commission Report to the Prime Minister, Planning Commission, New Delhi: Government of India, 7 March 1997.

IPCS Special Report, October 2009.

Look East Policy and North Eastern States, Ministry of Development for North Eastern Region (MDoNER), Government of India, 2011.

Ministry of External Affairs, Annual Report 1991–2, New Delhi: Government of India, 1992.

Ministry of External Affairs, Annual Report 1996–7, New Delhi: Government of India, 1997.

Report of the Committee Appointed to Investigate the Alleged Hardships Caused by the Compulsory Vaccination, under the Provision of Section 9 of the Burma Vaccination Law Amendment Act 1909 of Labourers Arriving in Rangoon by Sea, Rangoon Office of the Superintendent, Rangoon, Burma, 1918.

Report of the Working Group on Improvement and Development of Transport Infrastructure in the North East for the National Transport Development Policy Committee, 13 June 2012.

Research Project Report 2010, no. 7, Jakarta: ERIA, 2011.

Socio-economic Impacts of the Proposed Asian Highway on India's Northeast with Special Reference to Assam: A Preliminary Study, coordinated by Annanda Charan Bhagabati and Abu Nasar Saied Ahmed, OKD.

Thai-India Directory, 2011–12, Bangkok: Thailand-India Chambers of Commerce, 2012.

'Transforming the Northeast: Tackling Backlogs in Basic Minimum Services and Infrastructural Needs', *High Level Commission Report to the Prime Minister*, New Delhi: Planning Commission, Government of India, 7 March 1997.

Secondary Sources

Periodicals

Adas, Michael, 'Immigrant Asians and the Economic Impact of European Imperialism: The Role of the South Indian Chettiars in British Burma', *Journal of Asian Studies*, vol. 33, no. 3, 1974, pp. 385–401.

Bhattacharyay, B. and Prabir De, 'Promotion of Trade and Investment between People's Republic of China and India: Toward a Regional Perspective', *Asian Development Review*, vol. 22, no. 1, 2005, pp. 48–73.

Bagchi, Indrani, 'Four Navy Ships in South China Sea to Mark Indian Presence', *The Times of India*, 24 May 2012.

———, 'Prime Minister Manmohan Singh to China's Wen Jiabao: Back off on South China Sea', *The Times of India*, 19 November 2011.

Bandopadhyay, Kshitish Chandra, 'China Doshyuder Haate' (In the Hands of Chinese Bandits), *Bharatvarsha*, vol. 26, pt I, no. 1, 1345BY (1938), pp. 261–5.

Bandyopadhyay, Amulya Chandra, 'Javadwiper Mahabharata' (The Mahabharata of Java: A Story), *Bharatvarsha*, vol. 18, no. 2, 1337–8BY (1930–1), pp. 601–5.

Basu, Anath Nath, 'Santiniketane Chainik Sudhi Su Simor Abhyarthana' (Welcoming the Noble Tsu Simo in Santiniketan), *Prabashi*, vol. 28, pt II, Chaitra 1335BY (1928), pp. 368–70.

Basu, Bharat Kumar, 'Korea', *Bharatvarsha*, vol. 18, pt I, 1337BY (1930), pp. 273–88.

Basu Ray Chaudhury, Anasua et al., *Driving Across the South Asian Borders: The Motor Vehicle Agreement Between Bhutan, Bangladesh, India and Nepal*, Occasional Paper 59, New Delhi: Observer Research Foundation, September 2015, pp. 1–22.

Bhaumik, Subir, 'Look East through Northeast: Challenges and Prospects for India', *ORF Occasional Paper 51*, New Delhi: Observer Research Foundation (ORF), June 2014, pp. 1–34.

Bose, Nandalal, 'Chin Japaner Chithi' (Letters from China and Japan), *Prabashi*, vol. 28, pt I, no. I, 1339BY (1932), pp. 784–7.

Brunner, Hans-Peter, 'What is Economic Corridor Development and What can it Achieve in Asia's Sub-regions?', Asian Development Bank (ADB) Paper Series on Regional Economic Integration, no. 117, Manila: Asian Development Bank, 2013, pp. 1–13.

Business Standard, 'Modi Aims Subtle Barbs at Neighbour over South China Sea', 14 November 2014.

Byron, Rejaul Karim and Md Fazlur Rahman, 'Transit gets operational', *The Daily Star*, 14 June 2016.

Chakraborti, Tridib, 'India-Vietnam Relations: Transcendence from 'Gaze' to Action', *World Focus*, vol. 35, no. 12, December 2014, pp. 51–60.

Chatterjee, B.R., 'Mahabharata and the Wayang in Java', *Modern Review*, vol. XXXXVI, no. 7, 1929, pp. 658–62.

Chattopadhyay, Suniti Kumar, 'Javadwiper Pothe' (On the Way to Island Java), *Prabashi*, vol. 28, pt I, 1335BY (1928), no. 1, pp. 142–5; no. 2, pp. 266–73; no. 3, pp. 480–7; no. 4, pp. 594–602.

Chaturvedi, Banarasidas, 'Three Letters on Greater India, Indians Abroad', *Modern Review*, vol. XXXXVII, nos. 1–6, 1930, pp. 136–9.

Chirathivat, S., 'Thailand's Greater Mekong Sub Region: Role and Potential Linkages to South-West China and Northeast India', *Millennial Asia,* vol. 1, no. 2, 2010, pp. 171–95.

Das, Tarak Nath, 'Value of Cultural Propaganda in International Relations', *Modern Review*, vol. XXXXVII, no. 3, 1930, pp. 287–91.

Deccan Herald, 'India Needs Policy to Look East, Link West: Narendra Modi', 25 September 2014.

Denoon, David B.H., and Evelyn Colbert, 'Challenges for the Association of Southeast Asian Nations (ASEAN)', *Pacific Affairs*, vol. 71, no. 4, Winter 1998–9, pp. 505–23.

The Economic Times, 'New Silk Route? China Plans Kunming-Kolkata Railway Link', 18 June 2015.

Fujimura, Manabu, 'Cross-border Transport Infrastructure, Regional Integration and Development', ADB Institute Discussion Paper, no. 16, November 2004, pp. 1–21.

Ghosh, Kalimohon, 'Japaner Grihadharmaneeti' (The Internal Policy of Japan), *Prabashi*, vol. 13, pt I, Baisakh 1320BY (1913), pp. 29–33.

Gogoi, Dilip, 'East through Northeast: India and Southeast Asia in the new Asia', in *Beyond Borders: Look East Policy and North East India*, Guwahati: DVS Publishers, 2010, pp. 34–62.

Gupta, Monindrabhusan, 'Chin Chitrakalar Itihash' (History of Chinese Painting), *Prabashi*, vol. 24, pt II, no. I, 1331BY (1924), pp. 81–9.

The Hindu, 'China, India Fast-track BCIM Economic Corridor Project', 26 June 2015.

Inderfurth, Amb Karl F. and Ted Osius, 'India's "Look East" and America's "Asia Pivot": Converging Interests', *U.S.-India Insight*, vol. 3, no. 3, March 2013, pp. 1–3.

Jaffrelot, Christophe, 'India's Look East Policy: An Asianist Strategy in Perspective', *India Review*, vol. 2, no. 2, 2003, pp. 35–68.

Kaur, Amarjit, 'Indian Labour, Labour Standards, and Workers Health in Burma and Malaya, 1900–40', *Modern Asian Studies*, vol. 40, no. 2, 2006, pp. 425–75.

Labbeton, J.V.H., 'Javanese Dances, Gleanings', *Modern Review,* vol. XXXIX, no. I, 1926, pp. 219–21.

Maitra, Ganesh Chandra, 'Brahma Prabasher Chitra' (Description of Life in Burma), *Bharatvarsha*, vol. 14, pt I, no. 3, 1334BY (1927), pp. 75–86.

Mohan, Raja C., 'India's Geopolitics and Southeast Asian Security', *Southeast Asian Security*, Singapore: Institute of Southeast Asian Studies, 2008, pp. 43–60.

Muni, S.D., 'Review of Baladas Ghoshal, ed., *India and Southeast Asia: Challenges and Opportunities*', in *Contemporary Southeast Asia*, vol. 19, no. 2, New Delhi: Konark (in association with India International Centre), September 1997, pp. 209–12.

Mustafa, Gholam, 'Chine Musalman' (The Muslims of China), *Bharatvarsha,* vol. 18, pts 1, 2, 7–8, 1337BY (1931), serially pp. 966–9, 55–8.

Mustafizur, Rahaman et al., 'Connecting South Asia and Southeast Asia: A Bangladesh Country Study', Asian Development Bank Institute (ADBI) Working Paper Series, September 2014, pp.1–32.

Nag, Kalidas, 'Bharat Maitri Mahamandal' (India's Great circle of Friendship), *Prabashi,* vol. 26, pt I, Baishakh 1320BY (1913), pp. 365–78.

———, 'Dwip Bharater Natyakala' (The Drama of Island Bharat), *Prabashi,* vol. 29, pt I, no. 6, 1336BY (1929), pp. 897–902.

———, *Art and Archaeology in the Far East-French Contribution, Modern Review,* vol. XXXXVII, no. 1, January 1930, pp. 63–8.

Naidu, G.V.C., 'Wither the Look East Policy: India and Southeast Asia', *Strategic Analysis*, vol. 28, no. 2, April–June 2004, pp. 331–46.

Newsweek, 'U.S. Warship Sails Past South China Sea Islands in First Such Challenge to China under Trump', 25 May 2017.

Osada, Noriyuki, 'An Embryonic Border: Racial Discourses and Compulsory Vaccination for Indian Immigrants at Ports in Colonial Burma, 1870–1937', *Social Science Research on South East Asia*, 2011, vol. 17, pp. 145–64.

Patel, Nathoobhai D., 'Medicine in Modern India and Japan', *Modern Review,* vol. XXXX, 1926, pp. 167–70.

Pattanaik, Jaipati K., 'Should the Stilwell Road be Reopened?', *Economic and Political Weekly*, vol. 51, no. 15, 9 April 2016, https: //www.epw. in/journal/2016/15/reports-states/should-stilwell-road-be-reopened.html, accessed 12 August 2017.

Roy, Hemendralal, 'Shyamrajya' (The Kingdom of Shyam), *Prabashi*, vol. 24, pt II, no. 1, Kartik 1331BY (1924), pp. 64–73.

Roy, Prafulla Chandra, 'Nabya Chin O Bangala' (New China and Bengal), *Prabashi,* vol. 29, pt II, no.1, 1336BY (1929), pp. 80–91.

Sahidul, Khokon Hasan, 'Indo-Bangladesh Transhipment Formally Begins Today', *India Today*, 17 June 2016.

The Sangai Express, 'Business Conclave with Myanmar Sangai Fest Explores Free Trade Regime Idea', 23 November 2013.

Sarkar, Benoy Kumar, 'The Eternal Chinese Question', *Modern Review*, vol. XXXVII, no. 1, 1925, pp. 174–80.

Sarkar, Jadunath, 'Indian Influence on the Art of Indo China', *Modern Review,* vol. XXXIX, no. 1, 1926, pp. 39–43.

———, *Hindu Influence on Further India*, *Modern Review*, vol. XXXX, July 1926, pp. 4–7.

Sen, Jamini Kanta, 'Chainik Chitrakalar Chhayapoth' (The Shadowy Path of Chinese Painting), *Bharatvarsha,* vol. 26, pt I, no. 5, pp. 579–87.

Smith, Anthony L., 'ASEAN's Ninth Summit: Solidifying Regional Cohesion, Advancing External Linkages', *Contemporary Southeast Asia*, vol. 26, no. 3, 2004, pp. 416–33.

Sorcar, P.C., 'Japaner Pothe' (On the way to Japan), *Bharatvarsha*, vol. 25, pt 2, 1344BY (1937), pp. 62–9.

Tagore, Rabindranath, 'Chin O Japaner Bhraman Bibaran' (Description of Travels in China and Japan), *Prabashi,* vol. 24, pt II, no. 1, Kartik 1331BY (1924), pp. 89–90.

———, 'To the People of Japan'*, Modern Review,* vol. XXXVII, no. 1, 1925, pp. 4–7.

———, 'Unity of Chicago', quoted in Foreign Publications, *Modern Review,* vol. XXXII, no. 7, 1927, pp. 94–5.

———, 'Dhyani Japan' (Spiritualism in Japan), *Prabashi,* vol. 29, pt I, no. 5, 1336BY (1929), pp. 533–5.

———, 'Brihattara Bharat' (Greater India), in *Kalantor*, 1937, repr., Calcutta: Visva Bharati Granthan Vibhag, 2002, pp. 300–9.

Thongkholal, Haokip, 'India's Look East Policy: Its Evolution and Approach', *South Asian Survey*, vol. 18, no. 2, 2011, pp. 239–57.

Tiezzi, Shannon, 'The New Silk Road: China's Marshall Plan?', *The Diplomat*, 6 November 2014.

Vickery, M., 'Champa Revised', Asia Research Institute Working Paper Series, no. 37, Singapore: Asia Research Institute, National University of Singapore, 2005, pp. 3–98.

Wahyuni, Sri, 'ASEAN-India FTA signed in Bangkok', *The Jakarta Post,* 14 August 2009.

Articles in Edited Books

Anderson, W., 'A Growing Congruence of Interests with Korea', in *India's Foreign Policy: Retrospect and Prospect*, ed. S. Ganguly, New Delhi: Oxford University Press, 2010, pp. 175–205.

Basu, Pratnashree, 'Looking East through the Northeast: Challenges and Viabilities', in *North East in India's Look East: Issues and Opportunities*, ed. Imankalyan Lahiri and Pahi Saikia, New Delhi: Varti Publications, 2015, pp. 250–60.

Bezbaruah, M.P.s comments on 'Northeast Region of India within India's LEP' published in *India's Look East-Act East Policy: A Bridge to the Asian Neighbourhood*, Proceedings of International Relations Conference, Pune: Symbiosis Institute of International Studies, Symbiosis International University, 2014, pp. 1–72.

de Casperis, J.G. and I.W. Mabbett, 'Religion and Popular Beliefs in Southeast Asia before *c.*1500', in *The Cambridge History of Southeast Asia*, vol. I, ed. Nicholas Tarling, Cambridge: Cambridge University Press, 1992, pp. 276–340.

Cao, Sy Kiem, 'East Asian Economic Integration: Problems for Late-Entry Countries', in *East Asian Visions: Perspectives on Economic Development*, ed. Indermit Gill et al., Washington: World Bank and Institute of Policy Studies (Singapore), 2007, pp. 128–41.

Chakraborti, Tridib, 'Disparate Priorities: Explaining the Penumbra of India's Look East Policy', in *India and ASEAN: Foreign Policy Dimensions for the 21st Century*, ed. K. Raja Reddy, New Delhi: New Century Publications, 2005, pp. 52–93.

Chakraborti, Tridib, 'Modi's "Act East" Policy: Its Blueprint and the Future Promenade', in *Modi's Foreign Policy: Challenges and Opportunities*, ed. N.N. Jha and Sudhir Singh, New Delhi: Pentagon Press, 2016, pp. 303–20.

Chen, Hangao, 'Cooperation and Prospects of Yunnan-India Trade', in *India and China in an Era of Globalisation: Essays on Economic Cooperation*, ed. Jayanta Kumar Ray and Prabir De, New Delhi: Bookwell, 2005, pp. 111–21.

Chirathivat, S. and C. Sabhasri, 'Thailand', in *National Strategies for Regional Integration: South and East Asian Case Studies*, ed. J. Francois et al., London: Anthem Press and Asian Development Bank, 2009, pp. 383–481.

Chirathivat, S., 'China's Rise and Its Effects on ASEAN-China Trade Relations', in *China, the United States and Southeast Asia: Contending Perspectives on Policies, Security and Economics*, ed. E. Goh and S. Simon, New York: Routledge, 2008, pp. 38–55.

Chutintaranond, Sunait, 'Indian-Thai Relationship in Cultural dimension: The Issue of Indianization vs Localization', in *Connectivity and Beyond:*

Indo–Thai Relations through Ages, ed. Lipi Ghosh, Kolkata: The Asiatic Society, 2009, pp. 78–87.

Das, Samir Kumar, 'Between South and Southeast Asia: Recasting India's Northeast in the Age of Globalization,' in *Society, Politics and Development in Northeast India*, ed. Ashok Kumar Ray and Satyabrata Chakraborty, New Delhi: Concept Publishing, 2008, pp. 149–65.

Ganguli, Debarati and Suchandra Ghosh, 'The Greater India Society and R.C. Majumdar's Perception of India-Myanmar Relations', in *India-Myanmar Relations: Historical Links to Contemporary Convergences*, ed. Lipi Ghosh, New Delhi: Paragon International Publishers, 2016, pp. 75–86.

Ghosh, Lipi, 'Indian Revolutionaries and Subhas Chandra Bose in Thailand: The Era of Plaek Phibul Songgram', in *Connectivity and Beyond: Indo–Thai Relations through Ages*, Kolkata: The Asiatic Society, 2009, pp. 154–79.

Ghosh, Suchandra, 'Champa: A Politico-Cultural Study', in *Ancient Indian Trade and Cultural Relations with South East Asia*, ed. Chittabrata Palit, Kolkata: Calcutta Chamber of Commerce and Maulana Abul Kalam Azad Institute of Asian Studies, 2013, pp. 88–101.

Intal, Ponciano S. et al., 'Integrating Myanmar with Its Western and Northern Neighbours: A Shared Vision through the Promotion of Sustainable Agricultural Development', in *Agricultural Development, Trade and Regional Cooperation in Developing East Asia*, ed. P.S. Intal, Jr et al., Jakarta: ERIA, 2011, pp. 625–69.

Kawai, M. and G. Wignaraya, 'Policy Challenges Posed by Asian Free Trade Agreement: A Review of the Evidence', in *A World Trade Organization for the 20st Century: The Asian Perspective*, Glos: Edward Elgar Publishing, 2014, pp. 182–238.

Kimura, F. et al., 'ASEAN-India Connectivity: A Regional Framework and Key Infrastructure Projects', in *ASEAN-India Connectivity: The Comprehensive Asia Development Plan, Phase II, ERIA Research Project Report 2010*, no. 7, ed. F. Kimura and S. Umezaki, Jakarta: ERIA, 2011, pp. 1–56.

Kulke, Hermann, 'The Concept of Cultural Convergence Revisited: Reflections on India's Early Influence in Southeast Asia', in *Asian Encounters: Exploring Connected Histories*, ed. Upinder Singh and Parul Pandya Dhar, New Delhi: Oxford University Press, 2014, pp. 3–19.

Laishram, Rajen Singh, 'Knowledge and Development Disparity in the Frontier Provinces of China and India', in *Perspectives: Asia-Pacific,* Proceedings of the Fifth Biennial International Conference, Kolkata: Indian Association for Asian and Pacific Studies, 2012, pp. 514–30.

Legge, J.D., 'The Writing of Southeast Asian History', in *The Cambridge History of Southeast Asia*, vol. I, ed. Nicholas Tarling, Cambridge: Cambridge University Press, 1992, pp. 1–50.

Malik, Preet, 'India's Look East Policy: Genesis', in *Two Decades of India's Look East Policy: Partnership for Peace, Progress and Prosperity*, ed. Amar Nath Ram, New Delhi: Manohar, 2012, pp. 23–8.

Pusalkar, A.D., 'Cultural Interrelation between India and the Outside World before Asoka', in *The Cultural Heritage of India*, vol. I, ed. Suniti Kumar Chatterjee et al., Kolkata: Ramkrishna Mission Institute of Culture, 2001, pp. 144–59.

Schwever, Anne-Valérie, 'Le dynastie d'Indrapura (Quảng Nam, Viet Nam)', *Southeast Asian Archaeology 1998* (Proceedings of the 7th International Conference of the European Association of Southeast Asian Archaeologists, Berlin, 31 August–4 September 1998), ed. Wibke Lobo and Stefanie Reimann, Centre for South East Asian Studies, University of Hull, Special Issue & Ethnologisches Museum, Staatliche Museen zu Berlin, Stiftung Preussischer Kulturbesitz, 2000, pp. 205–17.

Shekhar, Vibhansu, 'Thailand's Look West Policy: Opportunities and Challenges for India's Northeast', in *Beyond Borders-Look East Policy and North East India*, ed. Dilip Gogoi, Guwahati: DVS Publishers, 2010, pp. 166–88.

Singh, Upinder, ed., 'Politics, Violence and War in Kamandaka's Nitisara', in *Rethinking Early Medieval India*, New Delhi: Oxford University Press, 2011, pp. 293–324.

Southworth, William A., 'The Coastal States of Champa', in *Southeast Asia from Prehistory to History*, ed. Ian Glover and Peter Bellwood, London: Routledge, 2004, pp. 209–33.

Wright-Neville, David, 'Southeast Asian Security Challenges', in *Strategy and Security in the Asia–Pacific*, ed. Robert Ayson and Desmond Ball, NSW: Allen and Unwin, 2007, pp. 210–15.

Authored Books

Acharya, Amitav, *The Quest for Identity: International Relations of Southeast Asia*, Singapore: Oxford University Press, 2000.

———, *Constructing a Security Community in Southeast Asia: ASEAN and the Problem of Regional Order*, London: Routledge, 2001.

Ali, Daud, *Courtly Culture and Political Life in Early Medieval India*, Cambridge: Cambridge University Press, 2004.

Aung San Suu Kyi, *Burma and India: Some Aspects of Intellectual Life under Colonialism,* Simla: Indian Institute of Advanced Study, 1990.

Bhattacharjee, Dhrubajyoti, *India's Vision on Act East Policy*, New Delhi: Indian Council for World Affairs (ICWA), 2016.

Bhattacharya, Swapna, *India Myanmar Relations 1886–1948*, Kolkata: K.P. Bagchi & Co., 2007.

Bhattacharyay, B.N. et al., *Infrastructure for Asian Connectivity*, Cheltenham: Edward Elgar Publishing, 2012.

Bhoumik, Subir, *Look East through Northeast: Challenges and Prospects for India,* New Delhi: Observer Research Foundation, 2014.

Brunner, Hans-Peter, *North East India: Local Economic Development and Global Markets,* New Delhi: Sage Publications, 2010.

Chakraborti, Tridib, *India and Kampuchea: A Phase in Their Relations: 1978–81*, Calcutta: Minerva Associates, 1985.

Chakravarti, N.R., *The Indian Minority in Burma: The Rise and Decline of an Immigrant Community*, London: Oxford University Press, 1971.

Chandra, Bipan et al., *India since Independence*, revd edn, New Delhi: Penguin, 2008.

Chaudhury, Anasua Basu Ray and Pratnashree Basu, *India-Bangladesh Connectivity: Possibilities and Challenges*, New Delhi: Observer Research Foundation, 2015.

Chirathivat, S., *Prospering Thailand-India Economic Partnership Mekong-Ganga Policy Brief*, New Delhi: Research and Information System for Developing Countries, 2009.

Coedes, G., *The Making of South East Asia*, tr. H.M. Wright, London: Routledge and Kegan Paul, 1966.

Datta-Ray, Sunanda K., *Looking East to Look West: Lee Kuan Yew's Mission India*, New Delhi: Penguin, 2009.

De, Prabir., *ASEAN-India Connectivity Report: India Country Study*, Delhi: Bookwell, 2012.

Desai, W.S., *India and Burma: A Study*, Calcutta: Orient Longman, 1952.

Funston, John, ed., *Government and Politics in Southeast Asia*, Singapore: Institute of Southeast Asian Studies, 2001.

Ghosh, Santidev, *Jiboner Dhrubatara* (Guiding Star of Life), Kolkata: Ananda Publishers, 1996.

Grare, Frederic and Amitabh Mattoo, eds., *India and ASEAN: The Politics of India's Look East Policy*, New Delhi: Manohar, 2001.

Guha, Ramachandra, ed., *Makers of Modern India*, New Delhi: Penguin, 2010.

Harrison, Brian, *Southeast Asia: A Short History*, 3rd edn, repr., New York: Macmillan, 1967.

Higham, Charles, *Early Cultures of Mainland Southeast Asia*, Bangkok: Art Media Resources, 2002.

Infrastructure for a Seamless Asia, Tokyo: Asian Development Bank Institute, 2009.

Golzio, K.H., ed., *Inscriptions of Champa,* Aachen: Shaker Verlag, 2004.

Kangle, R.P., *The Kautiliya Arthasastra*, pt I, Delhi: Motilal Banarsidass, 1986.

Kimura, F. et al., eds., *ASEAN-India Connectivity: The Comprehensive Asia Development Plan, Phase II*, Jakarta: ERIA, 2011.

Ky, Phuong Tran, *Vestiges of Champa Civilization*, Hanoi: The Gioi Publishers, 2004.

Lee ,Yew Kuan, *From Third World to First: The Singapore Story: 1965–2000*, New York: Harper Collins, 2000.

Leifer, Michael, *ASEAN and the Security of South-East Asia*, London: Routledge, 1989.

Mahajani, Usha, *The Role of The Indian Minorities in Burma And Malaya*, Bombay: Vora & Co., 1973.

Majumdar, Ramesh Chandra, *Hindu Colonies in the Far East*, 2nd edn, Calcutta: Firma K.L. Mukhopadhyay Agents, 1963.

———, *Champa: History and Culture of an Indian Colonial Kingdom in the Far East 2nd to 16th Centuries AD*, repr, Delhi: Gyan, 2008.

Mitra, Raja Rajendra Lal, ed., *The Nitisara by Kamandaki*, tr. Sisir Kumar Mitra, repr., Kolkata: The Asiatic Society, 2008.

Myint-U, Thant, *Where China Meets India*: *Burma and the New Crossroads of Asia*, London: Faber and Faber, 2011.

Nag, Kalidas, *The Humanization of History, Memoirs*, vol. I, Kolkata: Writers Workshop Publishers, 1991.

Prarn, B.R., *A History of Rangoon*, Rangoon: American Baptist Mission Press, 1939.

Raja Mohan, C., *Crossing the Rubicon: The Shaping of India's New Foreign Policy*, New Delhi: Viking, 2003.

Rana, Kishan S. and Patricia Uberoi, *India's Northeast States: The BCIM Forum and Regional Integration*, New Delhi: Institute of Chinese Studies, 2012.

Sar Desai, D.R., *Southeast Asia: Past and Present*, 4th edn, New Delhi: Harper Collins, 1997.

Sikri, Rajiv, *Challenge and Strategy: Rethinking India's Foreign Policy*, New Delhi: Sage Publications, 2009.

Sircar, D.C., *Indian Epigraphical Glossary*, Delhi: Motilal Banarsidass, 1966.

Sridharan, Kripa, *The ASEAN Region in India's Foreign Policy*, Aldershot: Dartmouth Publishing, 1996.

Tate, D.J.M., *The Making of Southeast Asia*, vol. 1, Kuala Lumpur: Oxford University Press, 1971.

———, *The Making of Southeast Asia*, vol. 2, Kuala Lumpur: Oxford University Press, 1979.

Tinker, Hugh, *The Banyan Tree: Overseas Emigrants from India, Pakistan and Bangladesh*, London: Oxford University Press, 1977.

Wales, H.G. Quaritch, *The Making of Greater India*, 2nd edn, London: Bernard Quaritch, 1961.

Unpublished Dissertations

Chakraborty, Mohar, 'India's "Look East" Policy: The Foreign Policy Dynamics from ASEAN Orientation to "Move East"', unpublished Ph.D. thesis,

Department of International Relations, Jadavpur University, Kolkata, 2013.

Rai, Sarita, 'The Role of Indian Diaspora in India-Myanmar Relations', M.Phil. dissertation, Department of International Relations, Sikkim University, 2015.

Interviews

U Tun Htay, Port Officer, Senior Pilot, Myanmar Port Authority, Rakhine State, Sittwe Port, 25 March 2015.

Viswakarma, Anil, Project Incharge, Essar, Sittwe, Myanmar, 27 March 2015.

Websites

http://www.jstor.org/stable/27913351, accessed 26 June 2016.

http://www.aseansec.org/4308.htm, accessed 10 July 2009.

http://asean.org/?static_post=joint-press-release-the-first-asean-india-joint-cooperation-committee-meeting-new-delhi-14-16-november-1996, accessed 10 June 2016.

http://www.vifindia.org, accessed 14 June 2016.

https://www.mea.gov.in/Portal/ForeignRelation/India-ASEAN_Relations.pdf2013, accessed 14 June 2016.

http://www.mea.gov.in/incoming-isitdetail.htm, accessed 10 June 2016.

http://www.irconference.in/assets/IRC_conference_proceedings.pdf, accessed 11 June 2016.

http://www.deccanherald.com/content/432698/india-needs-policy-look-east.htm, accessed 12 June 2016.

https://uk.news.yahoo.com/u-warship-sails-past-south-072156038.html, accessed 2 July 2017.

http://www.aseansec.org/15159.htm, accessed 14 May 2014.

http://www.aseansec.org/20820.htm, accessed 14 May 2014.

http://www.cfr.org/india/india-balance-power/p10948, accessed 7 May 2014.

http://www.asean.org/news/item/overview-of-asean-india-dialogue-relations, accessed 2 October 2015.

http://timesofindia.indiatimes.com/india/PM-Manmohan-Singh-to-Chinas-Wen-Jiabao-Back-off-on-South-China-Sea/articleshow/10786454.cms, accessed 3 May 2014.

http://www.bbc.co.uk/news/world-asia-pacific-15578083, accessed 15 September 2015.

http://www.business-standard.com/article/economy-policy/modi-aims-subtle-barbs-at-neighbour-over-south-china-sea-114111400007_1.html, accessed 30 November 2014.

https://www.whitehouse.gov/the-press-office/2015/01/25/us-india-joint-strategic-vision-asia-pacific-and-indian-ocean-region, accessed 20 October 2015.

http://mea.gov.in/press-releases.htm?dtl/27019/Statement_on_Award_of_Arbitral_Tribunal_on_South_China_Sea_Under_Annexure_VII_of_UNCLOS, accessed 13 July 2016.

https://www.washingtonpost.com/world/asia_pacific/china-reports-progress-on-south-china-sea-code-of-conduct/2017/05/18/4b538176-3c3f-11e7-a59b-26e0451a96fd_story.html, , accessed 29 May 2017.

http://www.voanews.com/content/cambodia-urges-closer-asean-ties-with-china/1734944.html, accessed 2 October 2015.

21http://yaleglobal.yale.edu/content/asean-summits-china-tilt-portends-new-world-order, accessed 29 May 2017.

http://www.narendramodi.in/english-rendering-of-prime-minister-shri-narendra-modis-remarks-at-the-east-asia-summit-nay-pyi-taw-6881, accessed 20 October 2015.

http://www.mea.gov.in/in-focus-article.htm?24714/From+Looking+East+to+Acting+East, accessed 14 June 2016.

http://pmindia.gov.in/speech-details.php, accessed 15 October 2015.

http://www.mea.gov.in/outoging-visit-detail.htm, accessed 15 October 2015.

http://www.deloitte.com/assets/Dcom-India/Local%20Assets/Documents/India_ASEAN_FTA.pdf, accessed 13 October 2015.

http://www.aseanindia.com/press-release-ins-sudarshini/, accessed 13 October 2015.

http://www.ndtv.com/article/india/full-text-obama-s-address-to-parliament-65093, accessed 16 October 2015.

http://planningcommission.gov.in/reports/genrep/ne_exe.pdf, accessed 16 October 2015.

http://www.ipcs.org/pdf_file/issue/SR85-SEARPInterview-Sikri1.pdf, accessed 13 October 2015.

www.telegraphindia.com/1090203/jsp/northeast/story-1047528.jps, accessed 28 February 2013.

www.acd-dialogue.org, accessed 5 September 2013.

www.databank.nedfi.com, accessed 10 September 2013.

www.carnegieendowment.org/newsletters/SAP/pdf/july07/speech_east_policy.pdf, accessed 17 July 2013.

www.assamtimes.org/node/8046, accessed 13 September 2018.

http://www.thehindubusinessline.com/2002/04/10/stories/2002041000030800html, accessed 2 January 2013.

www.highbeam.com/doc/1G1-112071220,html, accessed 11 October 2013.

http://www.adb.org/sites/default/files/myanmar-energy-sector-assessment.pdf, accessed 11 October 2013.

http://www.adbi.org/files/2009.08.31.book.infrastructure.seamless.asia.pdf, accessed 13 October 2013.

http://www.neda.or.th/eng, accessed 14 October 2013.

http://www.adb.org/projects/41682-013/details, accessed 14 October 2013.

http://www.unescap.org/ttdw/ppp/PPP2007/bf_thailand.pdf, accessed 14 October 2013.

http://www.mdoner.gov.in/content/myanmar, accessed 26 October 2013.

http://www.mdoner.gov.in/content/sardp-ne, accessed 20 September 2015.

http://www.mdoner.gov.in/node/1505, accessed 20 February 2015.

http://www.thehindu.com/news/national/china-india-fasttrack-bcim-economic-corridor-project/article7355496.ece, accessed 11 September 2015.

http://manipuronline.com/look-east-policy/kaladan-multi-modal-project-in-myanmar/2010/12/19, accessed 10 June 2015.

http://articles.economictimes.indiatimes.com/2015-06-18/news/63567726 1 rail-corridor-new-silk-route-bangladesh-china-india-myanmar, accessed 15 September 2015.

http://www.thedailystar.net/backpage/transit-gets-operational-1239373, accessed 17 June 2016.

http://indiatoday.intoday.in/story/indo-bangladesh-transshipment-formally-begins-today/1/694040.html, accessed 17 June 2016, accessed 17 June 2016.

http://www.mea.gov.in/aseanindia/Speeches-Statements.htm, accessed 27 March 2016.

http://www.adb.org/news/speeches/opening-remarks-adbi-seminar-connecting-south-asia-and-southeast-asia, accessed 24 May 2013.

www.mdoner.gov.in/sites/default/files/.../Final_Report_13.6.2012.pdf, accessed 20 August 2013.

http://www.mdoner.gov.in/content/aspects-of-lep, accessed 9 November 2013.

http://thediplomat.com/2014/11/the-new-silk-road-chinas-marshall-plan, accessed 27 May 2016.

http://www.adb.org/sites/default/files/publication/156764/adbi-dp16.pdf, accessed 24 May 2013.

www.india-seminar.com/2005/550/550%20Sushil%20Khanna.htm, accessed 20 February 2017.

http://sasec.asia/web/index.php/en/projects/transport/transport-sector-overview, accessed 10 November 2013.

www.himalmag.com/2006/august/special_report_1.htm, accessed 28 March 2016.

http://www.mea.gov.in/Portal/ForeignRelation/Myanmar_May-2014.pdf, accessed 27 March 2016.

http://www.mea.gov.in/Portal/ForeignRelation/Thailand_11_01_2016.pdf, accessed 29 March 2016.

http://kanglaonline.com/2013/05/state-cm-meets-manipuri-communities-at-mandalay, accessed 28 March 2016.

http://www.thesangaiexpress.com/tseitm-30912-trip-to-china-ibobi-opens-
    investment-doors, accessed 28 March 2016.
http://www.business-standard.com/article/news-ians/india-myanmar-to-start-
    border-trade-through-mizoram-115031800425_1.html, accessed 28 March
    2016.
http://www.worldbank.org/en/news/press-release/2014/06/12/107-million-
    world-bank-project-to-connect-mizoram-with-bangladesh-and-myanmar-
    via-roads, accessed 28 March 2016.

Editors and Contributors

ANASUA BASU RAY CHAUDHURY is Fellow of the Observer Research Foundation, Kolkata, and recipient of Kodikara Award (1998–9) from the Regional Centre for Strategic Studies, Colombo. Her publications include *SAARC at Crossroads: The Fate of Regional Cooperation in South Asia* (2006), *State of being Stateless: An Account on South Asia* (co-edited, 2015), and *Women in Indian Borderlands* (co-edited, 2011).

ACHINTYA KUMAR DUTTA is Professor of History, the University of Burdwan, and former post-doctoral Commonwealth Fellow. His published titles include *Trauma in Public Health: Tuberculosis in Twentieth-century India* (2018); *Economy and Ecology in a Bengal District Burdwan 1880-1947* (2002); *Ethnicity, Nation and Minorities: South Asian Scenario* (co-edited, 2003); and *History of Medicine in India: The Medical Encounter* (co-edited, 2005).

TRIDIB CHAKRABORTI is Dean, School of Social Sciences, ADAMAS University, Barasat, West Bengal. He was a Visiting Professor of ICCR, Chair (2015) at Dublin City University, Dublin, Ireland. He specializes on South East Asia and Asia Pacific affairs. He has authored *India and Kampuchea: A phase in their relations, 1978-81* (1985) and edited many books on international relations.

KORNKARUN CHEEWATRAKOOLPONG is Associate Professor of Economics, Chulalongkorn University, Thailand. She is a coordinator of 'The Study of Thailand's Outward FDI', sponsored by Thailand Research Fund (TRF). Her recent publications include 'Trade Diversification and Crisis Transmission: A Case Study of Thailand' in *Asian Economic Journal* and 'Trade Linkages and Crisis Spillovers' in *Asian Economic Papers*.

SUTHIPHAND CHIRATHIVAT is Professor of Economics, Chulalongkorn University, Thailand, Chairman of Chula Global Network and Executive Director of ASEAN Studies Centre. His academic interests involve the issues related to international trade, investment, finance, regional integration and development, and emerging issues in Asia in relation to the global economy and society.

APARAJITA DHAR is Assistant Professor, Department of History, the University of Burdwan, West Bengal. She has specialized in different facets of social history of science and technology, medicine, and gender history. She has authored several essays on women and medicine and co-edited *Life and Culture in Bengal: Colonial and Post Colonial Experiences* (2011).

SUCHANDRA GHOSH is Professor, Department of Ancient Indian History and Culture, University of Calcutta. Her areas of interest are interactions with South East Asia and Indian Ocean Buddhist and trade networks. Her publications include *From the Oxus to the Indus: A Political and Cultural Study, c.300 BCE to c.100 BCE* (2017); *Exploring Connectivity: Southeastern Bengal and Beyond* (2015); and *Early India and Myanmar: Spheres of Interactions* (2017).

SARVANI GOOPTU is Professor in Asian Literary and Cultural Studies, Netaji Institute for Asian Studies, Kolkata. She is the author of *The Actress in the Public Theatres of Calcutta* (2015); and *The Music of Nationhood: Dwijendralal Roy of Bengal* (2018). She has been working extensively on nationalism and culture in colonial and postcolonial India.

MAN MOHINI KAUL is Professor (retired) Centre for Indo-Pacific Studies, School of International Studies, Jawaharlal Nehru University, has authored and edited a number of books and published several articles in academic journals, edited volumes, and newspapers. She has worked closely with some of the top regional institutions and policymakers in India, South East Asia, and South West Pacific.

RAJEN SINGH LAISHRAM is a member of faculty in the Department of Political Science, Manipur Central University. He is a recipient of the Ford Foundation DSA in international relations theory and Visiting Fellow at the Yunnan Academy of Social Sciences, China, under the Ford Foundation ASIA Fellows Program. He has published widely in reputed journals.

JATINDRA NATH SAIKIA is Principal, Golaghat Commerce College, Assam. He is the Editor-in-Chief of *Research Promoter*. He has worked extensively on India-Thailand relations under the scheme, India-Thailand Bilateral Scholar Exchange Programme, and published widely in reputed journals.

Index

www.ingramcontent.com/pod-product-compliance
Lightning Source LLC
Chambersburg PA
CBHW031537260326
41914CB00032B/1850/J